Why do Blackheath and Greenwich in southeast London have such world-class modern domestic architecture? Because, as Ana Sutherland here so well explains, these two adjoining communities are essentially housing suburbs linked to great historical creations. Blackheath and Greenwich envelop the world heritage site of Maritime Greenwich with its magnificent Royal Naval College, Queen's House, Greenwich Park and the flat expanse of the heath of Blackheath. The architecture of the area has since Tudor times been of outstanding quality, as to be expected when in the presence of such royal, now residual, splendour, of palace and grounds.

The only regional comparison to the fine developments of post-Second World War Blackheath and Greenwich are Hampstead and Highgate in North London. The twinning of these suburbs north and south of the River Thames bare comparison. Much of the resemblance boils down to the middle-class radical idealism of both areas. In the years between the two world wars, Hampstead was lauded as the breeding ground of British middle-class socialism, particularly in the arts and architecture. Here is where artists like Ben Nicholson and Barbara Hepworth lived, and the great German émigré architects Walter Gropius and Marcel Breuer found shelter in the modern block of Lawn Road flats, by the progressive British architect Wells Coates.

But not until the post-war years did a new generation of design adventurers drift south of the river. They may not have been as politically pioneering as the socialists of the 1930s, but they did come brimming with progressive post-Second World War middle-class values, yearning for an unhistorical, uncluttered, and sensuously modern aesthetic for life and living.

Blackheath and Greenwich, within easy distance of central London, offered the building space amongst their lush canopy of trees. Blackheath especially was a garden-filled landscape ready, for better or worse, to be built over. Large Regency house gardens and commercial vegetable gardens became ripe for housing developments. First and foremost, amongst these expansions, and very big at that with hundreds of dwellings, were the housing estates of Span, a company led by architect Eric Lyons working with local developer Leslie Bilsby. As rows of Span terraces and flats expanded across the Cator Estate in Blackheath, more and more professionals arrived: lawyers, designers, and architects aplenty. Architects found cubbyholes in the area, building plots for their creativity. Local architects like Peter Moro and Trevor Dannatt built now heritage-listed buildings. And outside architects came and left their mark; big names like the architects of the Barbican, Chamberlin, Powell & Bon, with their Vanbrugh Park Estate, and Patrick Gwynne with private residences on the Cator Estate.

But architecture is not always about what is fashionable or cutting-edge. So many enjoyable and liveable buildings are 'modern' in a historical context. Why should the baby be thrown out with the bath water? Can't we have the best of both worlds? So thought the architect Charles Bernard Brown, a strong opponent to modernism when the post-war building architectural world seemed to be so black and white ... Traditional versus new. A strong building conservationist, Brown loathed the new boxy modernism of Eric Lyons. Don't destroy! Rebuild! he advocated, and wisely so, as he sensitively infilled the bombed-out and redundant building sites of Blackheath. The Paragon is his masterwork makeover, its crescent of large houses sensitively divided up into flats. He even bought up the eighteenth-century architectural salvage of the Adelphi Terrace by the famous Adam brothers, which had been destroyed in the 1930s, and reinstated pieces like fireplaces and door frames into his flat conversions.

Ana Sutherland has done an incredible amount of fine research, not only digging in the library, but in speaking with architects, residents and descendants. Oral history is so important, and often overlooked, many researchers rather keeping to a hands-off approach. The post-war generation is still our period, within our living lives and memories. More than simply a dictionary of building entries, Ana weaves a story of relationships. Her work has brought forth the fascinating architectural connections which make Blackheath and Greenwich, with their own population of kindred designers, seem like an autonomous heavenly realm. Consequently, local residents have been granted dispensation to change the last line of William Blake's poem Jerusalem when singing it to the hymn tune of Hubert Parry, as:

> 'I will not cease from mental fight
> Nor shall my sword sleep in my hand
> Til we have built Jerusalem
> In Blackheath and Greenwich's green
> and pleasant land.'

Greenwich South Street 1951, Festival of Britain sign, pointing towards the Paragon, in Blackheath

This is primarily a book about people and their connections; then about buildings, homes and neighbourhoods. It is a historical survey of modern architecture in Blackheath and Greenwich, southeast London, comprising 64 buildings and groups of buildings by 38 different architects, with biographical information about each architect. It is also intended as a guide with associated maps for walks to see the buildings. Featured are works of national and international importance as well as works of local relevance, by architects that influenced a generation and those of more local significance. Unique bespoke homes, social housing, suburban estates, as well as a few larger public buildings, are all covered.

This book discusses buildings and once provocative models of architectural practice, illustrated by photographs, plans and elevations, to inform and inspire current and future generations of local residents, architects and students. More importantly, it aims to celebrate the work of a group of architects who changed the character of this particular part of southeast London in the second half of the twentieth century.

The content is the culmination of a long interest in modern architecture and the city, enriched by half a lifetime of living and raising children in a Span house in Blackheath. Like most surveys, it does not claim to be comprehensive. It encompasses buildings built between 1950 and 2000 and includes those that are considered to be the area's best or most interesting examples – buildings that are inspiring, moving, part of a body of work, innovative and responsive to context, or integral to the landscape. Most are a combination of all the above.

The choice of time frame reflects the work of a specific generation of British architects. Although some of these architects began their career before the Second World War, the majority of those featured here, started to build in the 1950s – notably a few even for the Festival of Britain. Others resumed building after the war. Their work has a distinctive style, which was shaped by post-war scarcity and the rationing of building materials along with the opening up of society to consumerism. Many of these architects contributed to British architecture well into the 1980s and 1990s, either through their own practices or by inspiring the work of others.

The biographies and building entries are not uniform in length or completeness. Where possible, previously under-represented architects have longer entries whilst those with monographs and easily accessible information have more summarised ones. Information about the less well-known architects has been sought from the architects themselves or from surviving family members and colleagues.

Post-nominals are omitted for simplicity. Most of the architects featured here were RIBA members, either as ARIBA (Associate, designation used until 1971), FRIBA (Fellow), HFRIBA (Honorary Fellow) or PPRIBA (Past President) and many were given honours (MBE, OBE, CBE, KBE).

The floorplans and elevation drawings that illustrate the building entries are diagrammatic and reflect the original design, not the current layouts, except where alterations have been made that are consistent with the original design intent. Two of the buildings featured were demolished and one unbuilt, but are included due to their importance and as part of a body of work.

The four women architects featured were part of a pioneering group, a minority in a profession then dominated by men, often remaining in the background. Many more women played crucial roles in the running of the practices listed and were responsible for their output and achievements. Effort was made to credit those as well as usually overlooked assistants and project architects, where possible.

The Introduction sets the scene for the survey that follows. It was written with Heidi Seetzen, who shares the same interests and has also lived and raised children in a Span estate. It provides a loose definition of modern architecture and identifies some of its more formal features. It then considers the character of these two contiguous districts – Greenwich and Blackheath – and how they were shaped by different architectural styles and opposing sentiments. Finally, it sketches out the social and planning context as a framework within which these architects practiced.

Buildings tell us about the times that produced them. Discovering the stories and connections of those who commissioned, designed and lived in these works of architecture have revealed past struggles, successes and failures. They have been a joy to unfold.

Villa Savoye, France, Le Corbusier, 1927

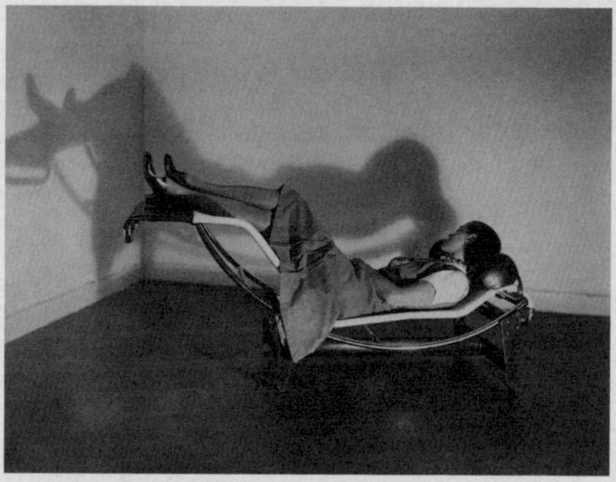

Charlotte Perriand in a chaise longue of her own design, 1929

Villa Mairea, Finland, Alvar Aalto, 1939

Bauhaus Dessau, Germany, Walter Gropius, 1926

Fallingwater, USA, Frank Lloyd Wright, 1937

Farnsworth House, USA, Mies van der Rohe, 1951

> 'To be modern is to find ourselves in an environment that promises us adventure, power, joy, growth, transformation of ourselves and the world – and at the same time threatens to destroy everything we have, everything we know, everything we are.'
> Marshall Berman, *All that is solid melts into air: the experience of modernity*, New York, 1982

What is modern architecture? For the purpose of this survey, modern architecture means buildings created following design principles set out by the pioneers of the modern movement. The movement had its origins in continental Europe and America during the inter-war period; it arrived in the UK in the 1920s and 1930s, then established itself confidently from 1945 onwards.

The idea of 'the modern' goes beyond architecture. Modernism was a true revolution in the arts, humanities, sciences and a whole way of life. Abstract art, cubism, surrealism and psychoanalysis all exemplify the way in which this new spirit revolutionised the world. The American philosopher, Marshall Berman, argued that to be modern is a very distinctive experience; one that is both exhilarating and destructive. Taking his cue, and the title of his book, from Marx's famous quote – *'all that is solid melts into air'* – Modernism or modernity was a break with the past that involved significant social change and upheaval.[1]

During the 1920s and 1930s, established social hierarchies in the UK were declining and the middle class was on the rise. New domestic arrangements were being formed and for many people there was a sense of freedom from more traditional ways of life. Social upheaval continued throughout the post-war years and translated into a desire for new forms of living, which found expression in those works by architects who embraced change.

> 'A motorcar is built with thought for style, that is, finish and elegance, but it is not built to look like a sedan or a stagecoach. To be concerned with style imitations and what the Americans call period design is not only irrational in itself, but it blocks the way to any possibility of true development. If you have your eye on that, you can't see this.'
> W. R. Lethaby, in Foreword to *The Modern House in England* by F. R. S. Yorke, 1920

Significantly, this also coincided with the emergence of new technologies and materials that enabled and inspired new ways of building. Cars, aeroplanes and ocean liners shaped modern life and became the inspiration for designers and architects. Le Corbusier (1887–1965) envisaged the house as 'a machine for living' – functional, stripped of unnecessary decoration, healthy, and beautiful in the same way that working tools, cars and ocean liners are beautiful. The ideas Corbusier explored in his book, *Towards a New Architecture*, first published in England in 1927, were highly influential for architects practising in Britain.[2]

> 'The most important thing to realise is that what drives the modern movement is a spirit of inquiry, it's a process of analysis and not a style. We worked with ideals.'
> Charlotte Perriand (1903–1999)[3]

In nineteenth-century Britain, Arts & Crafts architects had paved the way. They included Philip Webb, Norman Shaw, C. F. A. Voysey, Charles Rennie Mackintosh, Mackay Baillie-Scott and Edwin Lutyens[4], with their eye for detailing, care for craftmanship and sophisticated planning.

The three most influential masters of the first generation of modernists were Frank Lloyd Wright, Le Corbusier and Mies van der Rohe. Alvar Aalto's work in Finland was another key influence, as was the Bauhaus school in Germany, with many of its teachers and students finding refuge and work in Britain during and after the Second World War. This influx of architects from mainland Europe naturally led to an exchange of ideas. The creative catalysis it sparked was also fuelled by tours of Europe undertaken by British architects, including Wells Coates, F.R.S. Yorke, Jane Drew and Maxwell Fry.

The ideas formulated by the younger generation crystallised into a set of design principles. Le Corbusier's 'five points for a new architecture' are a useful reference and summary of the language and formal strategies found in the buildings of the period. These were: the use of pilotis; the free plan; roof gardens; free façade and the use of horizontal windows.

This new modernist language also concerned itself with careful composition and play with geometries, expressing the true nature of constructional materials and exploring new ones, including steel, concrete and glass. There was also a strong emphasis on purity – the rejection of applied decoration and the use of complementary internal fittings and finishes.

Although modern architecture initially saw itself as an absence of style, by the 1960s it had clearly become a style in its own right.

Genesta Road, Plumstead, London, Berthold Lubetkin, 1934

Willow Road, Hampstead, London, Erno Goldfinger, 1939

Nurses' home, St John's Hospital, Lewisham, London
Bertram Carter, 1937 (image from 1981, during demolition)

Selwyn Court, Lee Road, Blackheath, 1937

Greenwich Town Hall, Clifford Culpin, London, 1939

Over time, the pure and rational ideals that informed the early movement (functionalism and utilitarianism) evolved into a more formal style. Observers criticised the lack of picturesque form and humanistic values in modern buildings and some found these new spaces cold and difficult to live in.

Architect and historian, Charles Jenks (1939–2019), declared that Modernism was dead by the early 1970s. New labels came along, such as late-modernism and post-modernism. These embraced vernacular symbols and historic references, balancing technical innovation with traditional forms and materials. Other labels included brutalism with its monolithic use of concrete, and high-tech, where services and structure were exposed, as in Richard Rogers' Lloyds building in London and the Centre Pompidou in Paris.[5]

In Britain, the use of the vernacular was not entirely novel. Modernism had often found more gentle expressions here. This can be seen in the use of tile-hung surfaces, timber board cladding and stonework. There were very few examples of Mies van der Rohe's sleek style; most 'modern' houses and buildings combined modern and vernacular languages. For example, early Span estates included references to vernacular or traditional Kent building styles, with their timber cladding and tile-hung façades; later Span housing in the 1970s and 1980s featured pitched roofs, vertical and unusual shaped windows and the use of more organic site layouts.

> 'At this distance, with modernism being around a century old, it makes no sense to begin with the pure image, the unsullied blueprint, the clear-eyed visionary proposal, because millions of us live in the results.'
> Owen Hatherley, *Modern Buildings in Britain*, A Gazetteer, 2022

Social and Planning Context

> 'For six long years the individual had been subordinated to the nation's efforts to wage war. Now, without any feelings of guilt, individuals could express themselves as artists....'
> Rob Brazil, founder member of the Blackheath Art Society, 1947[6]

Many of the modern buildings in Blackheath and Greenwich were conceived, commissioned and designed against the backdrop of the changing landscape and building environment of post-war Britain.

More than 47,000 houses were destroyed in London during the Second World War. This necessitated wide-scale rebuilding. The ideas underpinning reconstruction and the specific proposals that framed these ideas, dated from the pre-war period. However, in the decades after the war the need for reconstruction was increasingly seized as an opportunity to implement modern principles for redeveloping Britain's inner cities.

Like so many other London neighbourhoods, Blackheath and Greenwich did not survive the war unscathed. In 1940, high-explosive bombs fell on Blackheath Road, killing 11 people and destroying a school in Maze Hill. In 1941, the Paragon and South Row were hit. In 1944, the area suffered more than 50 separate bombings and on 8 March 1945, just eight weeks before the end of the war, a V2 rocket attack resulted in the almost total destruction of Dartmouth Terrace and Wemyss Road, which included the Wesleyan Methodist church, the Blackheath High School, a post office and several shops on Montpelier Vale.[7]

Urban planning became an increasingly important discipline in the post-war years with people eager to discover how the metropolis could be rebuilt. In the midst of war, several influential planning documents had provided the foundation for a long-lasting consensus about the future development of London. Principal amongst these were the 1943 *County of London Plan*[8], the 1944 *Report of the Preliminary Draft Proposals for Post War Reconstruction in the City of London*[9] and the 1944 *Greater London Plan*[10]. All confronted the serious problems posed by the destruction of much of London's metropolitan core, the East End and stretching outwards, the damage to its nineteenth- and twentieth-century suburbs. With New Towns proposed outside a Green Belt, these schemes envisaged major population movements, coherent transport systems, industrial zoning, and a series of long-term environmental measures.[11]

In 1943, the government established the Ministry of Town and Country Planning and the following year passed the Town and Country Planning Act, later known as the 'Blitz and Blight Act', which established how the planning system was to work then and still continues today. Local authorities were given powers to compulsorily acquire bomb-damaged plots and the opportunity to get rid of slums. The Act specified the legal requirement to obtain planning permission. Following the socialist ideals of the period, the right to develop land was no longer a given of ownership. This was also the beginning of the listed buildings planning process.[12]

The Paragon no. 1 and 2 war damage, 1944

Blackheath Village V2 bomb war damage, 1945

Prefabs in St Germans Place, Blackheath 1951

After the second Town and Country Planning Act of 1947, every local authority in Great Britain was obliged to prepare a comprehensive local development plan. The London County Council's (LCC) plan was published in 1952 and included greater protection of open spaces while others were designated for redevelopment and housing. These enactments had great consequences for Blackheath and Greenwich.

Having published its own manifesto for the future in 1951, two years later the Blackheath Society challenged the LCC's proposals for the destruction of old housing stock near Hyde Vale and new housing developments facing the Heath near the Paragon, as well as more general threats to the area's green and pleasant surroundings from new developments, all of which went against its objectives of protecting the Heath, its historic fabric and the size of the village. Nevertheless, the LCC created two large housing estates on the Cator Estate: Pond Road of 1952, and Brooklands Park of 1958 – a modernist development with seven point blocks and a scale that prompted much local resistance.[13]

A number of LCC council estates were also built in Greenwich. These included Royal Hill, with its gentle brick point-blocks and the Maribor Estate, which completes the eighteenth-century crescent of Gloucester Circus.

Even before municipal developments arrived in Blackheath and Greenwich, the need for new housing and a reliable supply of food were already changing the Heath. Allotments were dug along Eliot Place. Nissen huts covered the Heath from All Saints Church to Shooters Hill Road, some of which were squatted. And in 1945, the LCC erected two rows of prefabricated houses opposite St German's Place designed by the avant-garde industrial architecture group ARCON. Other large sites of prefabs were the Hollyhedge Bungalows and Pond Road.

In the early 1940s, the government identified shortages of the materials needed for the rebuilding effort ahead. These shortages led to a dramatic slow-down in the pace of rebuilding, but also influenced the design and size of new houses. In Blackheath and Greenwich, these restrictions were noticeable in the immediate post-war building plans. For example, retaining Victorian foundations and parts of bomb-damaged structures, meant that a construction could be classified as a refurbishment, even if a significant part was rebuilt; otherwise, new domestic buildings were severely restricted in area. Local developer and builder Leslie Bilsby, for one, took advantage of this loophole, purchasing a large bombed-out Victorian villa at the end of Blackheath Park and commissioning the architect Patrick Gwynne to remould it into a chic modern residence. Bilsby later demolished the house and as a director of Span, replaced it with the Parkend estate in 1968. Span housing was shaped by these restrictions in its early years, with brickwork limited to small areas, substituted by wall tiles and painted timber cladding, and the cheaper aluminium sheet roofing chosen over slate or clay tiles.

Blackheath and Greenwich hold an interesting connection to the most important post-war social and architectural event, the 1951 Festival of Britain.[14] This summer celebration, intended to lift the mood of a nation suffering under post-war austerity, had its main site of pavilions and funfairs along the central south bank of the Thames, but it also spread out across the country to other cities and towns. The festival selected for awards, nineteen projects that contributed to the civic or landscape design and Charles Bernard Brown's restoration of the Paragon was a recipient. A blue plaque with the distinctive festival symbol adorns the Paragon's westernmost end, facing the Heath.

Several notable architects who lived in Blackheath and Greenwich and feature in this survey started their careers working in project teams for the Festival of Britain. Peter Moro, who built his now-listed house at 20 Blackheath Park in 1957, was part of the team that designed the Royal Festival Hall, with direct responsibility for its interiors. He recommended his former students from the Regent Street Polytechnic for projects on the South Bank site: Trevor Dannatt designed the Tea Bar in the industrial displays, while Gordon and Ursula Bowyer created the Sport Pavilion. Meanwhile, Patrick Gwynne, who would design three houses in Blackheath for Leslie Bilsby, produced the huge Crescent Restaurant at the Funfair Festival Pleasure Gardens in Battersea Park.

During the early 1960s Blackheath became a popular place to live, work or simply 'hang out' for musicians and artists. Celebrities who settled in the area included the blues musician John Mayall, Manfred Lubowitz from the band Manfred Mann, the journalist and critic Janet Street Porter and her husband Tim, an architectural photographer. Looking back on this period, the architect Walter Greaves' son, Henry, commented that: 'It's difficult to describe the vibe of living in Blackheath at that exciting time, as I had nothing else to compare it with, so it seemed totally normal to me – however, in retrospect, I realised that my parents were very progressive compared to my friends' parents and I was surrounded by modernism and fascinating people.[15]

1967 saw the introduction of the Conservation Areas Policy by the Civic Amenities Act. This changed the way in which developers could operate in order to safeguard whole areas of interest. In 1968, the Blackheath Conservation Area was designated by Greenwich and Lewisham councils as London's first conservation area.

The signs of drastic change did not only come from the new wave of modern buildings. A major motorway, 'Ringway 1', with a tunnel and flyover was planned to cut across and under Blackheath. Widespread outrage led to protests in 1962 and again in 1972, when the plans were finally halted. One of the key opponents to the proposals was MP James Callaghan, who then lived at 17 Montpelier Row and later went on to be Labour Prime Minister from 1976 to 1979. Across the Heath, the Greenwich Society (founded in the late 1950s) confronted the same dangers – plans for flyovers, cut-and-cover tunnels, the straightening and widening of historic streets. Thankfully, all large infrastructure plans were eventually abandoned.[16]

One major development, The Ferrier Estate, was built in neighbouring Kidbrooke between 1968 and 1972. Over many years 'The Ferrier' was poorly maintained, suffered from high levels of crime and acquired a bad reputation, although it was also marked by a strong sense of community and place. It was demolished between 2009 and 2012, as part of the Kidbrooke Vision – a development by Berkeley Homes.

In 1979, Margaret Thatcher's Conservative government succeeded James Callaghan's and the following year the Housing Act 1980 introduced the 'right-to-buy' policy, which together with the political drive to stop social housing programmes and wind down the new towns programmes, led to radical changes in the housing market. Thatcher's government reversed the achievements of previous decades during which the state had been both client and employer, choosing instead to promote private enterprise.

The final two decades of the twentieth century saw a slower pace of development in Blackheath, mainly due to the reduction of available sites. New homes were built on just a few mews streets, such as Langton Way and Heath Lane.

In neighbouring Kidbrooke and in Greenwich, large-scale new development schemes were planned and have now been completed. These included Kidbrooke Vision already mentioned and several higher-density masterplans and regenerations on the Deptford riverfront and Greenwich Peninsula, all of which were led by private enterprise.

At the domestic scale, the mid-century modern aesthetic and open-plan living have become increasingly fashionable – united by an interest in design and nostalgia for the supposedly plain and simple life of the 1950s. However, preservation of modern buildings presents many challenges – most of them concerning how to retrofit and improve insulation while also introducing local energy production efficiently. The poor construction of some of the post-war buildings is evident in their shallow foundations, extensive single glazing, exposed concrete structure, flat roofs, internal drainage, asbestos and more. Despite these challenges, there is now a drive to upgrade and renovate in order to preserve them for the future.

The Character of the Area

There are no exact geographical boundaries to this study. Instead, it focuses on three distinct areas – the Cator Estate, around the Heath, and Greenwich, the park and its surrounds.

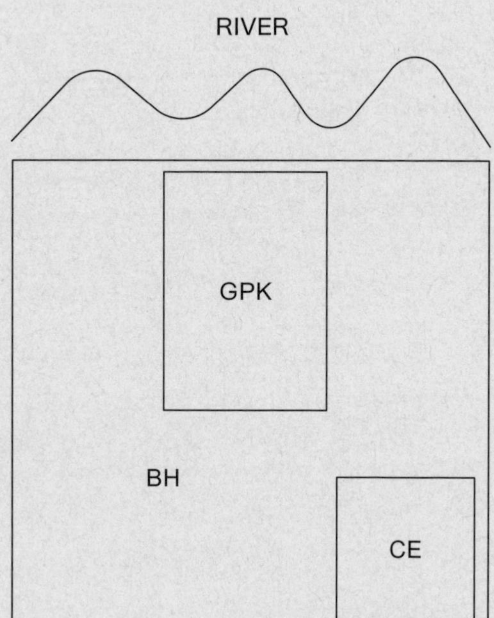

GPK – Greenwich Park
BH – Blackheath
CE – Cator Estate

The Cator Estate

> 'The original leafy layout has received another dimension, absent from almost everywhere else in London: the exhilaration of new and old together when both are good.'
> Ian Nairn, *Nairn's London*, 1966[17]

The Cator Estate is named after the timber merchant John Cator (1728–1806). He purchased the estate and Wricklemarsh House, a large mansion designed by the architect John James and built in 1723 for Gregory Page. Cator demolished the house around 1800. His primary residence was Beckenham Place; he initially used the Wricklemarsh estate mainly for its agricultural rental income but soon started to lease land for construction. His biggest project was with architect Michael Searles to create Blackheath's famous crescent The Paragon, completed in 1805. His other major legacy was the estate's tree-lined street pattern – a network of wide boulevards framed by grand houses, with Blackheath Park as its main artery.[18]

Today, the Cator Estate has a unique, leafy, park-like, almost country atmosphere. No commercial enterprises are allowed, the roads are not adopted and there is no public transport within its boundaries. Black cabs, coaches or vans are prevented from parking overnight and house sales are discreetly conducted without the visual intrusion of advertising boards. Its sense of separateness is further reinforced by the white gates at its main access points on Blackheath Park, Morden Road, Manor Way and Pond Road.

After the Second World War, the Cator Estate was ripe for residential development, having pockets of both agricultural land and war-damaged plots. These gave rise to a number of one-off houses as well as larger estates of terraces and flats. There are two predominant layouts: those that clearly follow the historic street frontage, and those that are more inward-looking, hiding away in former nursery gardens, orchards, allotments or mews.

Around the Heath

> 'There is a forgivable vagueness about demarcation, and people whose houses share mutual fringes are apt to temporise when asked where they live. They may well say, "Oh, in Greenwich – but up on the Heath" or else, "We are in Blackheath – over on the Greenwich side."'
> Felix Barker, in *Greenwich and Blackheath Past*, 1993[19]

The Heath is an open expanse of land that extends gently downwards through Greenwich Park, north towards the River Thames, with its southern slopes running down to the River Quaggy, on the Lee borders. Blackheath Village sits in a natural 'deep', or hollow, marked by a busy train station, rows of shops, bakeries, restaurants and estate agencies, as well as the Blackheath Halls and Conservatoire. Other 'deeps' to the north and east are the result of gravel mining in the early eighteenth century.[20]

On the southeastern edge of the Heath stands Morden College, with its 1695 magnificent quadrangle, chapel, library and associated newer buildings.[21] To the North lie the walls of Greenwich Park and Ranger's House.

The grassy heath, punctuated by only a few groups of trees, is a space of great natural value, an open ground for all sorts of activities: football matches, cycling, circuses and fairs, kite flying, picnics, dog walking, running, sunbathing and al fresco sex. There are four ponds, rich in wildlife, two of them are overlooked by pubs – The Princess of Wales and The Hare and Billet. The largest pond on South Row was used for model boating until recently but is now reserved for aquatic birds and flora.

Bisected by the A2, the old Roman route to Canterbury and the Kent coast, the Heath has long been a popular gathering place. Danes camped on its flat expanse in the 11th century and many royal ceremonies, pageants and protests have taken place here, as street names such as Wat Tyler Road still remind us. It was also an historically important place for many sports, most notably for the introduction of golf into England by James I in 1608. The Heath served as a gun base during the Second World War and currently provides the starting point for the London Marathon and a site for music festivals.[22]

The Heath and the village are both within the London Boroughs of Greenwich and Lewisham. The buildings covered in this survey also lie within two conservation areas – Blackheath and Blackheath Park, and the Maritime Greenwich World Heritage site buffer zone.

Greenwich, the Park and Its Surrounds

> 'So, I went to Greenwich and I was absolutely charmed by it. I thought, what a wonderful place that was. It had everything. And there was Blackheath village, there was Greenwich, there was the [Morden] College, there was the park, there was history, there was sort of social cohesion, beautiful buildings.'
> Peter Moro, 1996[23]

South Row from Pond Road, by Eric Lyons and Span, completed 1963

Pond Road Estate, by Albert Richardson for the LCC, completed 1954

Greenwich Park is a royal enclosure, the once-private park for the now long gone Greenwich Palace, a power-house of the Tudor dynasty where Henry VIII was born, where he married Anne Bolyen and where his children, Queen Mary I and Queen Elizabeth I were born. The park was walled by James I and Charles II built its first royal observatory in 1676, which has been in use ever since and where the prime meridian was established in 1884.

Maze Hill to the east and Crooms Hill to the west form the park's longitudinal boundaries. Both are lined with exquisite Georgian terraces and later buildings. Replacing the earlier palace, are three major landmarks – The Queen's House, the National Maritime Museum and the former Royal Hospital for Seamen, subsequently the Old Royal Naval College (now occupied by the University of Greenwich and Trinity Laban Conservatoire of Music and Dance).[24]

The Queen's House, a Palladian villa by Inigo Jones, was completed for Queen Henrietta Maria around 1635. The former hospital is a grand structure, which opened in 1705, with parts designed by Christopher Wren, Nicholas Hawksmoor and Thomas Ripley. The Maritime Museum was opened in 1937 in one of the former hospital buildings.

Other notable buildings outside the park walls are St Alfege Church (1714) in Greenwich town centre, by Nicholas Hawksmoor, Vanbrugh Castle at the top of Maze Hill (1719) by John Vanbrugh, and the eighteenth-century Ranger's House backing onto the park at the top of Crooms Hill.

In 1939, Greenwich gained another significant building – the Town Hall at the foot of Royal Hill, designed by Clifford Culpin (1904–1988), with its carefully detailed brickwork and square landmark tower. It shows the influence of 1930s Dutch modernism, especially Hilversum Town Hall by Willem Dudok.

Since the 1980s, the views from Greenwich and Blackheath have changed dramatically. First with the development of the Docklands to the west and the London City Airport (open in 1987) to the east, then the Isle of Dogs to the north, the continuous rise of Canary Wharf, and more recently the North Greenwich Dome and Peninsula regeneration to the east. New transport connections provided by the Docklands Light Railway were completed in 1987. Maritime Greenwich became a UNESCO World Heritage Site in 1997.

Opposing Forces

Today, the architecture around the Cator Estate, the Heath and Greenwich Park is a rich mixture of different periods and styles. Modern buildings have been integrated and are valued as a group of architectural treasures that contribute to the area's unique appeal. This has not always been the case, but is the result of a number of complementary and opposing forces – different stylistic sensibilities that embraced either revivalism or modernism, the conversion of older buildings and new approaches to conservation and restoration.

Four early modern buildings of note are Selwyn Court, The Lawns, St John's Hospital Nurses' Home and Greenwich Town Hall. Selwyn Court, the Art Deco block of flats with shops at ground level, at the corner of Lee Road and Lee Terrace, was built on the site of the gothic revival Blackheath Proprietary School for Boys (1831–1907). The Lawns are two Art Deco blocks of flats designed by Messrs Joseph (the architects for the Shell Mex House, 80 Strand, 1932). St John's Hospital Nurses' Home at the top of Lewisham Hill by Bertram Carter (1896–1986) was completed in 1938 but unfortunately demolished in the late 1980s. The fourth building is the former Greenwich Town Hall.

In 1937, the Blackheath Society was formed in response to the construction of Selwyn Court. The Greenwich Society was formed in the late 1950s to oppose proposed roadways schemes that threatened historic street patterns.[25] The creation of the Societies was indicative of residents' strongly held appreciation of the area's historical architecture. This was also reflected in the very few examples of pre-war modern architecture around Blackheath and Greenwich.

The predominant styles were revivalist. Neo-Tudor was the domestic style of Britain and can be found throughout Blackheath and Greenwich. Neo-Georgian was also particularly popular for both private and public buildings during the first half of the twentieth-century, perhaps the finest example being John Roan School (1928) in Maze Hill by Percy B. Dannatt and Banister Fletcher.[26] Even after the Second World War the Neo-Georgian style was seen as an appropriate and acceptable style for the area. Chesterfield Gardens on Wellington Grove, at the top of Crooms Hill, is another local Neo-Georgian scheme, built in the late-1940s for the Beaver Housing Society. It comprises a series of flats and maisonettes arranged around a communal lawn.

The large Pond Road housing estate by Albert Richardson (1880–1964) was designed

Looking north over Blackheath Village, the Heath and Greenwich Park to the towers of Canary Wharf

in a Georgian manner for the LCC, and includes Rycuff Square and Fulthorp Road, completed in 1954. Arranged in a series of squares and lawns, together with three blocks that form a subtle curve, these mirror, in plan, the nearby Paragon's crescent form, with a nod to the Woolwich Barracks. However, the Pond Road estate also explores modern concepts of layout, including deck access and maisonettes.

There is a striking stylistic contrast between the Pond Road estate and neighbouring South Row built only nine years later by Span with an exposed concrete structure, flat roofs and large floor-to-ceiling windows. Similarly, at the top of Maze Hill, the brick and columned Parkside, built in 1957 contrasts with the modern concrete blocks of Vanbrugh Park Estate completed in 1963 by Chamberlin, Powell & Bon, the architects of the Barbican Estate.

Blackheath's most noted conservation architect and revivalist was Charles Bernard Brown (1910–1990), who was responsible for the repair and conversion of the bombed grand houses of The Paragon into flats (a ten-year project 1947–1957)[27], and adjacent Colonnade House and Paragon House. He even purchased architectural salvage from demolished Adelphi Terrace near Charing Cross, built by the Adam brothers in 1768. As a result, the entrance to Paragon House in Pond Road features an ornate Adam door surround, while many of Brown's flats are adorned with neo-classical chimneypieces. A staunch Georgian, he also graced Blackheath with numerous brick residences, including rows of substantial houses on Parkgate as well as fine conversions of villas into flats, including 133 Blackheath Park, and conversions of stables and coach houses into dwellings, such as 55 Blackheath Park and Cator Manor on South Row.[28]

Modernists often praised Georgian architecture for its pure geometry and lack of ornament, but they generally considered Neo-Georgian buildings, and other historical revival styles, to be pastiches and unoriginal.[29] Architects in the revivalist styles and those in the modern camp often had to compete against each other for the same sites. Modernists often lost out in the face of opposition from the general public, government and local amenity groups. However, in Blackheath and Greenwich there were plenty of occasions when modern developments were successful, as this book demonstrates.

By the 1980s modernism was firmly entrenched. The same period also saw the arrival of post-modernism, which then incorporated elements of classical architecture, a good example being 6 Paragon Place with a bullseye window in a pediment. Restoration and conservation of the older buildings in the area also became a priority with stronger heritage legislation and architects now receiving appropriate training.

Local historian and author Neil Rhind[30] (1937–2024) has made a significant contribution to the conservation movement in Blackheath and Greenwich. He was the author of many books, articles and reports on the two areas, and was a leading member of the Greenwich Historical Society, The Blackheath Society and Blackheath Preservation Trust. The Trust, which was active from 1938 to 2016, purchased and restored more than 30 heritage buildings during this period. Key regeneration projects were the fifteenth-century Poplar Cottage, 80 Charlton Road, SE3 (Civic Trust Award), the late-seventeenth century Boone's Chapel, Lee High Road (Grade I listed), the eccentric Vanbrugh Castle (Grade I listed), by Gordon and Ursula Bowyer, and the Victorian Blackheath Halls.[31]

For many years Neil Macfadyen (1927–2017) was the principal consultant architect for the Blackheath Preservation Trust. He worked on the restoration of Eastnor House in Lloyds Place (Civic Trust Award), the bomb-damaged Blackheath Literary Institute in Station Yard (now Martin House), Blackheath railway station and behind it, Chapman House. New buildings in the eighteenth-century manner included 1 Lloyds Place and Eastnor Garden House, in Tranquil Vale.

From 1995 onwards, a major conservation and regeneration project repurposed the grand Baroque complex of the Old Royal Naval College. Threatened by sale to private developers under the Conservative government, strong local, heritage and public opinion through 'political, ideological and financial manoeuvres'[32] secured the buildings for the use of Greenwich University and Trinity Laban Conservatoire of Music and Dance. The sensitive conservation and restoration of the Wren, Hawksmoor and Ripley buildings, together with infill structures by architect Trevor Dannatt and his partner David Johnson, has brought a youthful, dynamic and inclusive character to Greenwich.

> 'The impending chaos of our urban skylines and the lack of any vision for what our cities might become is in contrast to a brief mid-century era when there was a vision and, even if it might have ultimately been wrong, it was at least intended for us, to make life better.'
> Edwin Heathcote[33]

Walking Through the City

Much of the research for this survey was carried out by walking or cycling through Blackheath and Greenwich; experiencing architecture from the perspective of an urban pedestrian is very much at the heart of the project. The cultural theorist and urban observer, Walter Benjamin, advocated becoming 'lost in the city' in order to unlock its secrets.[34] Similarly, the French philosopher, Michel de Certeau, observed that in walking through the city we often create our own spatial stories.[35]

Cities are always both real and imagined: created in time by different individuals and teeming with the experiences and lives of all its inhabitants. Walking through the streets of a city we observe how past visionaries imagined we should, or could live, and also how those ideas have embedded into everyday life, more or less successfully. Modern buildings were designed and built with a particular idea of social and domestic life in mind – a new way of living and new forms of community. These built visions were not always appreciated at the time. Their edges have now been softened, as buildings have settled into the landscape, became more familiar to us, and some of these values have been lost while others had become part of our contemporary world.

‘The most striking concentration is the 97 (architects) at Blackheath, a postal district over-architected to the tune of 38 to the square mile (14.7 per square kilometre). Perhaps the most useful way to visualise this is to imagine these 97 architects spread uniformly as possible in a triangle pattern over SE3, at a mean spacing of one every 307 yards (208 metres). One rather promising line of investigation suggests that to lure and entrap architects you need either Span or Georgian, or best of all, a mixture of the two, as at Blackheath.’

Thomas Peatfield (ed.), ‘Architects Galore’ in *SLSA newsletter* (South London Society of Architects – a branch of the London region of the RIBA), 1 May 1973

Distribution of Members of the SLSA by postal districts, February 1973, by Roy Bond, membership secretary

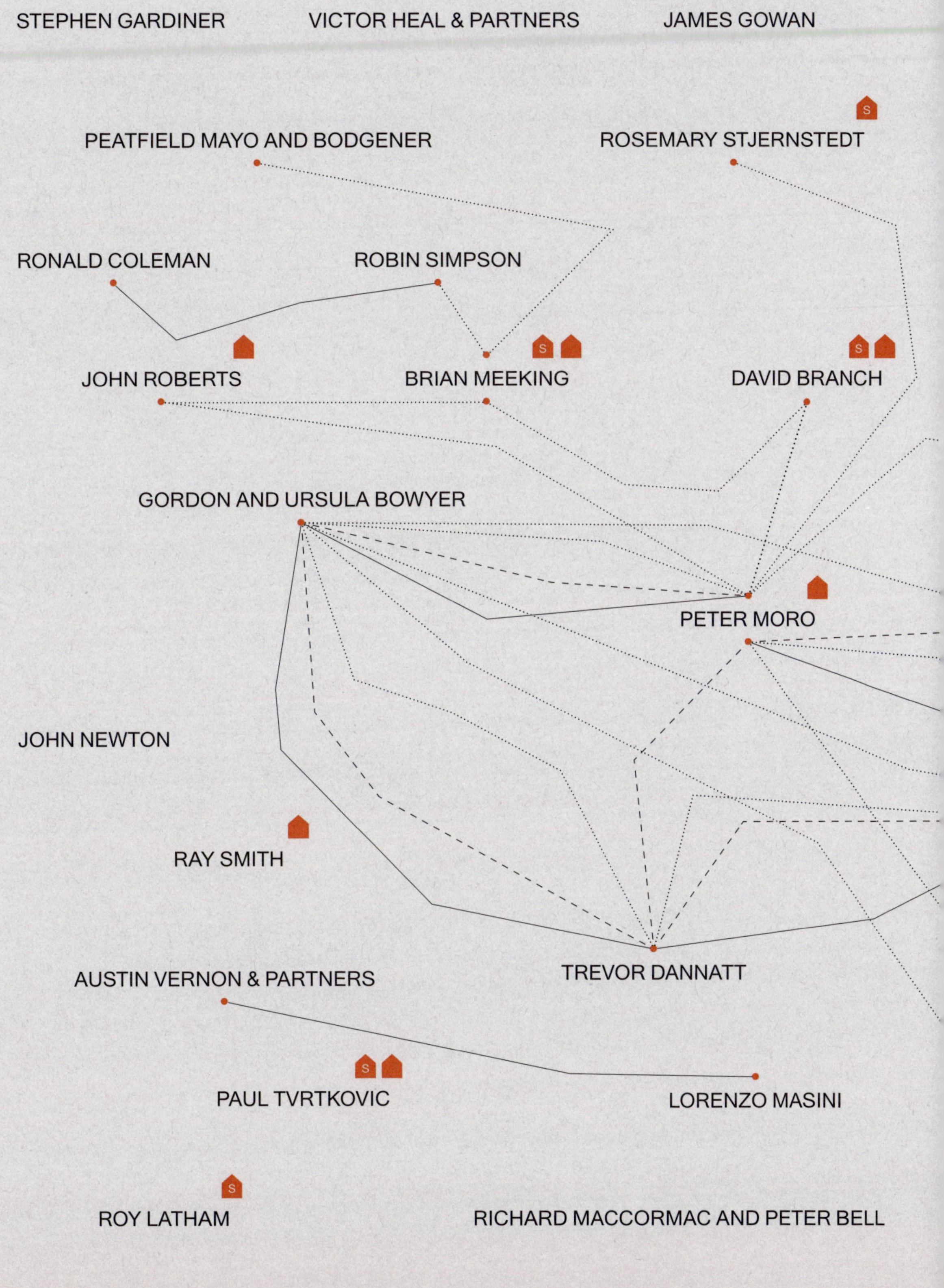
STEPHEN GARDINER
VICTOR HEAL & PARTNERS
JAMES GOWAN
S
PEATFIELD MAYO AND BODGENER
ROSEMARY STJERNSTEDT
RONALD COLEMAN
ROBIN SIMPSON
S
S
JOHN ROBERTS
BRIAN MEEKING
DAVID BRANCH
GORDON AND URSULA BOWYER
PETER MORO
JOHN NEWTON
RAY SMITH
TREVOR DANNATT
AUSTIN VERNON & PARTNERS
S
PAUL TVRTKOVIC
LORENZO MASINI
S
ROY LATHAM
RICHARD MACCORMAC AND PETER BELL
Work
Student / Teacher
Friends

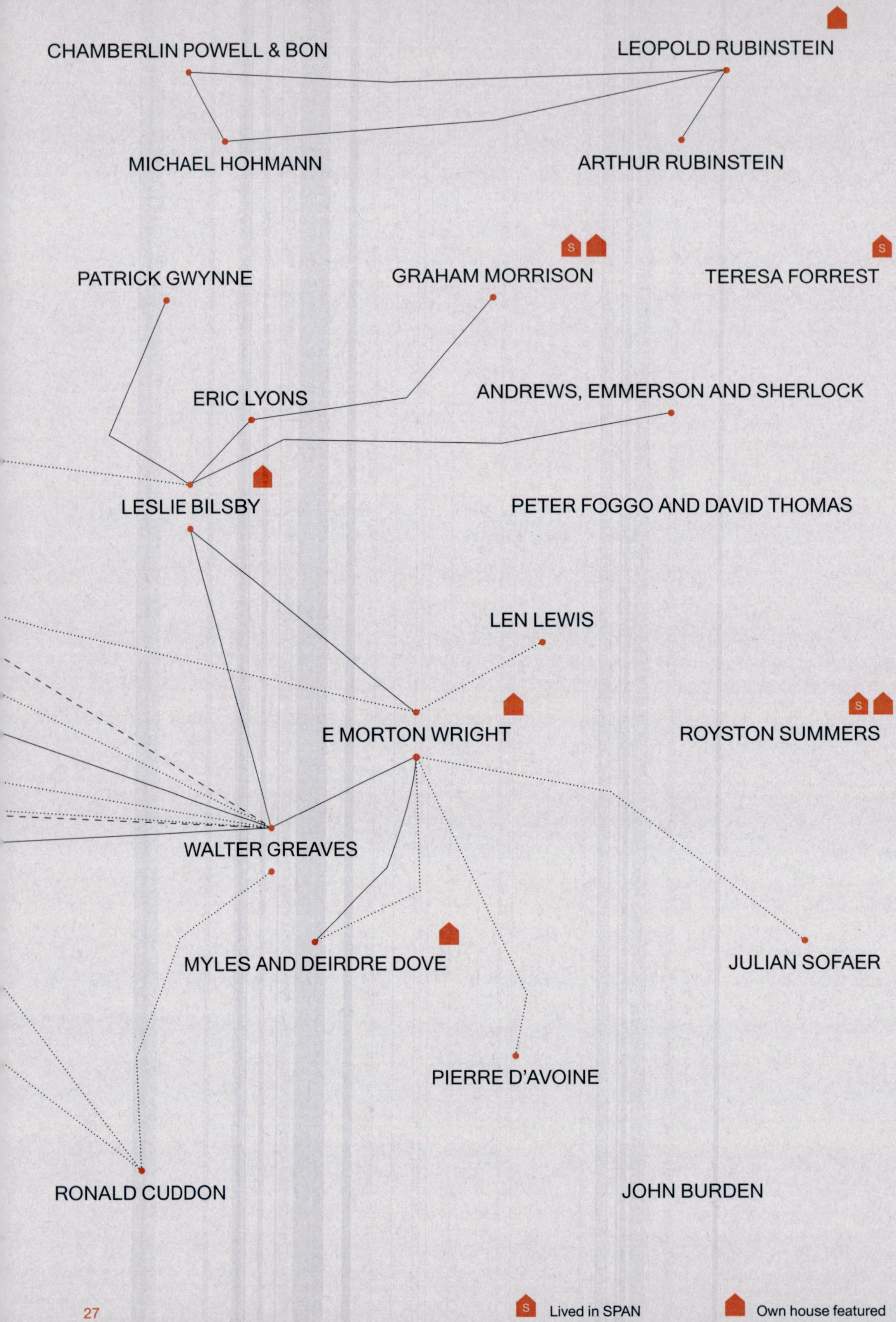
CHAMBERLIN POWELL & BON
LEOPOLD RUBINSTEIN
MICHAEL HOHMANN
ARTHUR RUBINSTEIN
PATRICK GWYNNE
GRAHAM MORRISON
TERESA FORREST
ERIC LYONS
ANDREWS, EMMERSON AND SHERLOCK
LESLIE BILSBY
PETER FOGGO AND DAVID THOMAS
LEN LEWIS
E MORTON WRIGHT
ROYSTON SUMMERS
WALTER GREAVES
MYLES AND DEIRDRE DOVE
JULIAN SOFAER
PIERRE D'AVOINE
RONALD CUDDON
JOHN BURDEN
S
Lived in SPAN
Own house featured

ARCHITECTS AND PROJECTS

01	Allies and Morrison	Oak Yard, The Keep
02	Andrews, Emmerson & Sherlock	6–16 Morden Road and 14–18 Morden Road Mews
03		Rangers Square
04	Arthur Rubinstein	85–104 Vanbrugh Park
05	Austin Vernon & Partners	Church Army Chapel
06	Brian Meeking	66 Greenwich Park Street
07		Greenwich Theatre, Crooms Hill
08		6 Paragon Place
09	Chamberlin, Powell & Bon	Vanbrugh Park Estate
10	David Branch	8 Meadowbank
11	E Morton Wright	24 and 26 Morden Road Mews
12		Christ Church Forum, East Greenwich
13	Eric Lyons (Leslie Bilsby and Span)	The Priory, Priory Park and Park Row
14		Corner Green and 24–33 Corner Green
15		The Keep
16		Spangate
17		Hallgate, The Hall, Foxes Dale and Brooklands Park
18		The Plantation and Parkend
19		South Row
20		The Lane and Streetfield Mews
21		Holm Walk
22	Gordon and Ursula Bowyer	17 and 17a Montpelier Row
23		2 Langton Way
24		Lyndale Close
25	James Gowan	Trafalgar Road Housing
26	John Burden	St Michael and All Angels Church Hall
27	John Newton	10 and 11 Park Row
28	John Roberts	4–7 Rocque Lane
29	Julian Sofaer	Meridian West, Diamond Terrace
30	LCC, Rosemary Stjernstedt	Brooklands Park Estate
31	Len Lewis	85 Brooklands Park
32	Leo Rubinstein and Michael Hohmann	11 Westgrove Lane
33	Lorenzo Masini	5a–5e St Germans Place
34	Myles and Deirdre Dove	57a Blackheath Park
35		129 Maze Hill
36	Patrick Gwynne	115 Blackheath Park
37		House in Blackheath, unbuilt project
38		10 Blackheath Park
39		22 Parkgate
40	Paul Tvrtkovic	14 Baizdon Road
41	Peatfield, Mayo and Bodgener	81–88 Ashburnham Grove
42	Peter Foggo and David Thomas	31 Langton Way
43	Peter Moro	20 Blackheath Park
44	Pierre d'Avoine	Chatfield House, 21 Westgrove Lane
45	Ray Smith	21 Park Vista
46		37 Park Vista
47	Richard MacCormac and Peter Bell	4 and 4a Langton Way
48	Robin Simpson	35a Hyde Vale
49	Ronald Coleman	28 and 30 Heathway
50	Ronald Cuddon	47a Blackheath Park
51	Roy Latham	40 Heath Lane
52	Royston Summers	North Several, Orchard Drive
53	Stephen Gardiner	16 Baizdon Road
54	Teresa Forrest	17 Langton Way
55	Trevor Dannatt	Blackheath Congregational Church
56		Blackheath Quaker Meeting House
57		Greenwich Building Society
58		8 Lloyds Place
59	Victor Heal and Partners	Sweyn Place
60	Walter Greaves	11a Morden Road Mews
61		64 Corner Green
62		9 and 11 Manor Way
63		21 Morden Road
64		1–3 Rocque Lane

Graham Morrison (b.1951) studied architecture during the 1970s under Leslie Martin at the University of Cambridge and as the winner of the Brancusi Prize travelled to Finland to study the work of Alvar Aalto. While a student he heard of Eric Lyons and Ivor Cunningham of Span and subsequently took up his first job in their office in East Moseley, southwest London.[36]

In the early 1980s he settled with his family in The Plantation, one of the Span estates in Blackheath. Later, he built his own home, Oak Yard, between Corner Green and The Keep. Working with Eric Lyons and Ivor Cunningham, Morrison learned the value of systematic repetition in housing and the mutual benefits of a well-designed landscape as a setting for buildings.

Morrison met Bob Allies while they were both working for Martin Richardson on housing projects in Milton Keynes. Allies, who had trained at the University of Edinburgh, subsequently worked for Michael Brawne and Michael Glickman, before spending a year in Rome after winning a Rome Scholarship in Architecture in 1981.

Together they founded Allies and Morrison in 1984. The practice is now one of the largest architectural firms in the UK and has won numerous awards, including RIBA National Awards, Civic Trust Awards, and the 2015 AJ120 Practice of the Year award. The practice's portfolio is very broad, ranging from detailed furniture design to city masterplans, including the redevelopment of King's Cross and the London 2012 Olympic Park masterplan and legacy.

Allies and Morrison have successfully combined modern architectural design with a respect for heritage since their very first commission at The Mound, Edinburgh. Their restoration of the Grade I listed Royal Festival Hall was shortlisted for the Stirling Prize in 2008.[37]

Local projects	Oak Yard, The Keep	1992
	Queen's House restoration, Greenwich Park	2002
	Planetarium Building, Royal Observatory, Greenwich Park	2007
Other London projects, selection	Allies and Morrison studios, Southwark Street	2004
	Royal Festival Hall restoration, South Bank	2008
	Highbury Square, Islington	2010

Bob Allies and Graham Morrison

01	Project	Oak Yard, The Keep
	Architect	Allies and Morrison
	Completed	1992
	Client	Architect's own house

Oak Yard sits on a challenging site adjacent to the railway tunnel running between Blackheath and Kidbrooke.

As is the case with many of Allies and Morrison's buildings, it explores the language of traditional architectural elements, materials, and their layering – including a pitched roof, brick walls, gable end and projecting bays – but recast in a modern way.[38] Three primary elements – a slate roof, a solid brick enclosure and a projecting white rendered porch – refer to the late Georgian and early Victorian pedimented villas in Blackheath, but the roof floats freely over the gable ends, which exposes it as a pair of thin plates connected to a metal ridge pole.

The formal or regular elevation is to the garden and the informal elevation is to the front, with a picturesque composition of window shapes. In contrast to the traditional arrangement, the entrance is placed on the informal façade of the 'villa' whilst the 'pedimented' gable forms the side wall.

In 2007, a successive owner asked Allies and Morrison to convert the sauna and add a single storey garden room, an entrance canopy and a screen.

In an interview with the *RIBA Journal* in 2021, Graham Morrison, reflecting on his shared experiences with Bob Allies, said: 'I feel we were students at a perfect time. There was a questioning of the orthodoxy of modernism that both of us were trained in. We didn't really indulge in post-modernism, but we felt free to talk about history as being interesting and helpful, without worrying whether Le Corbusier would have approved. It gave us a very strong grounding.'[39]

 Oak Yard projecting bay and gable end from Corner Green

1992

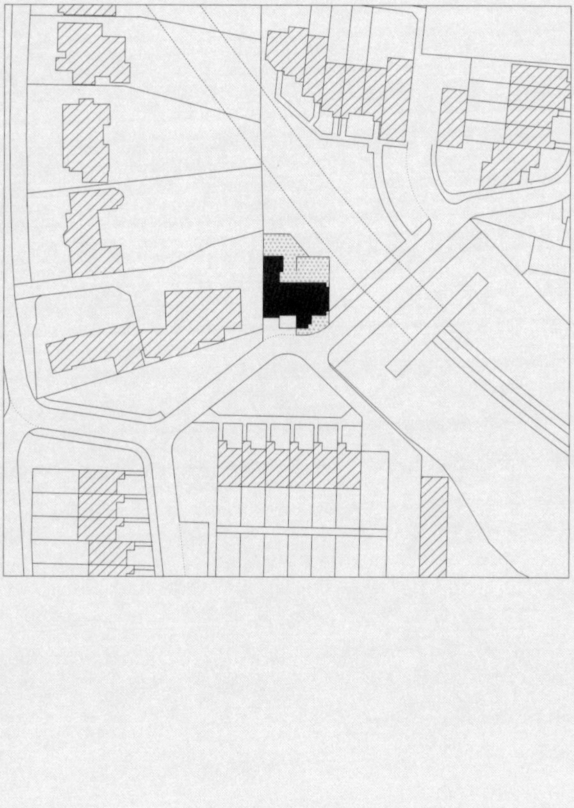

Site plan 1:2000 50m

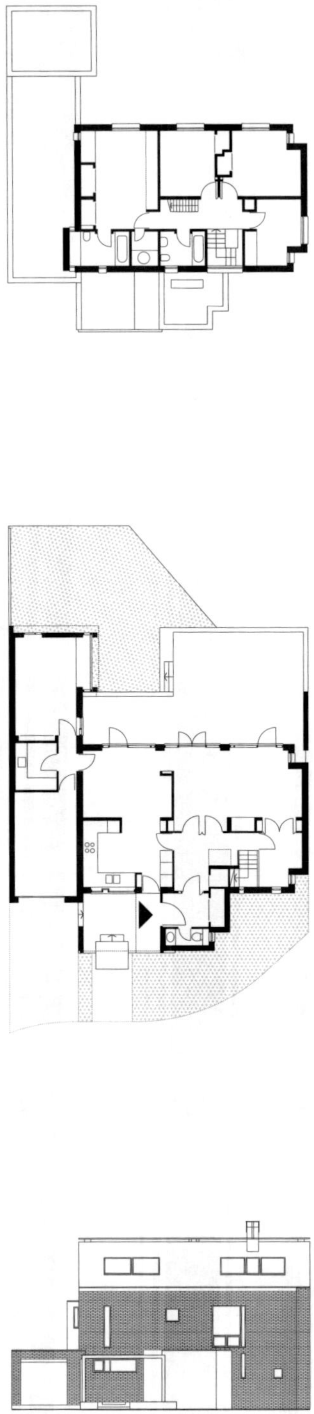

Top to bottom: first and ground floor plans; front elevation

10m

Andrews, Emmerson & Sherlock[40] completed a project for Span in Blackheath in 1964: 'Mordenrow' in Morden Road Mews and Morden Road; and for local developer Leslie Bilsby, Buckley House, a development of 10 flats in Kensington, in 1965.

The practice originated in the 1950s and comprised the architects Harley Sherlock, Malcolm Andrews, Alan Emmerson, Julian Keable and Harry Spencer, who had all met while studying at the Architectural Association. Sharing cooperative principles, they purchased two houses in Canonbury, Highbury, with financial support from the Government's war-damage repairs fund, which they connected, converted and refurbished for communal living and their office. To start with 'one person was fully employed at home while the other four obtained salaried jobs. At the end of each week, we put aside enough money to cover mortgage repayments and utilities, and we shared out the rest from a large cashbox labelled Income Pool'.[41]

During the practice's early days, inspired by the Span business model, the partners generated work opportunities by setting up companies (for example, Kemlock Developments) and housing societies (including Dean Housing Society Ltd) to buy and develop sites.

During the 1960s and 1970s, the practice focused on social housing, including projects for the LCC, GLC and London Borough of Islington. This work successfully demonstrated that designs inspired by the much-loved Georgian terraces and squares in central London could accommodate high densities just as well as tower block schemes. During this period, the practice operated mainly as Andrews Sherlock & Partners.

One of the practice's key partners was Harley Sherlock (1927–2014), an enthusiastic champion of city living. He published two books: *Cities are Good for Us* (1991) and *An Architect in Islington* (2006). Sherlock cared passionately about Britain's built environment and was particularly concerned that cars were invading and choking its towns and cities. He campaigned for increased investment in public transport and for more punitive measures to discourage car use.[42]

Local projects	Morden Road Mews and Morden Road	1964
	Quaggy Walk, Manor Way	1964
	Rangers Square, Greenwich	1970
	Armada Street, Deptford	
Other London projects	St Olave's Court, Bayswater	1961
	Tibbet's Close, Wimbledon	
	North Lodge Close, Putney	1962
	Inglemere Road, Forest Hill	
	Jackson's Lane, Highgate	1962
	Turpin's Green, Maidenhead	
	Popham Street, Islington	1968
	Blenheim Court, Holloway	
	The John Barnes Library, Islington	1971

Alan Emmerson and Harley Sherlock in their office at 18 Canonbury Park North, 1950s

02	Project	6–16 Morden Road and 14–18 Morden Road Mews
	Architect	Andrews, Emmerson & Sherlock
	Completed	1964
	Client	Span

The houses on Morden Road form a modern terraced block in a street of traditional large villas. Set back from Morden Road itself and accessed by a descending approach, the block comprises six houses of three storeys each, with integrated garages and entrances at the lower ground floor level. The gardens are accessed from a balcony and stairs at first floor level over a sunken patio.

The site connects with Morden Road Mews at the rear, forming another terrace of five, two-storey houses and an associated garage block.[43] While addressing the context and street frontage lines, the scheme differs from the Span estates designed by Eric Lyons in its lack of communal landscaped gardens and use of access ramps for the integrated garages. In the centre of the site, the garages forecourt has an underused strip of lawn, which was planned to be developed later as either further garages or studios.

Harley Sherlock wrote that his practice was appointed, 'possibly because Eric Lyons was over-committed not just in terms of architecture per se, but also on account of his increasing work at the RIBA.'[44] He also commented that the taller block of houses in Morden Road is 'fairly conventional except for their unusually dark bricks'. These bricks have now weathered to a softer grey. A winding wooden open-tread staircase links all floors.

The two-storey terrace, on Morden Road Mews, has an interesting layout with the dining rooms to the front, living rooms facing the rear garden, with the kitchens and similar open-tread staircases in the middle of the plan.

39 The three-storey terrace from Morden Road

Site plan

1:2500 50m

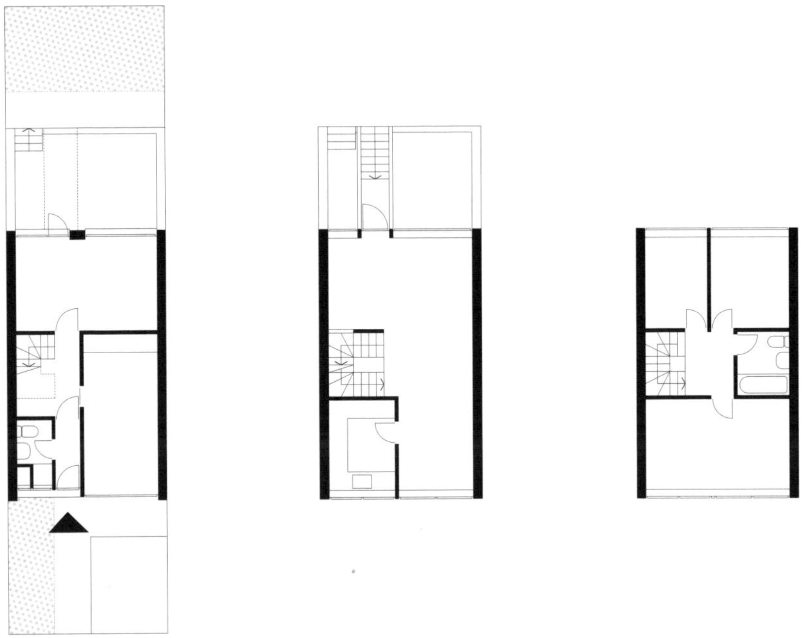

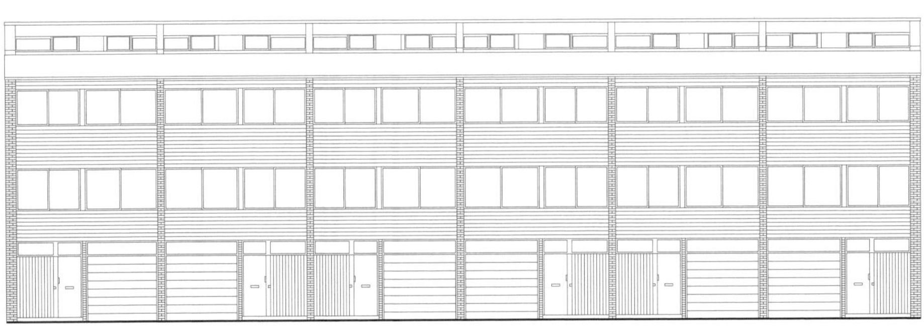

Above, left to right: ground, first and second floor plans
Below: Morden Road terrace elevation

10m

03

Project	Rangers Square
Architect	Andrews, Emmerson & Sherlock
Completed	1970
Client	Span
Awards	Civic Trust Award Commendation

A scheme of 33 cheerful and compact two-bedroom houses, arranged along three terraces around a central green. The land is a challenging steeply sloping site located off Hyde Vale, in Greenwich. The garages are segregated and accessed from a sunken entrance forecourt. The articulated elevations, pitched roofs, and entrance doors to these compact houses (57 square metres) are meticulously designed.

The site layout promotes social interaction and current residents enjoy social gatherings, including live music, on the large open green – a good place to watch the sun set, with uninterrupted views to Canary Wharf and the City.

The houses, which are only 3.2 metres wide, follow a layout that the practice had used before in its Putney North Lodge Close development. This minimum-frontage house type was originally devised in order to build to the required densities but avoid the use of high-rise blocks.[45]

The Civic Trust Award jury commented that, 'these houses were built on land for which planning permission had been granted for a six-storey block of flats; the change to a smaller scale is in itself a positive contribution to the character of the area.'

 The east block seen from the entrance court

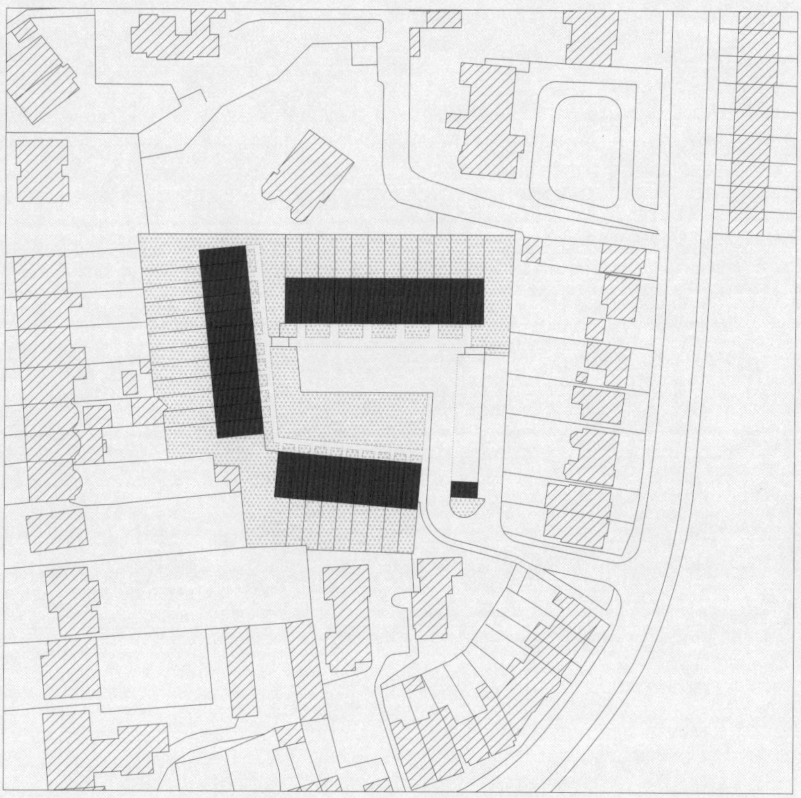

Site plan 1:2000 50m

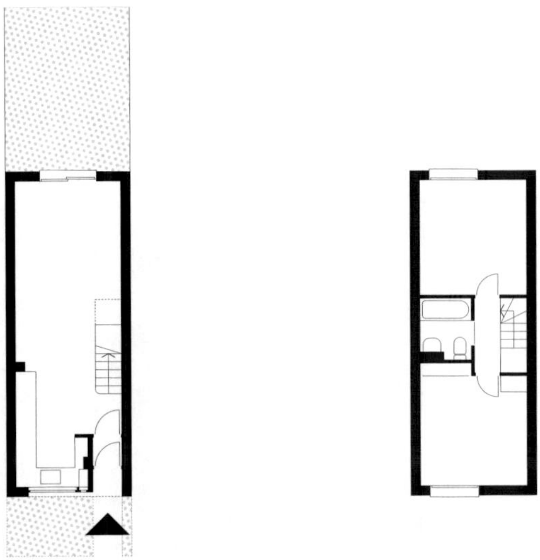

RANGERS SQUARE

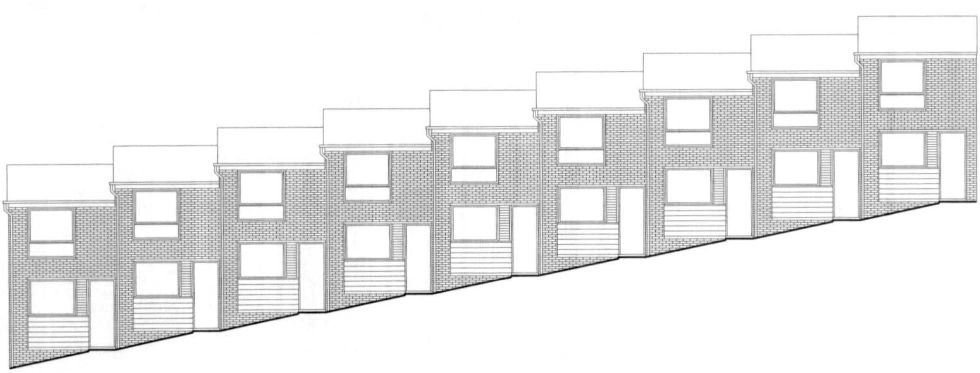

Above, left to right: ground and first floor plans
Below: east terrace front elevation

10m

1970

Arthur Rubinstein (b.1928), also known as Arthur Rubin, and his brother Leopold (1929–2012) studied architecture at Brixton School of Building. The Rubinstein family, originally from Germany, had been housed in the Jewish Temporary Shelter in Whitechapel.[46]

After completing his architectural studies, Arthur worked at Marshman & Warren, a practice in Bedford where he met Bernard Hartley (b.1934). The pair moved to London to set up a satellite office but after only one year, decided to set up on their own, establishing Rubinstein & Hartley, later known as Bernard Hartley & Partners, specialising in residential work, including projects for housing associations.[47]

Rubinstein & Hartley kept an office in Wimpole Street from 1965 to 1973, where both brothers worked briefly together. Arthur relocated to the US around 1968, living in Miami, Dallas, Boston and finally New York.[48] His brother Leopold remained in the UK and continued in practice with Hartley.

Local projects	85 – 104 Vanbrugh Park (attributed)	1967
Other London projects	100 – 105 Clarendon Road, Notting Hill	

04	Project	85–104 Vanbrugh Park
	Architect	Aurthur Rubinstein
	Completed	1967
	Client	Glamford Building Company

A terrace of twenty interlocking maisonettes arranged in ten bays. With its exposed concrete frame, fully glazed façade overlooking the Heath, and dark brickwork to the rear, the inventive plan of interlocking three-storey three-bedroom maisonettes is not apparent from the outside.[49]

The building reads as ten individual terraced houses, and may have been conceived as such, with the decision to divide them into maisonettes made on site at a late stage. The staircases are extremely constrained, and did not comply with the London Building Act, as a waiver in the original deeds shows.[50] The block lay empty for a few years after completion, perhaps because of the unconventional layout. However, by 1978, they were selling well.

Approaching each bay in the terrace there are two front doors: one serving the 'upper maisonette' and the other the 'pair maisonette'. This type of interlocked maisonette arrangement is rare in Britain but is used more often in France and the Netherlands. The two flat types are known to current residents as the 'uppers' and the 'lowers'. The ground floor is shared by both – each maisonette having an entrance hall, WC, garage and utility room. The first floor belongs to the lowers only. The second floor is shared again, the uppers having the Heath view, the lowers the rear view. The top floors belong exclusively to the uppers. Recently two maisonettes were united to create a larger townhouse.

85–104 VANBRUGH PARK

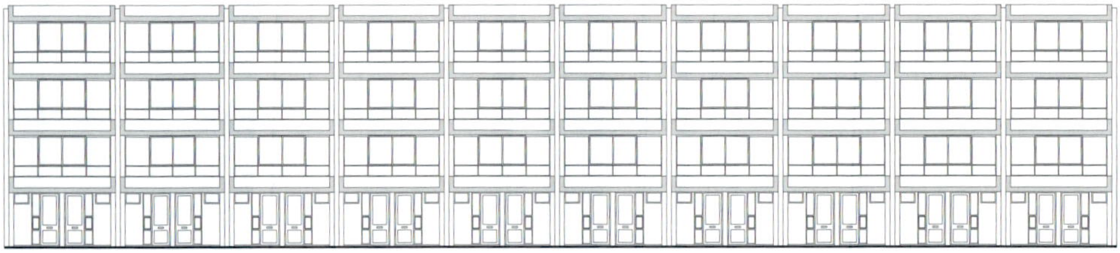

Above: the terrace from the Heath
Below: terrace front elevation

1:500 15m

1967

Site location

1:2000 50m

Interlocking floorplans: grey denotes the 'lowers' and white the 'uppers'
Top to bottom: third, second, first and ground floor plans

10m

Austin Vernon & Partners worked in Blackheath by chance. They were originally commissioned by the Church Army to design a training centre in Dulwich, but securing planning permission and support for this location proved difficult, so the charity found an alternative site in Vanbrugh Park, Blackheath, where it already had a base.[51]

Frederick Austin Vernon (1882–1972) was appointed as surveyor and architect for the Dulwich Estate in 1937. He founded Austin Vernon & Partners in 1948 with his nephew Russell Vernon (1916–2009). Russell Vernon had studied at the Bartlett and completed a town planning degree. He worked for Austin's architect-cousin George Vernon (1870-1942) before the Second World War.

The practice completed an extensive restoration of Dulwich Picture Gallery following severe bomb damage in July 1944.

Russell Vernon transformed the practice into a modern studio producing some of the best high-quality housing in Britain during the 1950s and 1960s. Working with developers and housebuilder Wates, they were responsible for more than 1,000 homes for the Dulwich Estate between 1957 and 1963. This ambitious development continued until 1978, with around 2,000 modern houses and flats built in total.[52]

Austin Vernon & Partners also completed a number of office and educational projects, including headquarters buildings for Otis Elevators and Lufthansa, and the striking Christison Hall at Dulwich College.

At its peak, Austin Vernon & Partners employed around 30 people. The practice closed in 1995.[53]

Local projects	Church Army Training Centre and Chapel, 27 Vanbrugh Park	1965

Other London projects	Housing at Dulwich Estate	1955–78
	Christison Hall, Dulwich College	1969
	Buildings at Alleyn's School	
	Buildings at James Allen's Girls' School	

E. T. Spashett, project architect, on the morning of the Chapel opening ceremony, 1965

05

Project	Church Army Chapel
Architect	Austin Vernon & Partners
Completed	1965
Client	Church Army
Status	Locally listed

The Church Army Chapel in Vanbrugh Park was opened in 1965 by Princess Alexandra and consecrated by Michael Ramsey, Archbishop of Canterbury. It was part of a larger development, the Wilson Carlile Training Centre. Carlile was the founder of the Church Army, an evangelical religious institution. The site was previously occupied by St Christopher's College for Training Sunday School Teachers from 1917 to 1932. The chapel was built on a quadrangle adjacent to a previous small chapel, part of the college.

The building is locally listed and notable for its roof design. It originally featured a central altar and, at the time of construction, the tallest metal spire in Britain. The chapel has a cross-shaped blue-glass window at the west end, which together with the yellow and textured glass vertical windows to the side walls, creates a filtered soft light and an otherworldly atmosphere. The pattern of the vertical windows is reminiscent of those used in Le Corbusier's La Tourette monastery in the south of France. The slit windows, running from floor to ceiling, are separated by concrete pillars faced on the outside with white mosaic tiles; the finish on the interior was originally white leather-cloth.[54] The furnishings and doors are of American black walnut and the entrance hall floor was a grey-green terrazzo.

The spire, unfortunately removed at some point before the 1980s, was a tall, slim, hollow aluminium cone, chosen for its lightness and strength and inspired by aeronautical engineering; the project architect, Ernst Trevor Spashett (1923–1994) having served in the Royal Air Force.[55] A small cross-piece on the top of the spire doubled as the hilt of a sword, representing the Church Army.

The chapel interior looking towards a structural pier

1965

The blue-stained glass cross on the west elevation

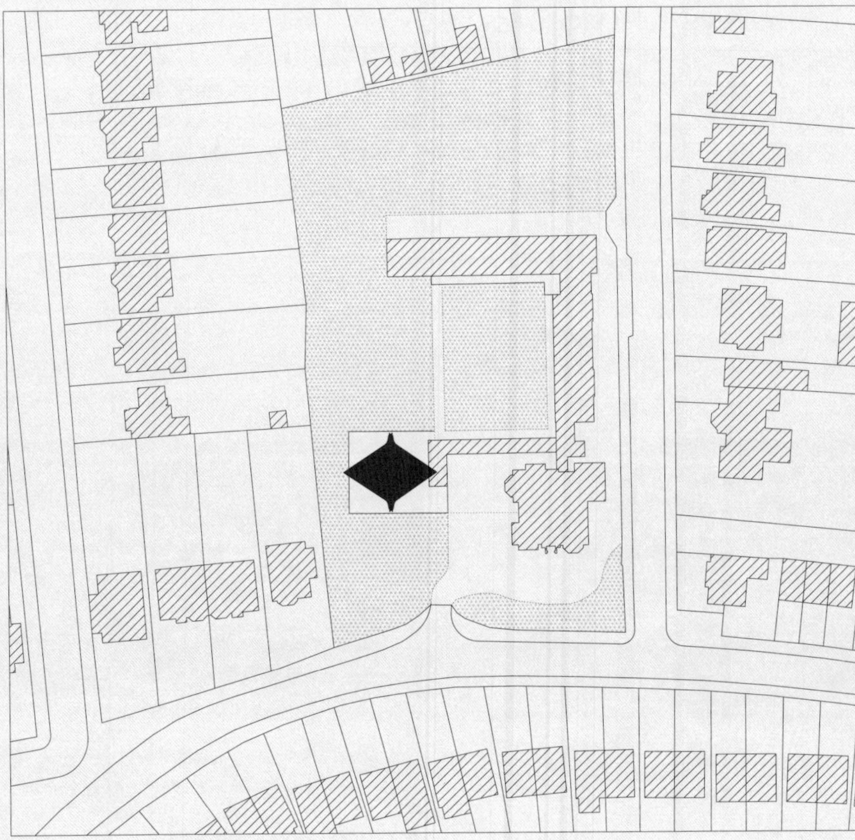

57 Site plan, as originally built 1:2000 50m

The chapel's striking saddle roof is, in geometric terms, a hyperbolic paraboloid which as a doubly ruled surface can be constructed from two rows of straight beams. It was built from three thin skins of timber laid in different directions, glued and nailed together, supported entirely by two buttresses visible externally. This early example of saddle roof construction in Britain had been influenced by the Commonwealth Institute in South Kensington (now the London Design Museum) designed by Robert Matthew, Johnson-Marshall and Partners in 1962, and by the Markham Moor A1 Petrol Station by Clark-Hall, Scorer and Bright in 1960.

The Chapel originally formed part of a larger training centre scheme arranged around a central quadrangle. The east side consisted of older buildings while the west side was open, with a new dormitory block forming the north side. This dormitory was a flat-roofed building of white brick and horizontal metal-framed windows, now much altered.

The chapel has been part of Blackheath High School since 1994 and is now used as a music room and dance studio. The original entrance block was demolished as part of a major refurbishment project in 2015.

External view complete with the spire in place, 1965

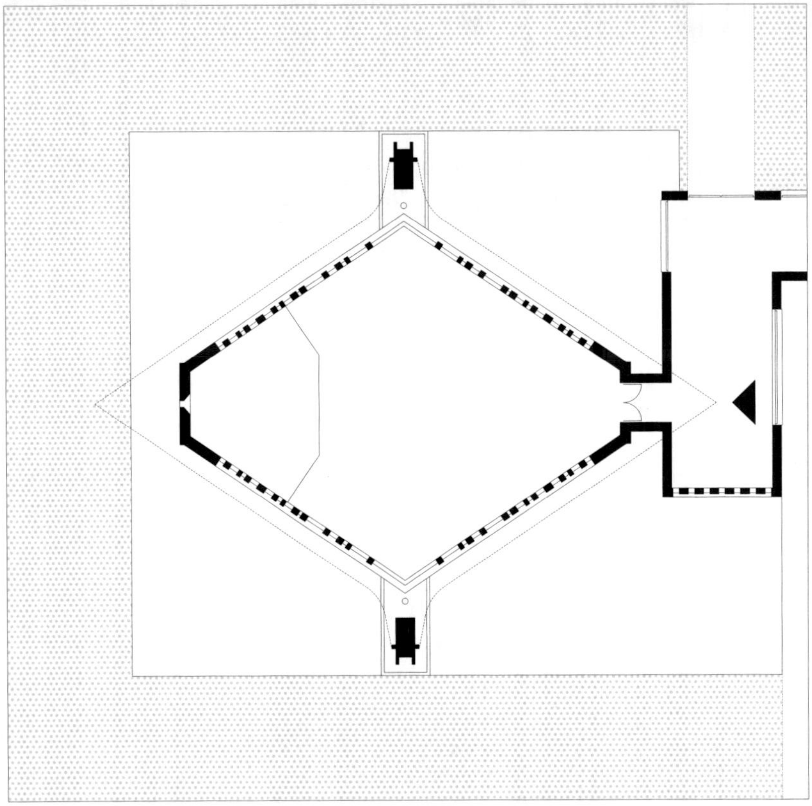

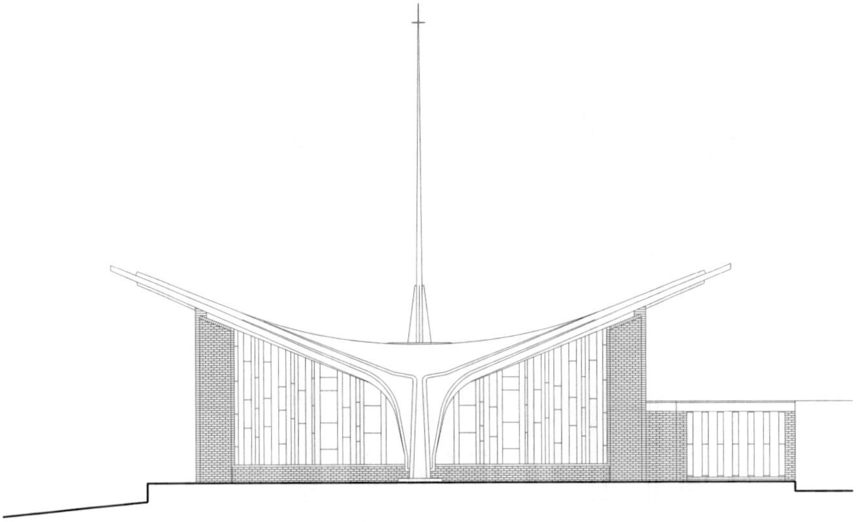

CHURCH ARMY CHAPEL

Above: ground floor plan,
as originally built
Below: south elevation,
as originally built

10m

1965

Brian Meeking (b.1930) ran an architectural practice at 41 Blackheath Road from 1958 to 1995. He employed a small team that eagerly sought out new opportunities and challenges, including the four distinctive homes that he designed for his family in Blackheath and Greenwich. The first of these, built in the early 1960s was at 66 Greenwich Park Street. It was followed by 144 Langton Way, 6 Paragon Place in 1987, and 12x Foxes Dale in 1993.

During his architectural training, Meeking served in the army and was posted to Nepal. While there, he helped design the British Gurkha Camp and took his final architecture degree.

Edna, his wife, studied art and actively supported his practice as an interior designer, project manager and trusted critic.

In addition to one-off houses, Meeking worked on several larger housing projects for Greenwich and Lewisham Councils, including the block of flats situated by the Sun in the Sands roundabout. He was also the architect and driving force behind the renewal of Greenwich Theatre.

After his retirement, Meeking designed a holiday home for his family in Menorca, Spain. Fittingly, the house was named Swan Song, although the Meeking family subsequently returned to Blackheath to a type T2 Span house.

Meeking, a keen sailor and boat builder, built three vessels himself – two in the Netherlands and one in the garden of 41 Blackheath Road.[56]

Local projects		
	66 Greenwich Park Street, Greenwich	1960s
	The Green Man music hall, Blackheath Hill[57]	
	141 – 159 Langton Way	1960
	92, 94 and 96 Langton Way[58]	1963
	142 and 144 Langton Way	
	Sun in the Sands, council housing block	
	The Old Priory, Priory Park[59]	
	6 Paragon Place	1987
	12x Foxes Dale	1993

Brian Mocking in his studio on the top floor of 6 Paragon Place

06	Project	66 Greenwich Park Street
	Architect	Brian Meeking
	Completed	Early 1960s
	Client	Architect's own house

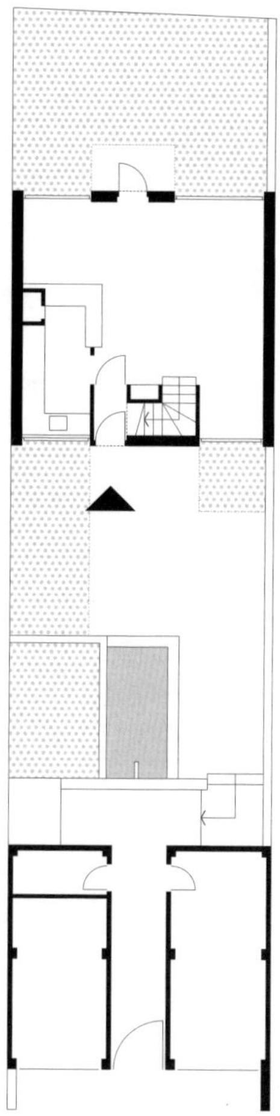

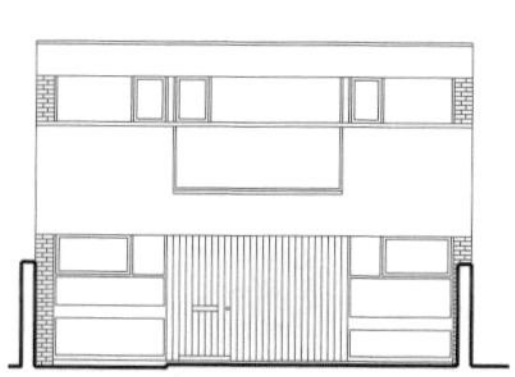

Above, left to right: ground and first floor plan
Below: courtyard elevation of the house

A flat-roofed two-storey building situated by the railway cutting and hidden behind a double garage and courtyard garden, it was an infill project on a 'site that nobody wanted'.[60]

The site layout and front courtyard garden complete with a pool and fountain, were inspired by Moroccan architecture, after a family holiday.

A bold design, the street frontage is a continuous wooden façade concealing a central door and passageway. Once in the courtyard, a wall of flint and concrete holding a waterspout, diverts the route via steps down to the courtyard and front door.

Inside, exposed floor structure and wall panelling continues the use of timber from the front. The footprint of the house is only seven metres square; the clever positioning of the staircase to the front and adjacent to the living room, creates a sense of openness and allows light from the large window above, to flood both floors.

This was to be the first of Meeking's many ventures in Greenwich and Blackheath – finding challenging sites, building unique homes and exploring the changing styles over the decades.

Courtyard view of pool and garage block

07	Project	Greenwich Theatre, Crooms Hill
	Architect	Brian Meeking
	Completed	1969
	Client	Greenwich Theatre Company
	Status	Part locally listed (Nevada Street elevation, 1871)

The current theatre building stands on the site of an old Victorian music hall dating from the 1870s. In 1898, it was called the Hippodrome and by the 1950s it had become a cinema; after which it was used as a warehouse before eventually falling into disrepair and standing derelict. Greenwich Council acquired it for demolition in 1962 but agreed to support the construction of a new theatre on the site, if there was sufficient local support.[61]

Greenwich Theatre sits at the foot of Crooms Hill, in a line of fine period terraced houses and wraps around the Rose and Crown public house on the corner, a hang-out for actors and theatre-goers.

The project benefited from extensive fundraising by the local community – most notably, music hall shows held at The Green Man pub (located at the corner of Dartmouth Row and Blackheath Hill, but now demolished). Brian Meeking sang in many of these productions – 'not many architects can say they sang to raise funds for their own buildings.'[62] John Cox, the opera director, devised the programme for these shows. They started out as weekend fundraising events, but became extremely popular and continued for many years, outlasting their original purpose. As Cox remembers, the project was 'important to us all' and carried some unifying 'political ideological appeal of the time, one that recognised the arts as important.'[63]

The fundraising campaign was an epic saga, featuring many dedicated citizens and led by actor and director, Ewan Hooper, who lived locally. Contributions were received from the Arts Council, the GLC and many other organisations and individuals.[64] Handmade ceramic name plates honouring the many donors are still on display on the top floor of the theatre. The names listed include local residents and businesses, schoolchildren and many celebrities such as John Lennon and Ringo Starr of the Beatles, as well as actors including Susan Hampshire, Constance Cummings, Pauline Collins, Cecil Day Lewis (who lived opposite), Fenella Fielding and Ned Sherrin.

GREENWICH THEATRE, CROOMS HILL

Side view of the stage

1969

The construction stage lasted two years, with the work completed in three phases as and when funding allowed. The first phase included a new façade on Crooms Hill, a foyer and a bar, followed by the structural works and waterproofing of the theatre hall and dressing rooms, and finally the fit-out and joinery. The original interior was bold, with bright orange auditorium seating contrasted by black and white furniture and decoration throughout. Joinery finished in white Formica and brown hessian completed the material palette.[65] The final cost was around £120,000. Don Sidonio, who ran a delicatessen near the Green Man pub and owned a fleet of local ice-cream vans, served as the project treasurer.

The theatre features a façade of striking vertical brickwork and aluminium windows on Crooms Hill; behind is a space that the art historian Nikolaus Pevsner described as a 'multi-storey exhibition-space-cum-foyer with boldly exposed concrete'.[66] The theatre foyer leads to a generous concrete staircase that doubles as an exhibition and gathering space. The Nevada Street elevation is a mixture of exposed concrete and brick walls with a raised loading door and winch.

At the theatre's heart is a mid-size auditorium of about 400 seats – an ideal size for mounting new productions, prior to transfer to the West End or larger venues across the country. From 1969 and for the next 28 years the theatre ran its own company, with Ewan Hooper as the first artistic director.

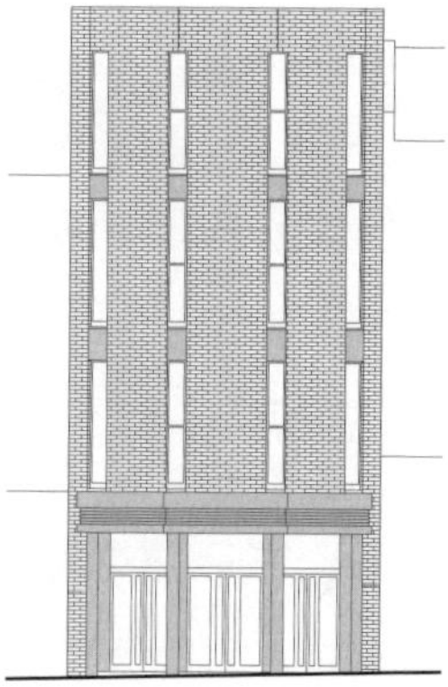

Left: the auditorium in-situ concrete balustrade
Right: west elevation

10m

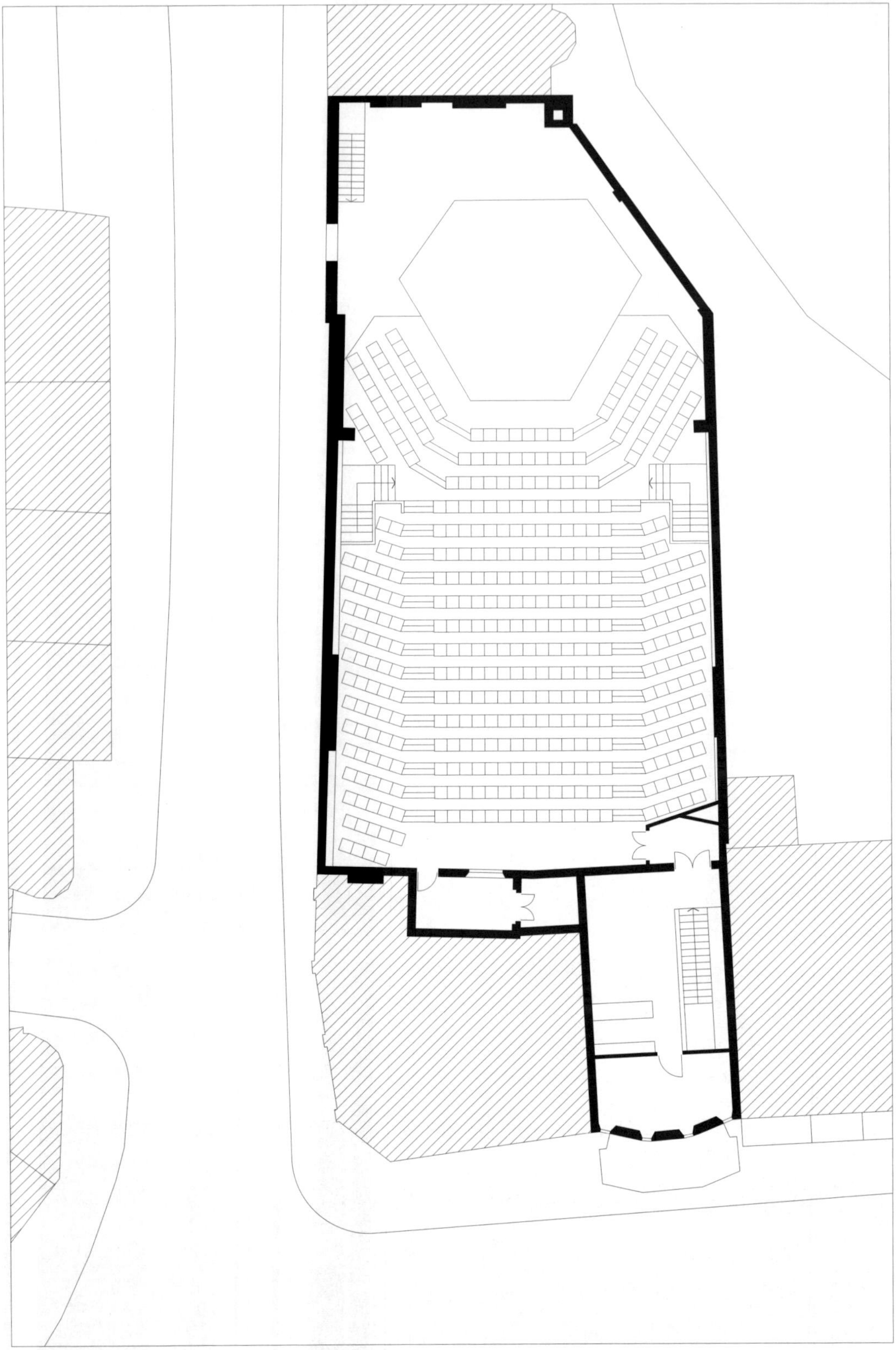

67 The auditorium floor plan in context

10m

1969

08

Project	6 Paragon Place
Architect	Brian Meeking
Completed	1986
Client	Architect's own house

A detached concrete and white rendered house on a steep slope, featuring a glass-walled top-floor room surrounded by a roof terrace. The floorplan is articulated by 45-degree chamfered corners. The site was originally part of a walled garden, with no access from the road, so parking is on an off-street drawbridge-like platform that doubles as an entrance forecourt.

Interviewed in 1993, Meeking explained how the site had presented a huge challenge to him and the three previous owners because the land fell away from the road so sharply.[67] His solution was to arrange the house over three storeys with living spaces and garage on the ground floor or street level, bedrooms on the lower ground, a conservatory and large roof terrace on the first floor, all connected by a wide spiral staircase.

The roof slab is cantilevered in part, its edges stiffened with upstand beams that form the balcony edges – effectively a lid – creating a spacious interior of uninterrupted ceilings. Fine shadow gaps, drips and chamfered corner details were all incorporated in the formwork.[68]

Meeking's inspiration for the design of the house came from the rendered domestic buildings seen on his holidays in Spain, Greece and Italy, where the usual construction method is in-situ reinforced concrete slabs and columns with hollow clay block infill and cement rendering on the external walls.

The contract was direct-labour and Meeking often worked on site with the building team, suffering several personal injuries, included some burnt fingers. 'It's my own fault,' he admitted. 'I shoved them in the cement. It's the sort of thing professionals don't do, but enthusiasts like me just get stuck in.'[69]

The garden elevation

6 PARAGON PLACE

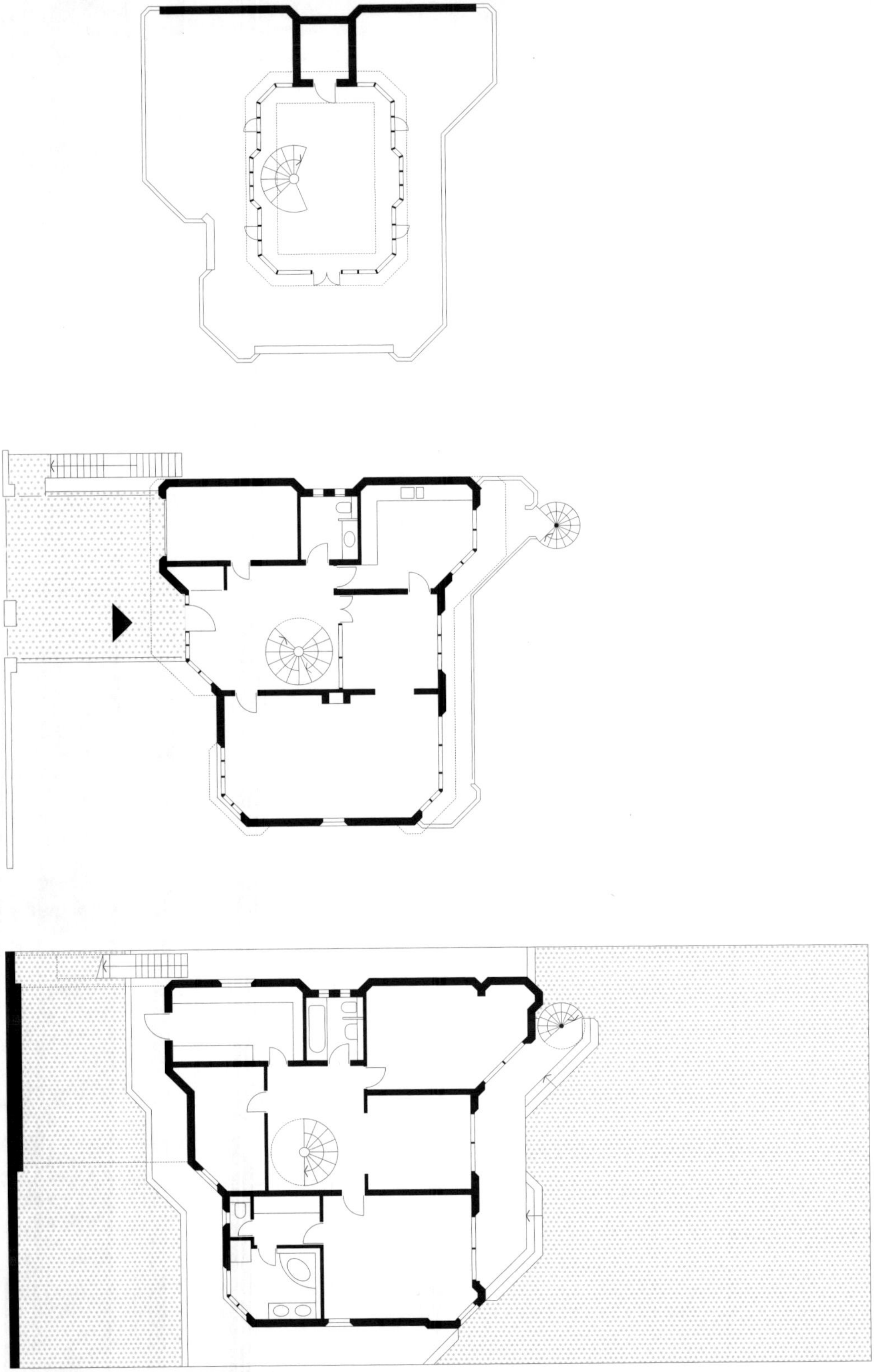

Top to bottom: first, ground and lower ground floor plan

10m

1986

Chamberlin, Powell & Bon, one of the UK's leading post-war architectural practices, designed only one project locally – the Vanbrugh Park Estate for Greenwich Council.

Peter 'Joe' Chamberlin (1919 – 1978), Geoffry Powell (1920 – 1999) and Christof (or Christoph) Bon (1921 – 1999) launched their practice in 1952 when Powell won the competition to design the Golden Lane Estate for the Corporation of the City of London and joined forces with his fellow teachers at Kingston Polytechnic. They had each entered the competition having agreed that should any of them win they would form a partnership to deliver the successful design.

Following completion of the Golden Lane Estate, the practice created the impressive Barbican development, an icon of Brutalist architecture encompassing the Barbican arts centre, residential blocks arranged around communal spaces, education facilities, a library and a retained medieval church.

As a large practice, Chamberlin, Powell & Bon undertook projects such as Bousfield Primary School in Chelsea, a city centre campus for Leeds University and New Hall College, Cambridge (now Murray Edwards College) with its domed refectory and vaulted library. Their work received the RIBA bronze medal in 1956 and 1957, a Ministry of Housing and Local Government medal in 1965, a Civic Trust commendation in 1973, and RIBA Architecture Awards in 1973 and 1974.

Local projects	Vanbrugh Park Estate, Greenwich	1965
Other London projects	Bousfield Junior and Infant School, South Kensington	1956
	House on Hendon Avenue, Finchley	1958
	Two Saints Comprehensive School, Elephant and Castle	1960
	Golden Lane Estate, City of London	1963
	The Barbican Estate, City of London	1983

Geoffry Powell, Christof Bon and Joe Chamberlin, 1953

09	Project	Vanbrugh Park Estate
	Architect	Chamberlin, Powell & Bon
	Completed	1965
	Client	Greenwich Council
	Status	Locally listed

The Vanbrugh Park Estate, together with the Golden Lane and Barbican estates in the City of London, form the three key housing schemes designed by Chamberlin, Powell & Bon. As Golden Lane Estate was completed in 1962 and construction of the Barbican started in 1965, the Vanbrugh Park Estate (1959–1965) bridges the two. The project was led by Powell, supported by Brian Frost and Mike Thomas.

Echoes of Golden Lane can be found in Vanbrugh Park, for example the layout of low-rise terraces around courts and a single tower at the edge of the site forming the focal point of the scheme. The main entrances to the estate and its refuse stores are marked by tall brick structures. The project also uses pre-cast concrete portal windows; a similar feature is used to house services in the Barbican estate.

The Vanbrugh Park Estate was commissioned in 1959. Greenwich Council chose the architects after considering 'a number of firms of high-standing'[70] because its own housing department was short-staffed. The scheme comprises terraces of two and three-storey houses, mews flats above garages and an eight-story block, Westcombe Court – all situated on the edge of the Heath, near Greenwich Park, not far from Vanbrugh Castle. The mix is 64 flats, 70 terrace houses and 42 mews flats above garages.

The architects explained that the tower block's location makes the most of the views to the north and renders it 'unassertive'[71] when seen from the Heath. The long wall of red reused bricks facing the Heath, refers to the historic park walls nearby.[72]

The low units are of painted exposed blockwork. Chamberlin, Powell & Bon favoured an undecorated finish, but this was not compliant with the London Building Act, so a sealant paint was required.

The finer details are reserved for the interiors, with most of the flats and houses benefiting from the imaginative use of clerestory windows and bold stoves with tubular flues, which together with open staircases, provide sculptural features – a nod to Alvar Aalto's own 1936 house-studio in Helsinki. The stoves are encased with blockwork, creating thermal mass for the slow diffusion of heat. Materials such as timber boarding, exposed blockwork and quarry tiles enrich the interior quality.[73]

VANBRUGH PARK ESTATE

 The tower seen from Combe Avenue

The central core and access walkways of the tower

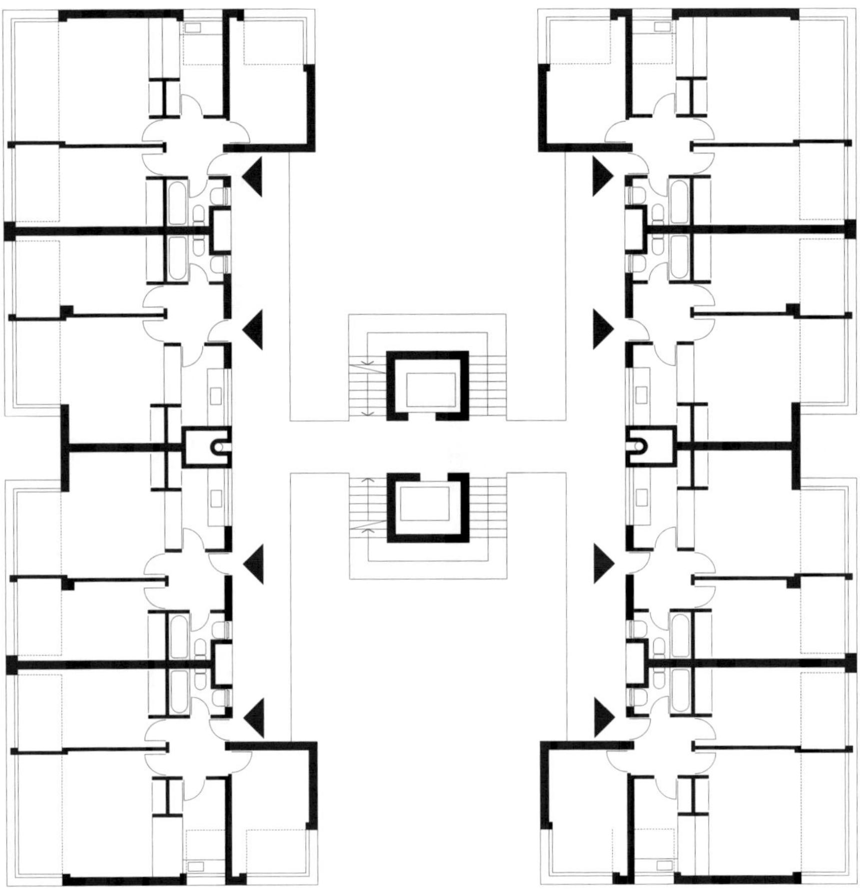

VANBRUGH PARK ESTATE

Tower plan

10m

1965

The tower Westcombe Court, has an open central staircase, lined with vertical tiling. The block's concrete walls, originally stained dark brown, were patchy in appearance because the successive coats created irregular bands and did not weather-down as hoped. This issue was later rectified by applying a light render.

The estate has not aged well. Much of the exposed blockwork has been painted or pebbled-dashed and residents have replaced windows and installed fences on an ad-hoc basis. Its long street frontages comprising garage doors are still forbidding but the elevated flats benefit from privacy from the road.

The landscape design, which integrated existing mature trees, consists of planted courtyards, play areas and clothes drying yards.[74] Most of these elements are still in place, however, a shallow pool at the base of Westcombe Court and a pedestrian bridge that crossed over Combe Avenue to link the tower to the Heath have both been lost. The street lighting was originally screened with elegant semi-circular concrete shades but these were compromised when Greenwich Council attached new fittings to the outside of the shades rather than inside them.

Today, the estate is marked by a renewed sense of community, with residents' initiatives under way to create a greener Vanbrugh Park by improving planting and softening the landscape within the shared spaces.

The estate provides an interesting contrast to Parkside, the adjacent development of neo-Georgian style buildings, arranged around central courtyard lawns, built in 1957, just 2 years before Vanbrugh Park was commissioned.

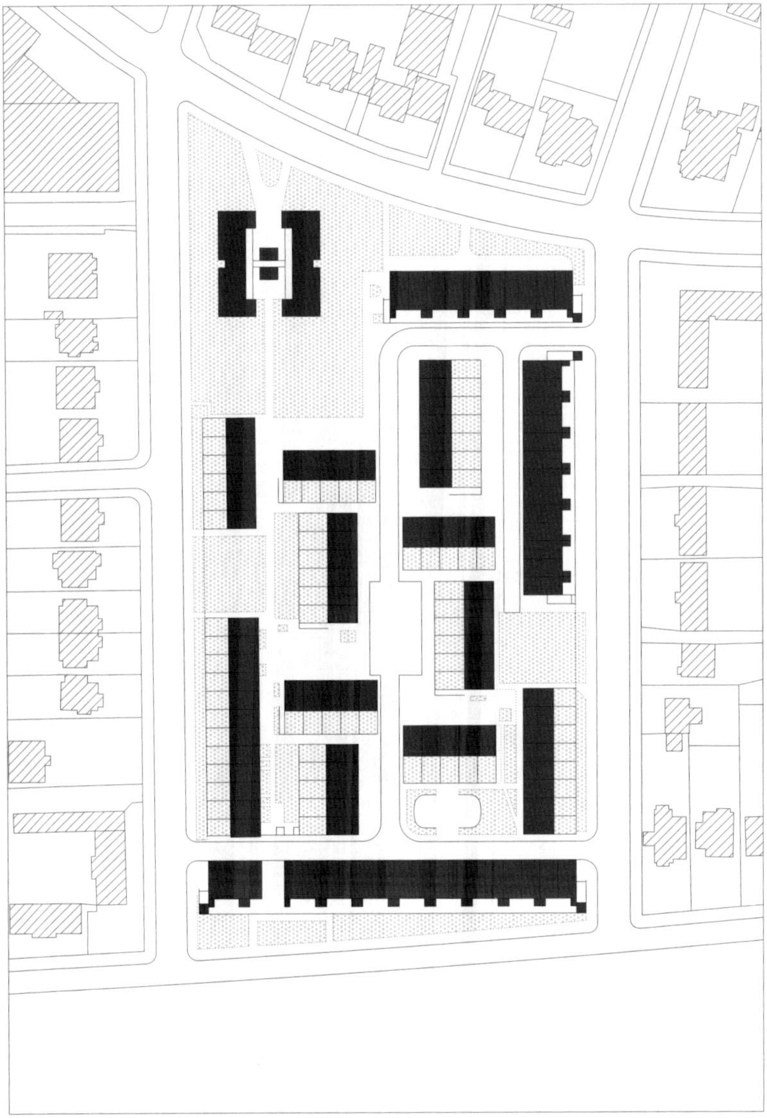

VANBRUGH PARK ESTATE

Site plan

1:2500 50m

1965

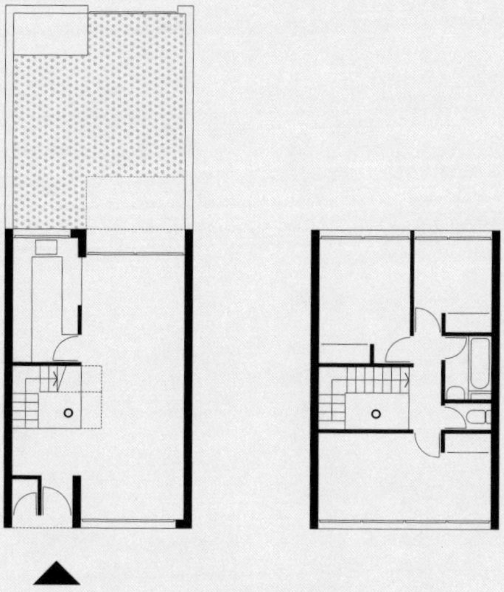

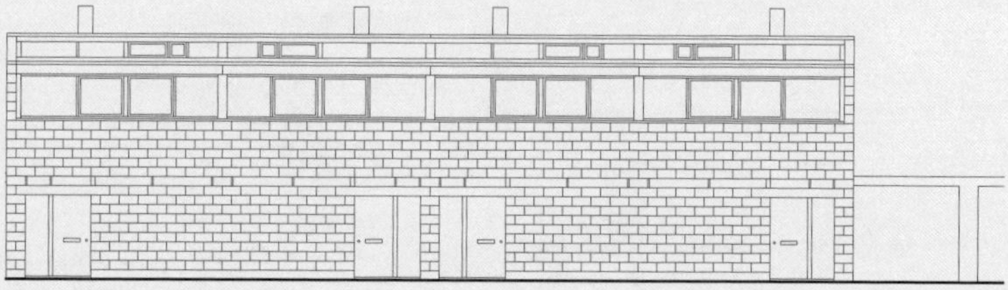

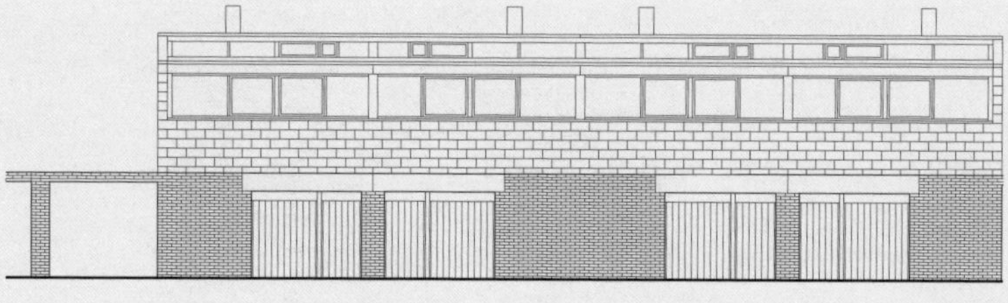

Above, left to right: ground and first floor plans
of a terraced three-bedroom house
Middle: terrace, front elevation
Bottom: terrace, garden elevation

10m

79 Interior of a three-bedroom house 1965

David Creighton Branch (1924–1998) and his wife Jean moved into a Span flat in Hallgate, Blackheath in 1959. When a corner site in nearby Meadowbank became available, they acquired the land to design and build a new family home. Branch was a close friend and neighbour of architects Brian Meeking and Peter Moro.

Branch started his architectural studies in 1940 at the South West Technical College but his studies were interrupted by war service. In the army he completed a two-year engineering course and was posted as an officer to India with the Royal Engineers. Returning to England in 1947, he worked for Seely & Paget (the architectural practice responsible for designing Eltham Palace in the mid-1930s) on war-damaged buildings and projects such as Eton College, Lambeth Palace and the Charterhouse in London. At the same time, he undertook his qualifications as an architect, graduating in 1956.[75]

In 1953, Branch joined forces with John Morgan, who he met at Seely & Paget. They practiced together for many years. Their practice became Morgan Branch Roberts in 1968 when David Roberts joined. Branch retired in 1986.

Morgan Branch Roberts specialised in commercial work for some of the largest international companies, including designs for clients in the pharmaceutical, cosmetics, and film industries. They also worked on residential schemes, shopping centres, cinemas and church buildings.

Local projects	8 Meadowbank (demolished)	1970
	11 Manor Way refurbishment	1993

Other projects	Eli Lilly Research Centre, Windlesham	1968
	Yardley factory, Basildon	1972
	Kodak Research Laboratories, Harrow	1975
	Roussel Laboratories, Swindon	1979

David Branch

10

Project	8 Meadowbank
Architect	David Branch
Completed	1970 (demolished circa 2015)
Client	Architect's own house

The site of 8 Meadowbank – originally the garden and orchard of the adjacent large villa, Park Lodge (1918) – was described by Branch as 'a dell in a wood'.[76] It was screened by a row of mature trees to the north and enclosed by the curve of the road to the south. The entrance to the house was approached via a drive and a protected sun trap formed between the house and garage wall.

A single-storey building, its internal spaces flowed from room to room and along the corridor to the bedrooms. Jean Branch, an accomplished artist, required space to hang her paintings, so all walls were whitewashed, with the exception of the study, where hessian-cladding added texture and warmth.[77]

In the enclosed courtyard, the only solid volume was the chimney breast to the living room, which doubled as an external barbecue and formed the heart of the house. The main bedroom and dining room had no external windows but faced onto the courtyard; the other bedrooms were arranged along a corridor which also overlooked the same central space.

The materials used in the house showed the influence of the commercial and large-scale projects undertaken by Morgan Branch Roberts, but with detailing on a smaller scale. This was reflected in the use of the steel frame structure, large aluminium windows, spandrel panels, and walls of exposed concrete blocks.

Jean Branch lived in the house until her death in 2011. The demolition of the building followed a bitter planning battle during which the Blackheath Park Conservation Group and many locals attempted, unsuccessfully, to secure listing for Branch's home, describing it as 'an urban rarity for its form'.

Providing a unique local example of a modernist house influenced by Mies Van der Rohe and the International Style, it was clearly a dissonant yet respectful building of huge cultural value and its demolition was a great loss for Blackheath.

The house built in its place was designed by Walkerbushe Architects and completed in 2017.

8 MEADOWBANK

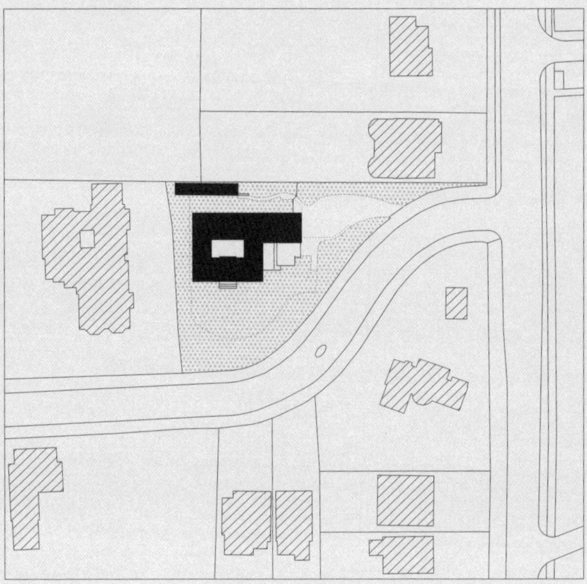

83 Site plan 1:2000 50m 1970

Above: steps between the garden and living room
Below: the central courtyard

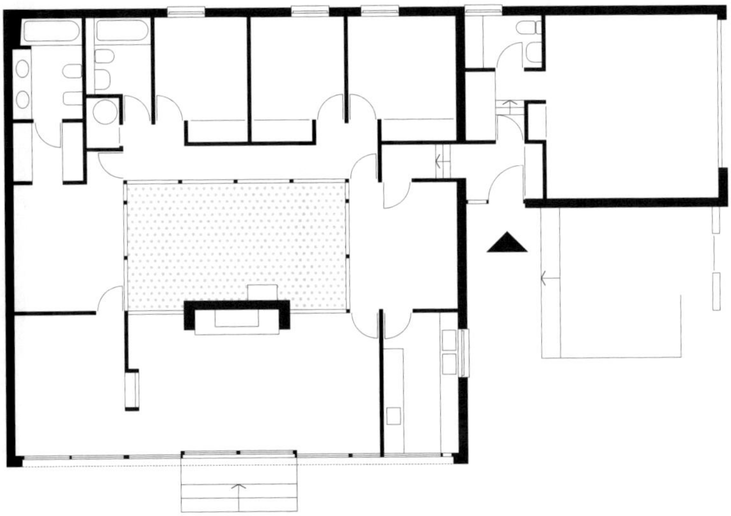

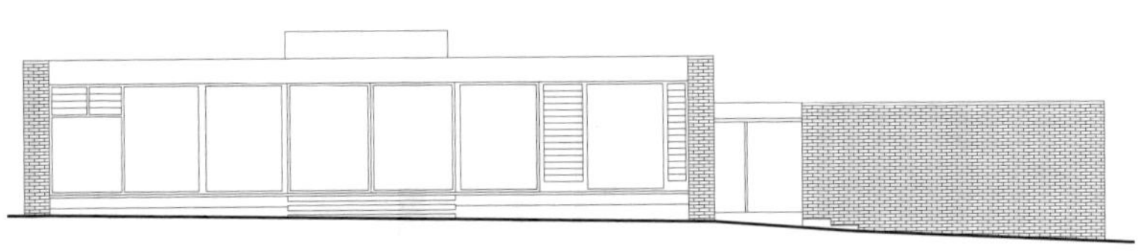

8 MEADOWBANK

Above: ground floor plan
Below: south elevation

10m

1970

E Morton Wright (b.1932) established a practice at his Greenwich home in 1965. In the early 1970s he purchased Meridian West – a house designed by Julian Sofaer, located off Diamond Terrace, and has lived and worked there ever since. Morton Wright was heavily involved in fundraising for the Greenwich Theatre project and always supported its activities.

Morton Wright studied at Thames Polytechnic, then worked at Richard Sheppard, Robson and Partners, where he was involved with several educational buildings and where he met neighbours Myles and Deidre Dove. He was the project architect for City University, Northampton Square, London.

He designed a variety of building types, including houses, extensions to schools (Leverstock Green and Nash Mills primary schools in Hertfordshire) and church conversions. He also designed a new church and community centre for Leytonstone United Free Church.[78]

He worked for The Hyde Housing Association for many years, designing social housing and sheltered accommodation for disabled residents. His projects included a scheme of 10 flats in Combedale Road, Greenwich, 16 flats in Lansdowne Lane, Charlton and flats in Silverdale, Sydenham.

When Walter Greaves moved from Blackheath to Sussex in 1968, he handed several projects over to Morton Wright, which had planning permission but still required detailing and working drawings for construction. These included 1 Leycroft Close, Canterbury, Kent, now Grade II listed and a pair of houses in Morden Road Mews.

Local projects		
	24 and 26 Morden Road Mews, construction stage	1968
	Extension to Meridian West, Diamond Terrace	1970s
	St Mark's Church alterations, 22 Greenwich South Street	
	46–50 Combedale Road, Greenwich	1985
	Christ Church Forum, Trafalgar Road	1989

E Morton Wright outside 26 Morden Road Mews, 1968

11

Project	24 and 26 Morden Road Mews
Architect	E Morton Wright
Completed	1968
Client	Leslie Bilsby

A pair of single-storey houses built in the rear garden of a large Victorian house at 24 Morden Road, with an associated block of seven garages, linked to and serving the flats in the Morden Road house. Both houses benefit from south-westerly walled gardens. Number 26 also has a narrow garden court to the south-east. Today, number 26 has minor alterations and extensions with the garage converted to accommodation. Number 24 has gained an additional storey

A distinctive feature of the houses are the curved brick walls that enclose the gardens and parts of the buildings. The walls are of exposed London stock brickwork with a special chamfered brick base and top. A band of slate hanging tiles sits above the walls enclosing the roof, their difference emphasised by a pronounced horizontal shadow gap to the top of the wall. Predominantly flat, each roof is articulated by two mono-pitched volumes, giving a sculptural form to the buildings' profiles that is not expressed internally, which suggests Bilsby, as developer, may have had to reduce costs at some stage.

Initially a scheme by Walter Greaves, the curved brick walls are characteristic of Greaves' designs and can also be seen at 11a Morden Road Mews and 1 to 3 Rocque Lane.

No. 24 entrance patio on completion

Above: the approach mews lane with no. 26 and 24 to the right
and 24 Morden Road beyond
Below: the curved garden wall to no. 26

1968

11

E MORTON WRIGHT

Ground floor, as originally built

10m

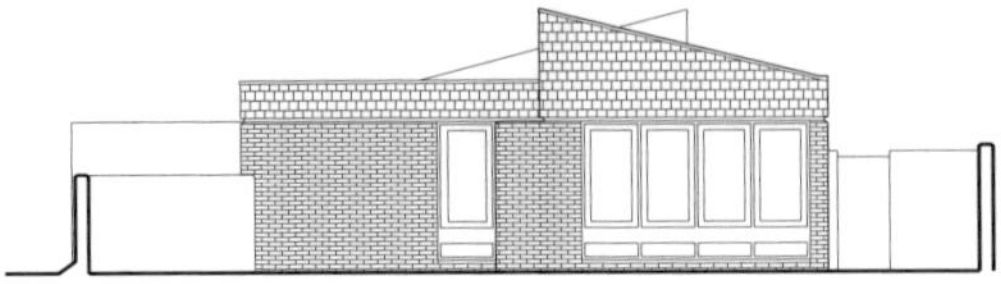

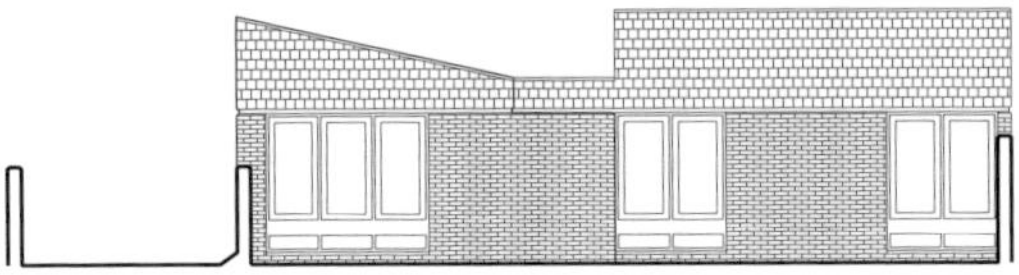

24 AND 26 MORDEN ROAD MEWS

Top to bottom: no. 26 and no. 24 garden elevations and no. 24 during construction

10m

1968

12

Project	Christ Church Forum, East Greenwich
Architect	E Morton Wright
Completed	1989
Client	Church of England

E Morton Wright worked on this project for more than 20 years, developing the brief with various charities and community groups and working with the parish to raise the necessary funds. Early on, it became clear that it would not be possible to accommodate the required amount of space within the original church volume, so he proposed that a new hall should be built at the eastern end of the site and the existing building divided into three floors, to maximise its use by charity groups. All spaces were designed to be fully accessible to disabled and wheelchair users.[79]

The original church structure dates from 1849 and was built as an outreach from St Alfege Church in West Greenwich. The new Christ Church Hall was dedicated in 1989 with the complete development accommodating the main hall, an upstairs chapel, parish office and a peace garden. It is of exposed blockwork walls with a fine roof of timber and steel trusses, similar to the Quaker Meeting House in Blackheath village designed by Trevor Dannatt. In plan, the walls of the new church hall are rotated by 45 degrees in relation to the street, disengaging the new structure from the original church building and allowing the light to filter indirectly into the space. Morton Wright was also responsible for bespoke furnishings such as the chairs and the altar.

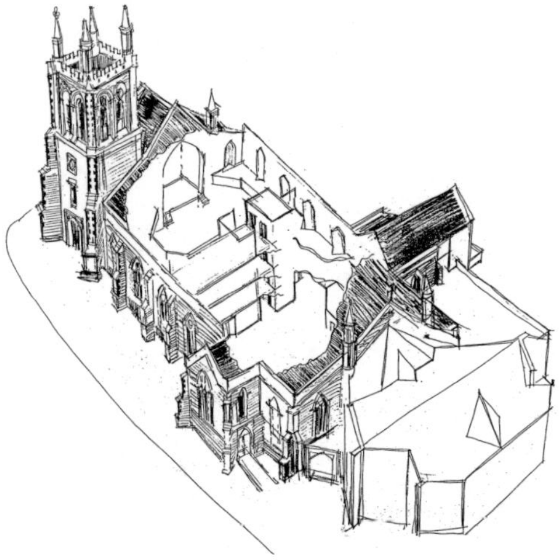

Cutaway perspective drawing illustrating the floors added to the original church and the new hall to the east, by E Morton Wright

93 The altar seen from the gallery

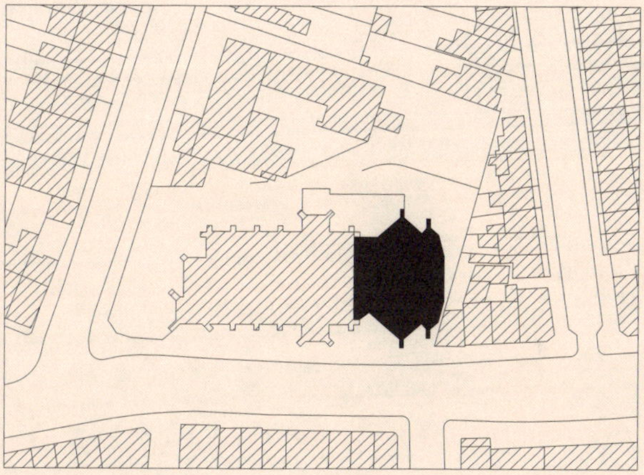

Site plan 1:2000 50m

95 Interior of the new church

1989

Eric Lyons (1912 – 1980) and the development company Span were responsible for a wave of change that created the largest and most influential set of modern buildings in Blackheath between the mid-1950s and early 1980s. In Blackheath, on the Cator Estate, Span was responsible for 483 dwellings on 21 different sites.

Lyons was born in Highbury, north London. He attended evening classes at Regent Street Polytechnic from 1929 to 1932, where he met Geoffrey Townsend. After qualifying he worked for several practices, most notably with Maxwell Fry and Walter Gropius, the German émigré founder of the Bauhaus.[80]

In 1938, Lyons and Townsend began working together. During the Second World War, Lyons registered as a conscientious objector and designed factories and hostels for the cinema architect Harry Weedon. After the war, he resumed his practice with Townsend, and later set up office in the grounds of his home, Mill House, East Molesey, near Hampton Court, which he purchased in 1955.

By 1957, Townsend and the builder-developer Leslie Bilsby, had formally created Span Developments, with Lyons acting as its lead architect. Lyons was joined by the architect Ivor Cunningham, who became a partner in 1963 and was initially responsible for landscape design.

Lyons designed housing schemes for Span in Blackheath, Beckenham, Twickenham, Teddington, Putney and Cambridge. His own practice, Eric Lyons and Partners, was involved in designing high-density housing estates for local authorities in London and Southampton. At New Ash Green, Kent, from 1963 onward, Lyons created a new town of 500 dwellings and a town centre with 57 shops. The scheme was never fully completed – primarily because the government withdrew support for its social housing component – and marked the end of the Lyons-Span collaboration in 1969. After a break of about six years, Span reconstituted and Lyons' practice was involved in further schemes until the mid-1980s.

Span was extremely successful and Lyons was socially and politically motivated. He was elected President of the RIBA between 1975 and 1977, during which time he lobbied the government to build better housing.

Local projects	The Priory	1954–55
	Hall 1	1955–57
	Priory Park	1956–57
	The Keep	1956–57
	T3 Houses, Foxes Dale	1957
	Hall 2 – including Dale Close	1956–57
	Hallgate	1957–58
	Corner Green	1958–59
	The Plantation	1962
	South Row	1960–63
	Park Row	1963
	Spangate	1962–64
	The Lane	1960–64
	Brooklands Park	1960–64
	Hall 4 – Halldale	1964–67
	Parkend	1965–67
	Holm Walk	1975–78
	24–33 Corner Green	1978–79

Other projects	Parkleys, Ham	1954–59
	New Ash Green, Kent	1967–69
	Mayford, Oakley Square, Camden	1971
	Vilamoura Marina, Portugal	1971–74
	World's End estate with H. T. Cadbury-Brown and Partners, Chelsea	1977

Eric Lyons, 1961

Leslie Bilsby (1910–1990) was born in Lincolnshire. He attended evening classes at Regent Street Polytechnic where he studied painting. However, his interests turned towards architecture and design and he went to work for Whiteleys Department Store in London as their design consultant. In 1937, he set up his own building and furnishings company and worked with modern architects that included Wells Coates, Denys Lasdun, Patrick Gwynne and Ernö Goldfinger. His company was the contractor for 2 Willow Road, Hampstead (1939), Goldfinger's own house, which is now Grade II listed and owned by The National Trust.

After serving as an infantry officer during the Second World War, he worked for the developer-turned-architect Charles Bernard Brown (1910–1990), completing restoration and conversion projects in Blackheath and Greenwich, including The Paragon and Colonnade House.

A supporter and promoter of modern architecture, Bilsby was instrumental as a developer for the Span estates. He commissioned and lived in four homes on the Cator Estate; three designed by Patrick Gwynne and one by Walter Greaves. He also commissioned an unbuilt design by Gwynne.

Bilsby was made an Honorary Fellow of the RIBA in 1981 for his achievements and contribution to the profession.[81]

Local buildings commissioned by Bilsby	115 Blackheath Park by Patrick Gwynne (demolished 1966)	1949
	Unbuilt project by Patrick Gwynne	1960
	21 Morden Road by Walter Greaves (demolished 2006)	1968
	10 Blackheath Park by Patrick Gwynne	1969
	22 Parkgate by Patrick Gwynne	1979

Leslie Bilsby and Eric Lyons, 1962

Span changed the character of Blackheath, building on pockets of undeveloped land, including the gardens of large villas, nurseries and spaces created by the demolition of bomb-damaged houses. Span's modern homes added to the rich architectural character of the area, attracting architects, designers, planners and professionals in the growing media industries. Over a period of 30 years, Span built 21 developments in Blackheath, comprising 176 flats and 307 houses.[82]

Span was a development company, founded in 1957 by architect and businessman Geoffrey Townsend, Ernst Haynes and builder-developer Leslie Bilsby, with Eric Lyons as the lead-consultant architect. The name Span was chosen because it sounded contemporary and also referred to spanning 'the gap between the suburban monotony of the typical spec development and the architecturally designed, individually built residence.'[83] Span specialised in housing for the middle classes and, before ceasing operation in 1984, created 73 schemes in southern England, comprising more than 2,000 dwellings.

In 1964, Ian Nairn writing about the Blackheath Span estates in his guide *Modern Buildings in London* asserted that 'If Eric Lyons is the modern Nash, then this is his Regent's Park'.[84]

Span's company embossed stamp

Span Guiding Principles[85]

- Imaginative layouts and dynamic spatial arrangements. The different plans were each given a type (T) designation, e.g. TQ, T10, etc.
- A generous communal landscape, of equal importance to the buildings
- Design for both privacy and social opportunity, blurring the private and public realms
- Landscaped spaces to encourage the opportunity for informal play, as opposed to formal play areas
- A strong positive identity of place
- Introverted schemes, prioritising people over vehicles
- Seclusion, tranquillity and safety
- Community self-management by residents' committees[86]

By following these principles, Span created estates that are innovative and beautiful, enhance their context and are long-lasting. They targeted customers of a certain social class:

> 'The Span house is positive, modern, elegant and practical. A Town house, conceding nothing to Subtopia[87] [indifferent suburban housing of previous decades]. It is quiet, warm, spacious and adult. Built for people who like children and music and laughter, who like entertaining, good talk, Sundays that dawdle between the *Observer* and the *Sunday Times*, and better than average food.'[88]
> in Span T8 house, promotional brochure

> 'I found our neighbours, mostly people much like ourselves – Spock and Span, as someone called us – rather congenial, even the straightforwardly monogamous ones. You need neighbours in life. We had a social circle, some fellow Spanners, some rather more Georgian, and we all dinner-partied back and forth, agreeably enough.'[89]
> in *Among Others*, Michael Frayn

Span succeeded in creating places that most people enjoy. Many residents who bought their houses when they were first on the market, did not move, and if they did, moved to another Span. The shared garden spaces bring residents together and the Span sense of community is strong.

But not everything about Span is ideal. Committee structure envisaged by Lyons as an ideal of estate self-management and neighbourhood self-regulation does not always work that well in practice. Personal tensions or difficult decisions sometimes create antagonisms between Span dwellers, as they do in any other shared freehold block of flats or housing estate. The compact house types have proven a challenge to fit out and maintain, especially over the past 20 years or more, as domestic appliances and new technologies demand additional space. And their thin build is a challenge for today's fuel-consuming society.

> 'The aim is to create an overall unity that avoids regimentation, provides a sense of freshness, enhances rather than eradicates the natural features of the site; that ensures that estates look mature from the outset and retain an informal, intrinsic dignity that will still communicate itself fifty years from now.'[90]
> in *Span – living with new ideas*

13

	The Priory, Priory Park and Park Row
Architect	Eric Lyons

Project	The Priory
Completed	1956
Mix & Typology	61 flats, Types A, B and C
Status	Locally listed
Awards	Civic Trust Award and RIBA Award

Project	Priory Park
Completed	1957
Mix & Typology	4 houses, Type T2

Project	Park Row
Completed	1963
Mix & Typology	9 houses, Type T10

The three-storey blocks of flats at The Priory and the four two-storey terrace houses that comprise Priory Park, were some of the first developments built by Span in the local area. Situated among mature trees and meandering paths, The Priory's shared entrance areas are enhanced by distinctive wayfinding graphics, set in the Clarendon typeface. The architectural historian Nikolaus Pevsner described the estate as, 'low blocks happily grouped around informal courtyards, with vistas through open ground-floor lobbies'.[91]

Span struggled to gather the building resources necessary at the start of their activities and Wates was commissioned to deliver the flats.

The Priory was featured in a 1969 BBC documentary *Omnibus: The more we are together* in which the architectural critic, Iain Nairn identified the use of tile-hung cladding as a reference to vernacular Kentish architecture.[92] Tile-hanging became a standard feature on early Span housing and was so stylistically successful that it spread across Britain in housing that attempted to replicate the Span look. Nairn wrote: the Priory 'is in the same style as Ham Common but on a sloping site which gives a chance for a marvellous effect of interlocking squares, thickly planted.'[93]

The original site, which included two large houses, Heathfield and The Priory, was at first allocated for high-rise redevelopment in the late 1940s, as part of the Greater London Plan. Following public opposition, the appeal inspector ruled in favour of a private development of two storeys only.[94] The tower of an original small church, which gave its name to the development, still survives, at the corner of Parkgate and Priory Park as a folly incorporated into a modern house designed by Brian Meeking.[95]

Park Row was built on the site of two houses, numbers 59 and 61 Lee Road. It is a small scheme of nine houses arranged in two terraces, aligned with both Lee Road and Priory Park.

Covered main entrance with wayfinding

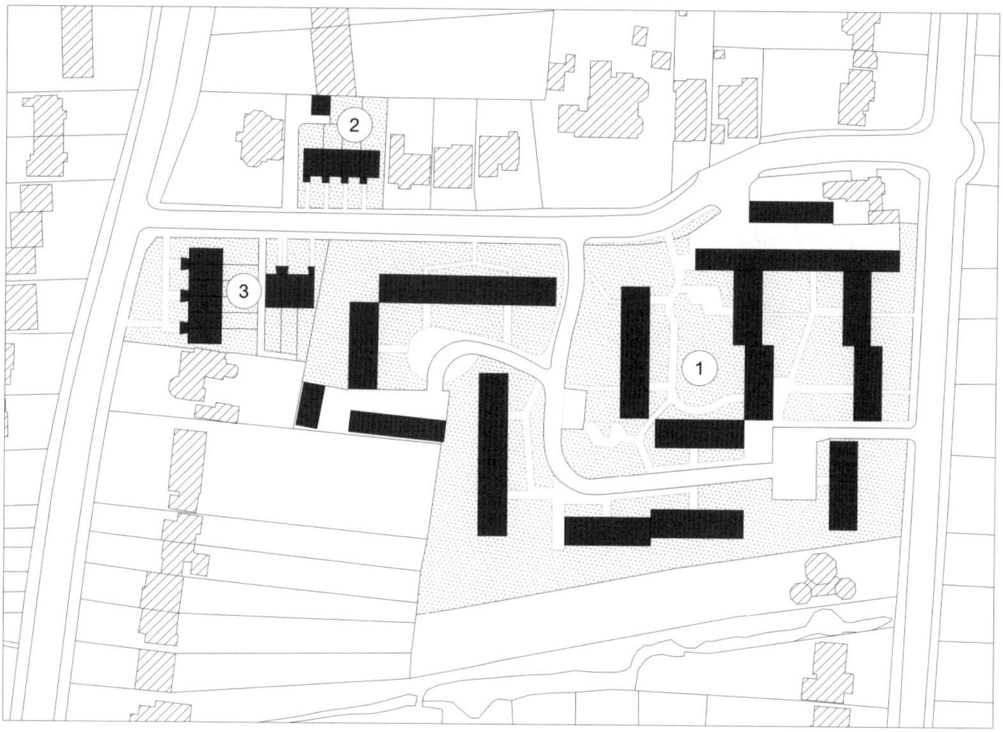

Site plan
1 The Priory
2 Priory Park
3 Park Row

1:2500 50m

 The Priory communal garden

	Corner Green and 24–33 Corner Green
Architect	Eric Lyons

Project	Corner Green
Completed	1959
Mix & Typology	23 houses, Type T7 and T8
Status	Locally listed

Project	24–33 Corner Green
Completed	1979
Mix & Typology	10 houses, Type A and B

Built on the site of allotments, the first phase of Corner Green is notable for its open layout, which is based on the traditional English village model of houses grouped around a central green, with the grassy landscape, designed by Ivor Cunningham, continuous up to the front doors. In order to achieve this, the garages are segregated on the site's periphery. The terraced houses have flat roofs and elevations composed of vertical brick bands alternating with panels of white painted timber boarding and windows.

As in most Span estates the house types, here T7 and T8, are designed to 'offer flexibility of composition, allowing the units to be arranged to suit the particular nature of a site. The blocks are offset from one another to adapt to the contours and boundaries of the site and create a sense of enclosure.'[96]

Eric Lyons particularly enjoyed the layout and planting of Corner Green and 12 years after its completion judged the development to 'have survived (or matured) as the best of all Span schemes.'[97] On the central green, a mature tree dominates – it was planted in 1959 by the Ministry of Housing to celebrate the construction of the one millionth house in the post-war period by private enterprise.[98] Another feature that pleased Lyons when he revisited Corner Green was the choice of London stock brickwork, with its familiar and soft tones.

In 1978–79, Lyons designed a set of ten houses, in two terraces, on an open site between the 1950s developments of Corner Green and The Keep. Intended by Span to be called Corner Keep, the Post Office however insisted that the houses were addressed as a part of the Corner Green lane.

Like Holm Walk, its contemporary estate nearby, this scheme broke with the repeating rectangular and flat-roofed Span developments of the previous decades. Influenced by the picturesque seaside architecture of southern Portugal when designing the marina scheme in Vilamoura in the early 1970s, Lyons introduced a new mix into Corner Green, with two- and three-storey houses displaying steep dual-pitched roofs. Most striking are the window shapes, many of three sections, some with a drop in the centre making a T-shape, others to one side. The large communal garden lies over the Kidbrooke railway tunnel.

24–33 Corner Green from the communal garden

1979

Corner Green in the 1960s

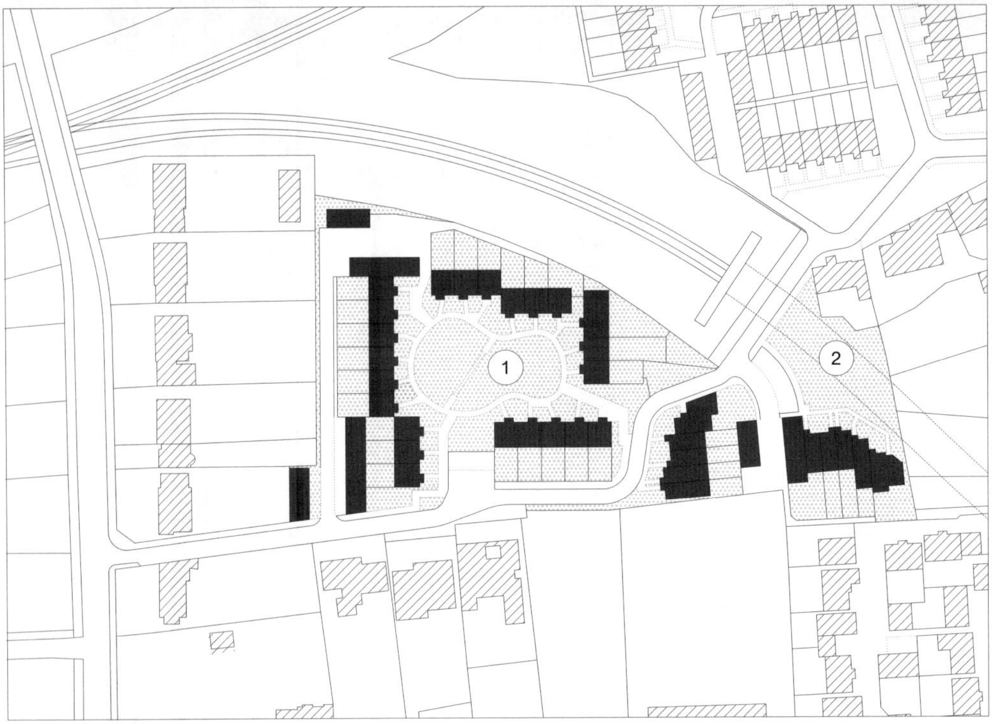

Site plan
1 Corner Green
2 24–33 Corner Green

1:2500 50m

1959, 1979

CORNER GREEN AND 24–33 CORNER GREEN

Corner Green communal garden

1959

15	Project	The Keep
	Architect	Eric Lyons
	Completed	1957
	Mix & Typology	44 houses, Type T2
	Status	Locally listed

The Keep southern terrace

Along with Corner Green, The Keep was built on land previously used as allotments. The estate features tile-hung two-storey terraced houses and provides much-appreciated allotments for the residents on a triangular piece of land alongside the railway cutting (previously the site of a pigsty).[99]

Revisiting the scheme in 1971, Eric Lyons commented, 'For me, the most unsatisfying scheme, a job that suffered from the participation of a planning officer who sent for tracing paper and a soft pencil and showed us how to improve the arrangement of the buildings on the site.'[100] In other words, the council officers forced Lyons to abandon his usual communal green spaces for a more typical suburban street layout. Cleverly, Lyons got around this with a fine landscaping design to soften the impact of the compromised scheme, with each front garden's planting and edging treatment contributing to the overall uniformity of the estate.

Ian Nairn commented: 'Corner Green is the better to look at, with a central square free of cars balanced between formality and freedom. But the Keep seems better to be in, paradoxically, just because the houses and cars are mixed together more, and the place is less of a set-piece.'[101]

THE KEEP

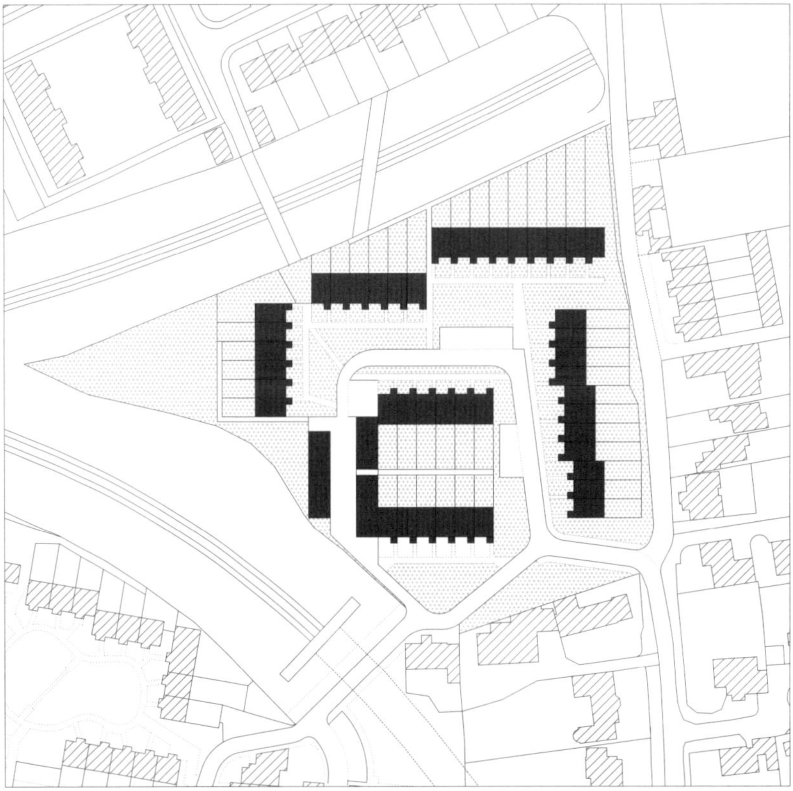

Site plan 1:2500 50m

16

Project	Spangate
Architect	Eric Lyons
Completed	1964
Mix & Typology	17 flats, Type Q

Built on the site of three houses dating from the 1820s that faced on to Lee Road,[102] Spangate is a block of flats situated at the western end of Blackheath Park. Its name derives from the nearby entrance gates to the Cator Estate and refers to the many Span estates within.

A 'pleasantly proportionate'[103] L-shaped, three-storey flat-roofed building enclosing a secluded garden, it is accessed by an open covered entrance with exposed pilotis. This allows views from the street through to the landscaped inner courtyard garden. There is no provision of balconies or private garden spaces, in a conscious decision to promote community living.

The garden features *Matriarch*, a fine sculpture by Frederick E McWilliam (1909–1992), which was installed in 2006 by the sculptor's daughter, a Spangate resident.

North elevation 1:500 15m

115 Site plan 1:2500 50m

1964

The kitchen hatch from the living room in a top floor flat

SPANGATE

Inner courtyard communal garden

1964

17

	Hallgate, The Hall, Foxes Dale and Brooklands Park
Architect	Eric Lyons

Project	Hall 1
Completed	1957
Mix & Typology	44 flats, Types A, B and C

Project	T3 houses, Foxes Dale
Completed	1957
Mix & Typology	3 houses, Type T3
Status	Grade II Listed

Project	Hall 2, including Dale Close
Completed	1958
Mix & Typology	41 houses, Type T2

Project	Hallgate, Blackheath Park
Completed	1958
Mix & Typology	26 flats, Types A, B and C
Status	Grade II Listed
Awards	Civic Trust Award

Project	Brooklands Park
Completed	1964
Mix & Typology	16 houses, Type T15

Project	Hall 4, Halldale
Completed	1967
Mix & Typology	13 houses, Type R

 The tile hung facades of the T2 houses

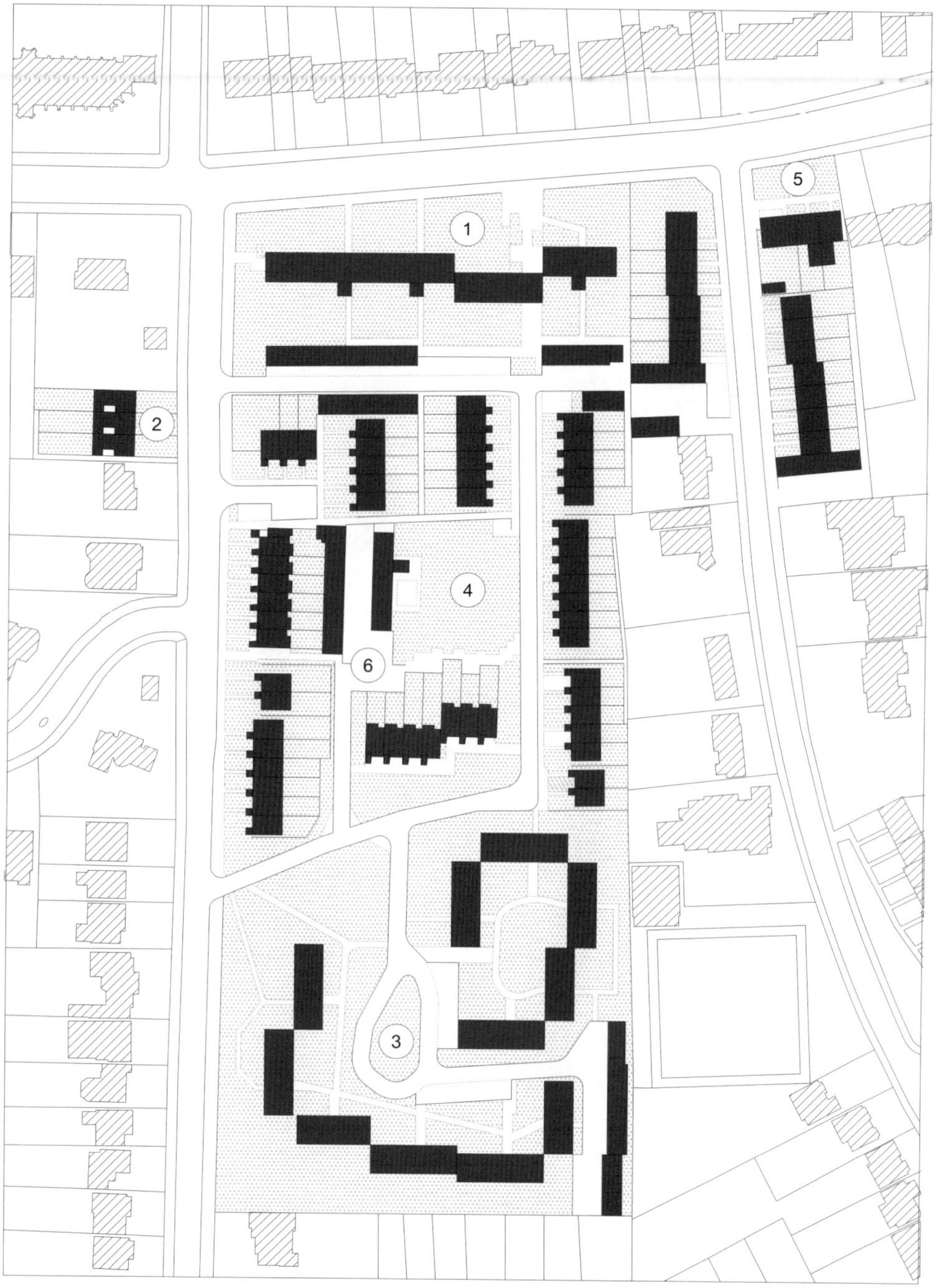

Site plan
1 Hallgate
2 T3 Houses
3 Hall 1
4 Hall 2
5 Brooklands Park
6 Hall 4

Hall 1 is one of the earliest Span developments in Blackheath, built on the site of the extensive gardens of The Hall, a small mansion from the early 1800s.[104] The development retained the topography of the sloping lawn and line of chestnut trees which originally formed a north-south avenue walk. The estate comprises eleven two-storey blocks of flats arranged informally to enclose communal gardens. Hall 2, completed a year later, offered two-storey family houses arranged in terraced blocks and features the tile-hung front elevations of the type T2 house used in The Keep in 1957.[105]

An annotated floorplan of Hall 2, circulated to residents in the 1960s, provides a snapshot of the early residents' professions and socio-economic status: of 39 residents, seven were architects and four civil servants. There was also a musician, a retired schoolmistress, an RAF pilot, a university lecturer, a journalist, an art dealer, a sales executive and a doctor. Notable residents were Walter Bor (1916–1999) – a LCC town planner who later led the team that developed Milton Keynes, and Rosemary Stjernstedt (1912–1998), who also worked at the LCC and later at Lambeth Council. Frank Knight, an architect partner at Fry, Drew & Partners lived there as did the historian and senior civil servant, Richard Sommerville (1906–1992). Bob Godfrey (1921–2013), an animator and director of children's TV shows, including 'Roobarb and Custard', lived at 6 Foxes Dale for many years.[106]

Hall 1 with Hall 2 to the left soon after completion

Hallgate from Blackheath Park

HALLGATE

17 The T3 houses form a short and delightful terrace along Foxes Dale. House number 2 was the show home and was selected by *House & Garden* magazine as their 'House of Ideas' for 1957. The T3 is the most spatially complex Span house type, with a roof terrace, inner patio garden and a spiral staircase connecting the three storeys.[107] Initially planned as a scheme of 19 units, only three were built. The others were to line Blackheath Park but Hallgate's flats were built instead. Listed at a cost of about £6,000 each, the T3s were expensive and proved unprofitable.[108] The adjacent site, extending on to Blackheath Park, was sold to Peter Moro to build his own house, after Leslie Bilsby had demolished the Victorian villa that stood there.

Hallgate, a three-storey block of flats, was built on the site of three older houses on the south side of Blackheath Park. Similar to the later Spangate block of 1964, Hallgate has an open passageway with exposed columns, forming, as the name suggests, the gate to The Hall estate beyond. Initially refused planning permission, Span fought hard for this scheme and permission was granted on appeal. To commemorate the victory, Lyons commissioned local sculptor Keith Godwin to create a sculpture set into the entrance wall. Called *The Architect in Society*, it portrays a figure that represents Lyons being crushed under the weight of the forces of 'society', which rejected modern architecture at the time. Godwin also created a sculpture for Span's Parkleys Estate in Ham.

The fourth and final part of The Hall is formed of two three-storey terraces. These Type R houses are of light yellow bricks and have more articulated façades and rooflines than the earlier Span blocks. 1 Foxes Dale was the development's show home and benefits from a wider end-plot and a unique garden designed by Ivor Cunningham and featured in *Modern Private Gardens* (1968, by Susan and Geoffrey Jellico) where it was described as 'an architectural setting for outdoor living' with its pergola, sculpture and conservatory; a striking butterfly glass roof, designed by Lyons and visible from the road.[109]

The Hall 4 was built on the site of two demolished villas – The Hall and Bellfield – and was yet another trigger in the ongoing conservation battle within Greenwich and Blackheath. Bellfield was designed by George Smith, the architect for Blackheath railway station and the church of St Michael's and All Angels. The Hall, was also a fine Georgian building. The Blackheath Society and Georgian Group both lobbied for their preservation but eventually lost the battle.[110]

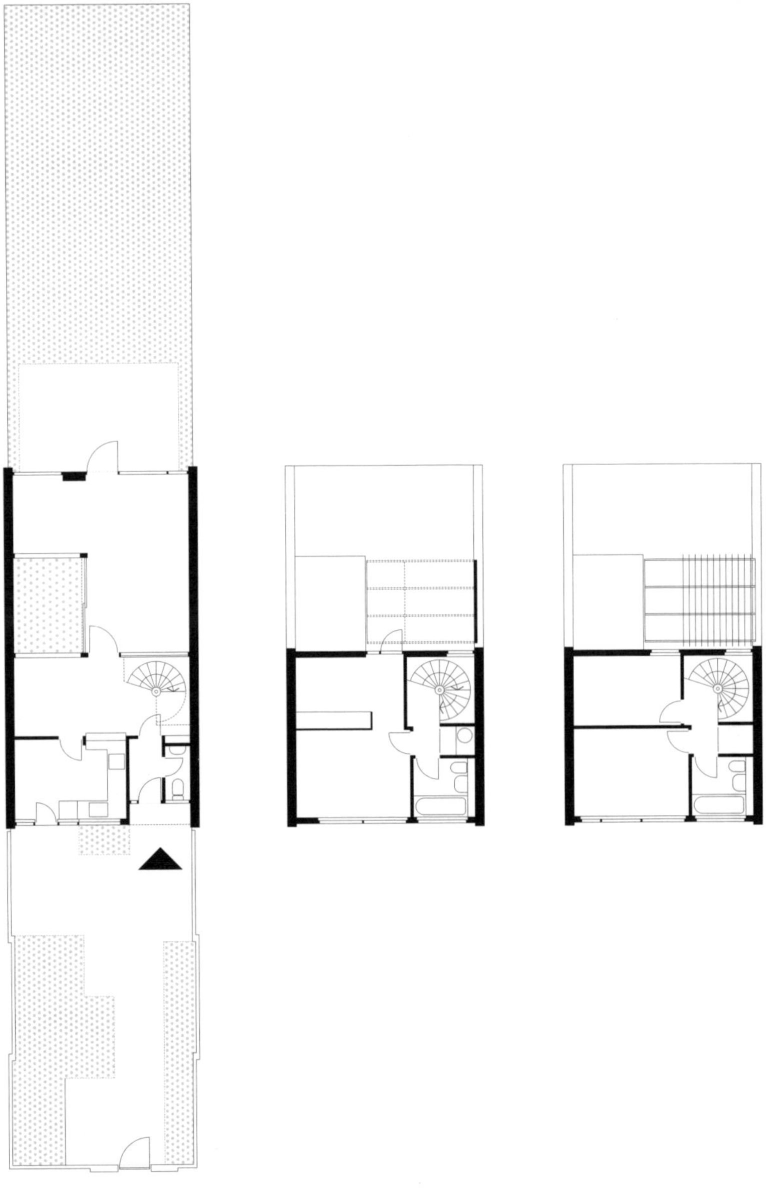

T3 Houses
Above, left to right: ground, first and second floor plans
Below: terrace front elevation

10m

T3 house spiral staircase
Opposite above: T3 house elevation from the front patio
Opposite below: T3 house living room and inner courtyard to the right

Hallgate main entrance

The Architect in Society by Keith Godwin at the Hallgate main entrance

Halldale show house conservatory, designed by Eric Lyons
Opposite above: Halldale, a first floor living room
Opposite below: Halldale, southern block seen from Hall 1

1967

18

	The Plantation and Parkend
Architect	Eric Lyons

Project	The Plantation, Morden Road
Completed	1962
Mix & Typology	34 houses, Type T7 and T8
Status	Locally listed

Project	Parkend, Blackheath Park
Completed	1967
Mix & Typology	19 houses, Type T2AX

Built on the site of the Copping's nursery garden, a local family business with a fruit shop on Lee High Road[111], The Plantation is accessed from a long drive and mostly hidden from Morden Road. The drive was created by demolishing an earlier house at number 17. The estate houses are of yellow stock brick, arranged around two greens and much-enjoyed landscaped communal gardens.

When Eric Lyons revisited the scheme in 1971, he voiced second thoughts: 'We talked ourselves into a daft landscape idea of a meaningless mounding of grass as well as a meaningless scooping out of the central area. I like to study trendy architectural tricks in landscape design and in architecture in order to avoid them and I am sorry that we fell for that crude one'.[112] Most residents and visitors would strongly disagree with him. Children enjoy rolling down the slopes of the lawns and those entering the estate enjoy its separation from Morden Road, enhanced by the mounding of grass that defines the setting of the play area.

Adjacent to The Plantation, but not physically linked to it, the Span estate, Parkend, marks the eastern extremity of the Cator Estate. It comprises larger type T2AX houses, which have both gated front patios and back gardens. This unusual Span house type expands on the front porch idea used in the earlier T2 and T2A houses, with a single-storey volume accommodating an entrance hall, WC and front workroom – frequently used as a home office or guest bedroom.

Parkend was built on the grounds of 115 Blackheath Park, the first of Leslie Bilsby's own houses on the Cator Estate. Originally a Victorian villa set in large gardens, it was severely bomb-damaged during the Second World War, so Bilsby appointed the architect Patrick Gwynne to transform it into a modern house in 1949. After moving to a new house, Bilsby demolished it in 1966 to make way for Parkend.

 Parkend at completion in 1967

1967

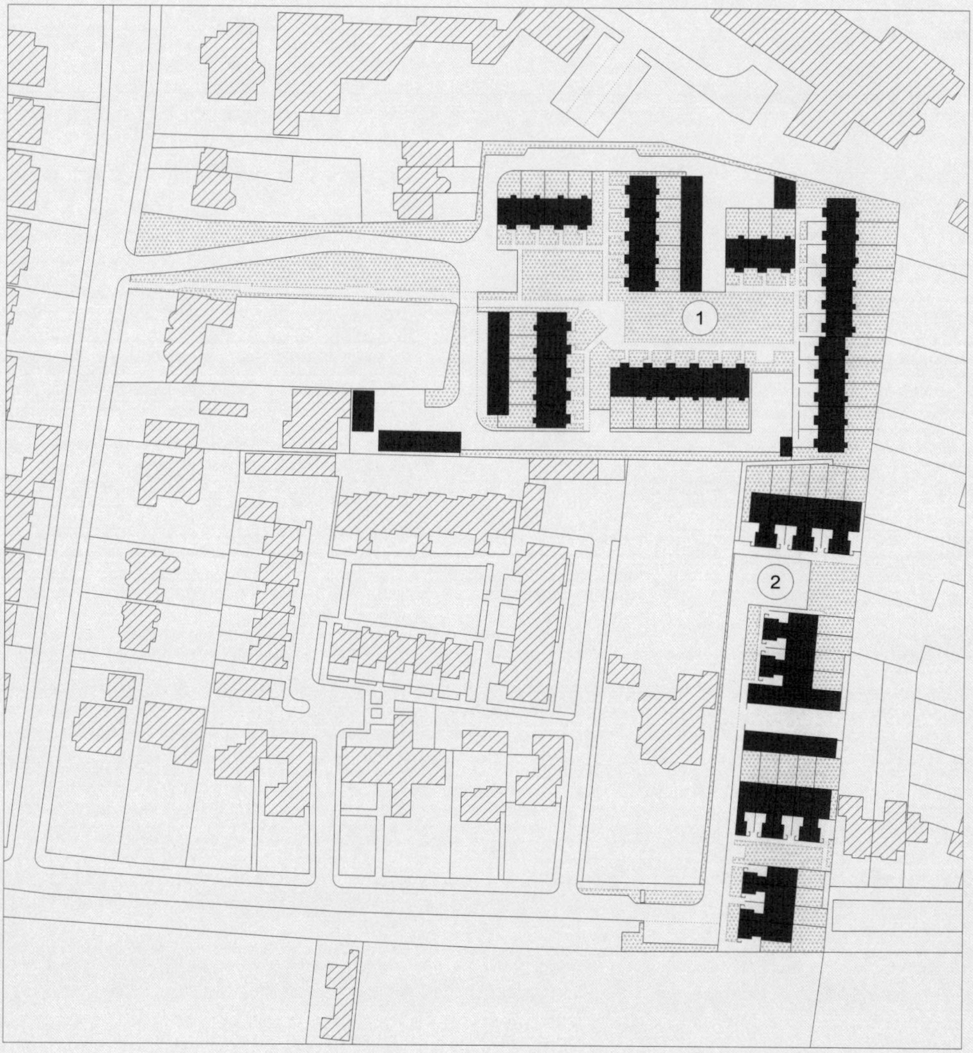

Site plan
1 The Plantation
2 Parkend

1:2500 50m

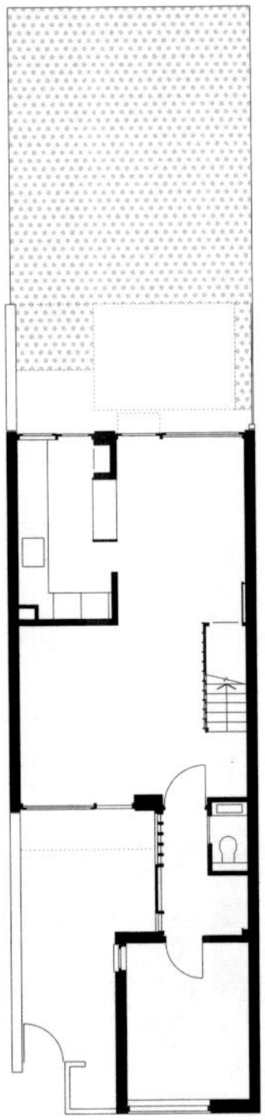

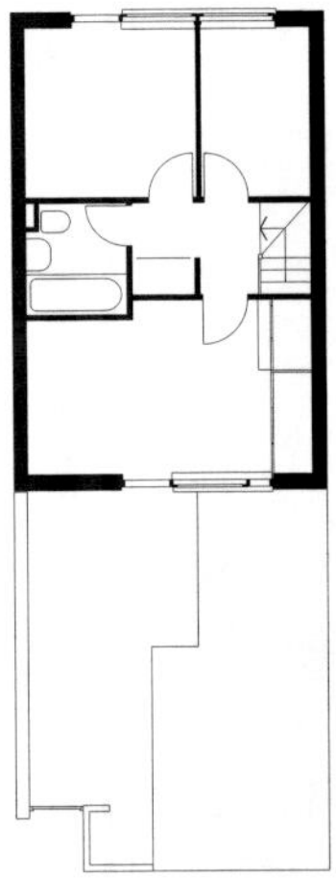

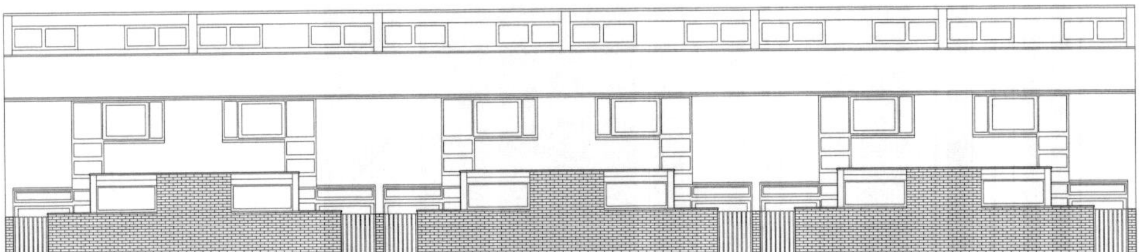

Above, left to right: Parkend ground and first floor plans
Below: Parkend northern block, front elevation

10m

THE PLANTATION AND PARKEND

1967

The Plantation communal gardens

THE PLANTATION AND PARKEND

1962

19	Project	South Row
	Architect	Eric Lyons
	Completed	1963
	Mix & Typology	10 houses and 23 flats Type Q
	Status	Grade II listed
	Awards	Civic Trust Award

South Row occupies a prominent site on the south side of the Heath, overlooking its largest pond. It sits between Colonnade House and the magnificent crescent of the Paragon, both by the architect Michael Searles from around 1800.

When the planning process for South Row started in 1959, the scheme met strong local resistance and was refused planning consent at a public inquiry. Despite these obstacles, planning permission was eventually granted and the scheme was completed in 1963. The architect Sir Hugh Casson was one of the influential individuals who supported Span during the inquiry, while the appeal inspector wrote that, 'a facsimile building would cast doubt upon the authenticity of the adjacent buildings and assume an importance which it could not justify or maintain.'[113]

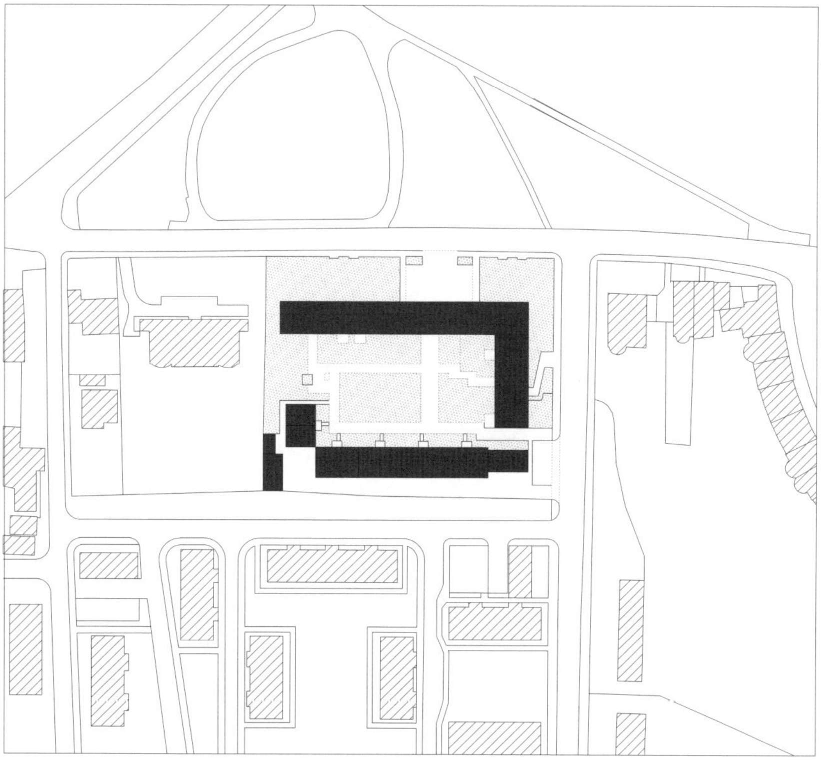

Site plan 1:2500 50m

Courtyard garden with the block of flats to the left and the terrace houses to the right

South Row in context: the Paragon and Cator Manor to the left, Colonnade House to the right; from Span's marketing brochure, 1963

SOUTH ROW

1963

The South Row saga started as the result of bomb damage and a plan proposed by the LCC in 1946 to buy the site and build a scheme of four five-storey blocks. At a public inquiry in 1947, concerns were raised and the part of the site fronting the Heath was removed from the compulsory purchase order. The hope was that all buildings along South Row could be restored or built as replicas.[114] However, with restoration work led by Charles Bernard Brown already underway at the Paragon and Colonnade House, it soon became clear that the cost of the proposed new facsimile building opposite the pond was not affordable.

The extensive site was then divided into two parts, with the Pond Road estate developed to the south for social housing. Designed by Albert Richardson, it was completed in 1954, based on a neo-Georgian style. Ivor Cunningham, Eric Lyons's partner acidly described the estate as 'vapid Georgian flats for the masses'[115], yet another sign of the needless conflict between traditional and modern. Perhaps this accounts for the high brick wall on South Row's southern boundary.

South Row is composed of two L-shaped blocks: a three-storey building facing the street with 22 flats and penthouse, and a terrace of 10 houses to the rear. Grouped around a landscaped court, with a direct connection towards both the Heath and Pond Road, the scheme feels both private and open. In Nikolaus Pevsner's words, 'the front to the Heath an uncompromising, well proportionate statement of international modern principles, the back, accessed through an open-ground floor lobby, with homelier Span weatherboarding'.[116]

One of the strongest Span estates in the area, both in its arrangement around a formal internal court and its structured façades, the elevations are organised using an expressed concrete frame with exposed columns and beams, infilled with elements of dark brickwork for the flats and white painted timber for the houses.

The flats have private balconies and the houses contain inbuilt garages at lower ground level. The main upper ground floor to the houses is accessed by sets of steps from the court, providing privacy and adopting a device historically used in traditional terraced housing, the piano nobile. Internally the houses have an open tread staircase and first floor gallery that both give a generous feeling of space despite their narrow plan.

Perspective of South Row published in 1960, after Span's successful planning appeal

The raised ground floor of the terraced houses, facing the communal courtyard garden

20	The Lane and Streetfield Mews
Architect	Eric Lyons

Project	The Lane
Completed	1964
Mix & Typology	39 houses, Type T10 and T15
Status	Locally listed
Awards	Housing Design Award, Civic Trust Award

Project	Streetfield Mews
Completed	1984
Mix	15 houses and 5 flats

The Lane occupies an unusual, narrow, crescent-shaped site off Blackheath Park. The design for this constrained site takes the form of a winding lane, with the houses grouped in small terraces. The landscaping by Preben Jakobsen (who worked for Span from 1961 to 1969) creates both open and more intimate spaces. Separate areas for garage blocks and a small play space are squeezed into odd pockets of space. The house types, T10 and T15, are mono-pitched, of dark brickwork to the ground floor and white-painted timber cladding to the first floor.

Adjacent is Streetfield Mews, the last Span development in Blackheath, built 20 years later and completed after Eric Lyons death in 1980, with the project led by Ivor Cunningham. The site was previously allotments with the major constraint of the railway tunnel below, emerging at its south-eastern end. The unbuildable portion of the site over the tunnel contributes to the development's semi-rural setting and provides a large open space that is currently used as allotments, a communal garden and a wild meadow.

The houses are of dark red brick with slated pitched roofs and five flats set above garages. Arrival is through a gatehouse terrace, which in combination with the use of circular windows and low roof lines, creates an organic, vernacular almost farm-like setting.

The Lane and one of the communal pocket gardens

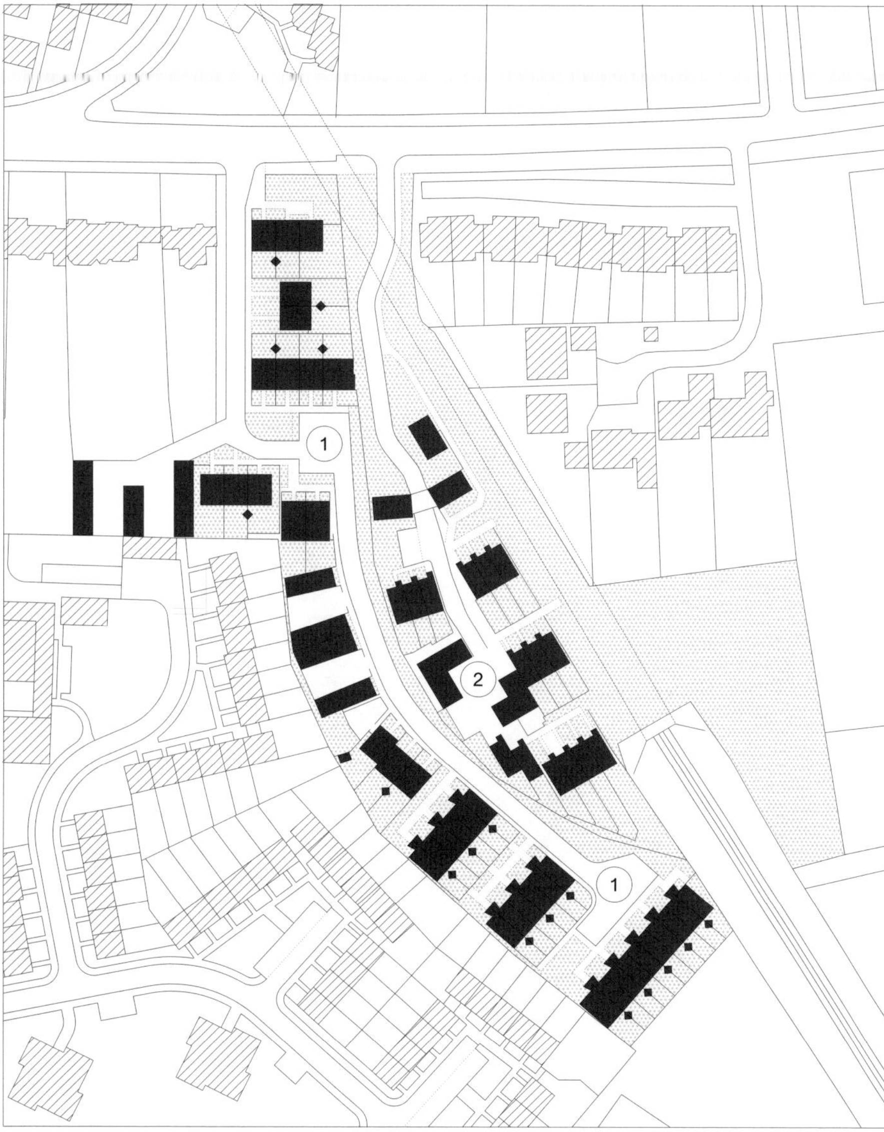

Site plan
1 The Lane
2 Streefield Mews

1:2500 50m

147 Streetfield Mews approach from Blackheath Park

1984

21

Project	Holm Walk
Architect	Eric Lyons
Completed	1978
Client	10 houses, Type A and B
Awards	Highly Commended Housing Design Award

A late Span development of 10 houses of dark brick with pitched tiled roofs and vertical windows. The house types are the same as nearby Corner Green, completed the year after, and share its use of irregular rooflines and two- and three-storey format.

The successful and unusual layout is heavily constrained by the railway tunnel which traverses the southern part of the site before crossing Blackheath Park to Streetfield Mews on the other side. The layout is composed of four small terraces placed organically along the invisible line of the tunnel below and aligning with Blackheath Park.

In contrast with the repetitive original Span schemes, the ten houses in Holm Walk are variants of house types A and B with eight different layouts overall. One of the houses benefits from an additional single storey room which was originally a glazed sales office. Its garden was designed by landscape architect Rosemary Alexander in the 1980s.

Situated above the railway tunnel, the communal garden is secluded and triangular in shape. It contains a large cork oak tree, more common on the Iberian Peninsula than in southeast London. Eric Lyons and his partners were working on a marina project at Vilamoura in Portugal while Holm Walk was under development, so perhaps the tree was brought from the Algarve as a seedling.

View from the communal garden

HOLM WALK

 Site plan 1:2500 50m 1978

Gordon (1923–2019) and Ursula (b. 1925) Bowyer moved to their home in Maze Hill, Greenwich in 1950, at the suggestion of Trevor Dannatt, the best man at their wedding in 1949. The Bowyers had both studied at the Polytechnic and met while working for Peter Moro, who was also their teacher. Gordon said of their training that, 'we benefited from the best teachers, as during the war there were no architectural commissions'.[117] After graduating, Gordon worked first with Richard Sheppard and then together with Ursula, took part in the Festival of Britain in 1951, for which they designed the Sport Pavilion.

Ursula (née Mayer) arrived in Britain with her family in 1937 as a German Jewish émigré. She entered the Polytechnic at just 16 – a move suggested to her mother by Moro, himself a German émigré. Ursula's first job was with Jane Drew (1911–1996) who always promoted women in architecture.

The Bowyer's office was initially in Blandford Street, near Baker Street. They shared this space and worked in a collaborative atmosphere alongside Trevor Dannatt, Margaret and Richard Finch, Peter Moro, Walter Greaves and Georgio Subiotto. Kenneth Grange was their graphic designer and Robin Day an important collaborator for furniture and furnishings. In the 1950s and early 1960s, they worked on residential commissions, which were never really profitable, so during the 1970s they shifted their focus to designing larger housing and commercial projects, for IBM, Max Factor and Vidal Sassoon, both in Europe and the US, as well as exhibition designs – for the RIBA and the British Museum, amongst others.

After starting a family, Ursula took on smaller projects locally. Her most noted work was the conversion of Vanbrugh Castle to four houses. She became closely involved with the Greenwich Society, working to establish the Blackheath Conservation Area. She also contributed to local campaigns; to save the fine Jacobean Charlton House and to secure university use of the Old Naval College buildings in Greenwich, alongside Trevor Dannatt.

One of the partners at the Bowyers' practice, Iain Langlands, also lived in the area and had worked for Span before joining the Bowyers in 1961.[118] With the arrival of Steve Batchelor, the practice became Bowyer Langlands Batchelor in the early 1980s, following the Bowyers' retirement.

projects

17 and 17a Montpelier Row	1958
2 Langton Way	1960s
Lyndale Close	1963
19 Morden Road Mews	1972
Hatfield Court, Heathway	1972
Vanbrugh Castle conversion, Maze Hill	1977

Ursula and Gordon Bowyer, 1953

22

Project	17 and 17a Montpelier Row
Architect	Gordon and Ursula Bowyer
Completed	1958
Client	James and Audrey Callaghan (for number 17)

This pair of three-storey houses was built on the site of a bomb-destroyed property.[119] It forms a modern in-fill between the early Victorian houses to the south, and the late-eighteenth century terrace to the north (now the Clarendon Hotel). Number 17 was designed for James Callaghan MP and his young family, who had been Bowyer's neighbours in Greenwich. Callaghan later served as Labour Prime Minister from 1976 to 1979. Number 17a was intended for the architects themselves, but they decided to remain at their home in Maze Hill.

Although initially conceived as a single house, for economic reasons the final scheme was for a pair. The two houses are mirrored in plan with garage, utility, cloakroom and study on the ground floor; living room, dining room and kitchen on the first floor; and the bedrooms above on the top floor. The first-floor living room benefits from open views over the Heath towards All Saints Church. Here large sliding doors create a flexible, open-plan and double-aspect living room. Originally the two rear gardens had no dividing fence and were enjoyed as a single shared space.[120]

When James Callaghan became Chancellor of the Exchequer in 1964, he and his family moved to 11 Downing Street. The architect Michael Mellish (d.2024), a partner at Peter Moro's practice, moved in with his family and lived there until his death. Mellish preserved the original windows and interiors, including the timber-boarded ceilings, large sliding glazed panels and fitted storage units that are all key to its character.[121]

After leaving 17 Montpelier Row, Audrey Callaghan commented: 'I do miss the house that was so expertly tailor-made… The rare kind of house that exactly suits one's way of life is like a second skin. It was a wrench to leave.'[122]

More recently, a pair of two-storey white-rendered houses, The Courtyard House and Stoneley, were built at the end of the long gardens. Designed by local architect Suzanne Brewer, they are accessed from Lynch Close. The Courtyard House was completed in 2005 for the architect's own use, and Stoneley followed two years later.

Above: garden front under construction
Below: 17 and 17a Montpelier Row soon after completion

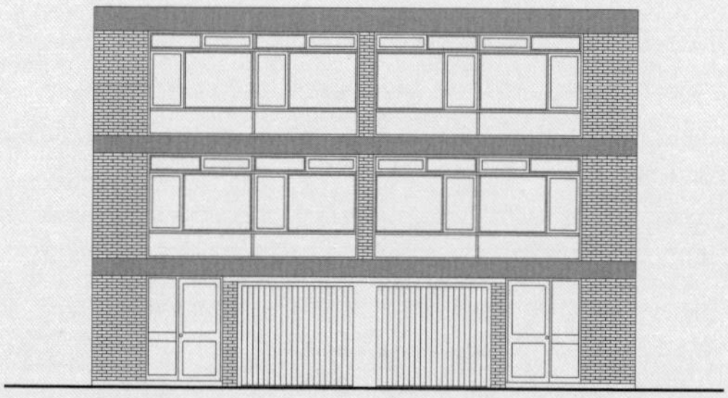

Front elevation

17 AND 17A MONTPELIER ROW

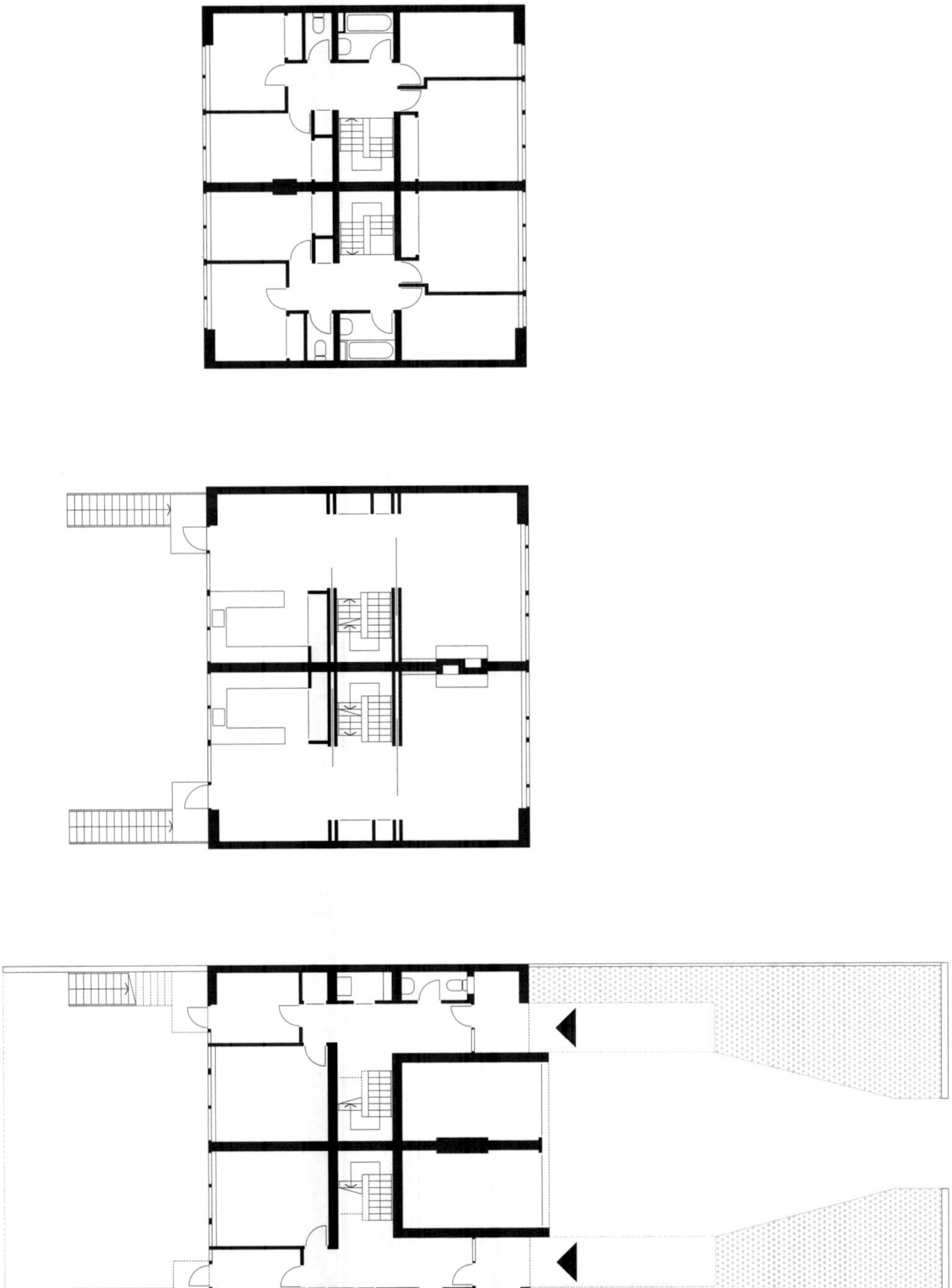

Top to bottom: second, first and ground floor plans

10m

1958

23

Project	2 Langton Way
Architect	Gordon and Ursula Bowyer
Completed	1960s
Client	George and Ann Dannatt

Originally a project by Trevor Dannatt for his brother George, Ursula Bowyer subsequently carried out further work on this small nineteenth-century coach house. Externally, the conversion includes a picturesque window facing the Heath and a striking new front door and window forming an abstract composition to the north face of the house. The refurbishment consisted of a new kitchen, dining area and an extended living space with a cleverly placed fireplace, slot window and integrated bookcase. A slight change of level adds character to the interior as does the use of exposed brick walls and floor-to-ceiling windows in the living room.[123]

The next owner, Graham Lane, took on the house in 1967. Lane was an associate at Denys Lasdun's practice, working on projects such as 26 St James's Place, a Grade II* listed block of flats in central London.[124]

Site plan 1:2000 50m

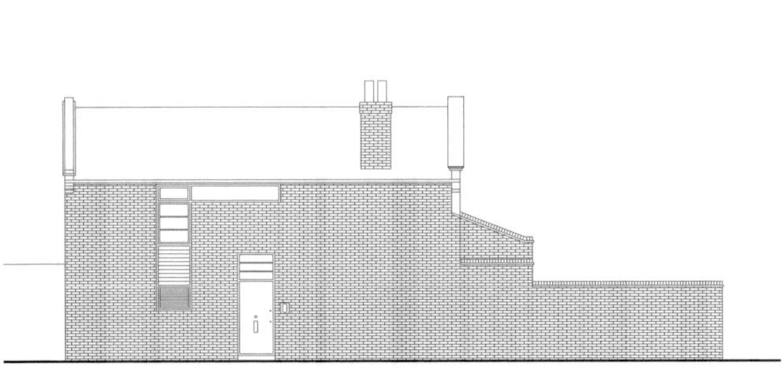

Above: the extension seen from the dining area in 1965
Below: street elevation

10m

Project	Lyndale Close
Architect	Gordon and Ursula Bowyer
Completed	1963
Client	Dannatt family

A terrace of five 3-bed houses and block of six garages, on a site in the garden of a large corner villa at 43 Westcombe Park Road.[125] The compact two-storey houses have richly articulated façades with projecting bays that create recessed entrances. The doorways form a simple asymmetrical composition with white glazed tile cladding to the WC on one side, and a small projecting canopy above.[126]

The terrace and garages create an L-shape on the site, with access to the houses via a mews-like lane on their northern side. Their rear elevations open towards private gardens to the south. As the garage block faces on to Foyle Road, the first impression, on approach, is a harsh one. Gated metal railings, added at a later date, add to the general sense of defensiveness. However, any sense of harshness is dispelled when one understands the clever layout of the plot and the quality of the secluded housing beyond.

Front elevation

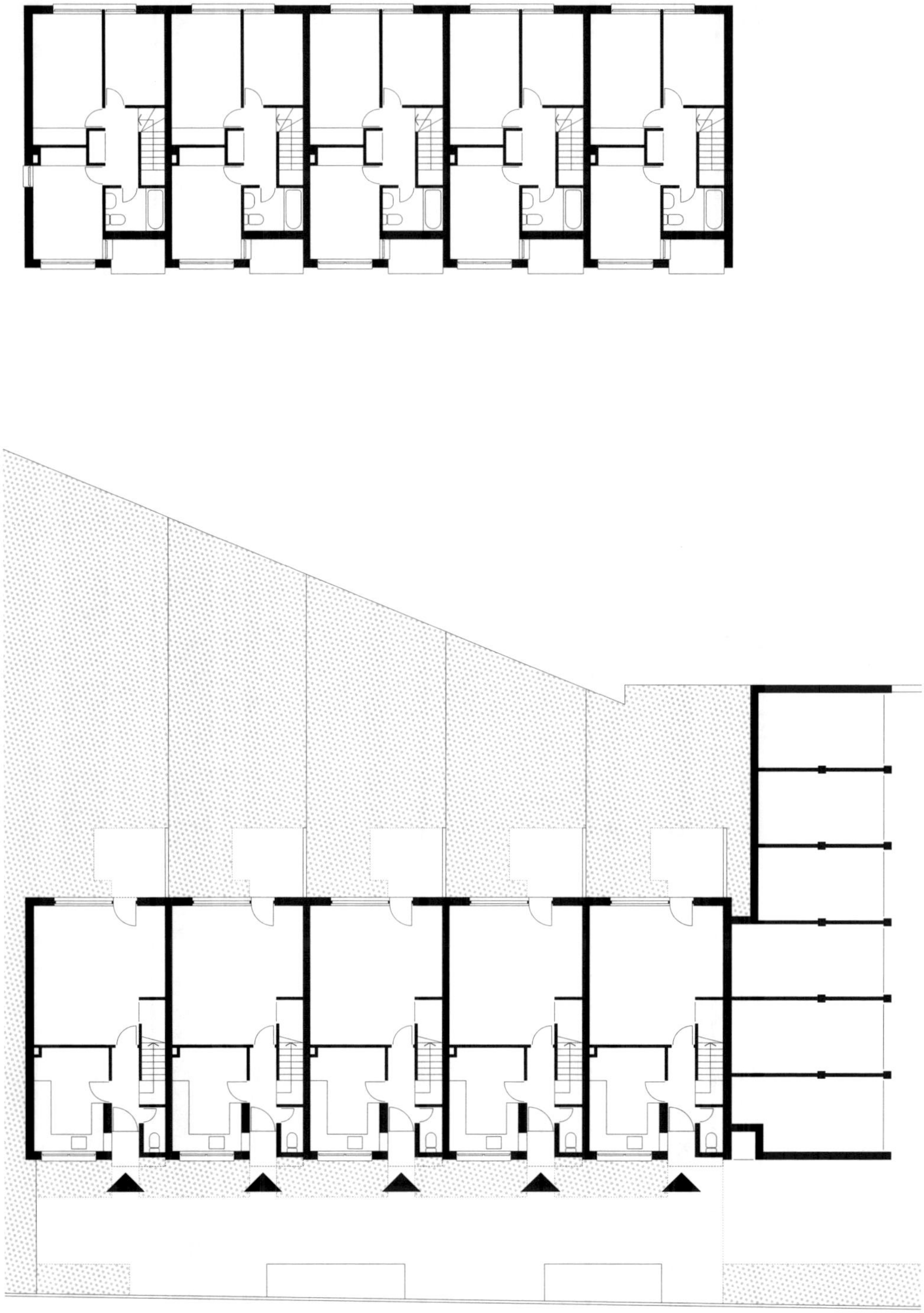

Above: first floor plan
Below: ground floor plan, as originally built

10m

1963

James Gowan (1923–2015) had no family or personal connection with Greenwich. However, he was interested in exploring social housing design and was commissioned by the GLC to deliver two local schemes: Corvette Square, off Trafalgar Road; and Creek Road, now part of the Meridian Estate.

Gowan was born in Scotland. He trained at the Glasgow School of Art (1940–42) and later at the Kingston School of Art (1946–48). During the Second World War he was an RAF radar operator based in Palestine. After leaving Kingston, he was employed by Philip Powell, of Powell and Moya, who had been his tutor. He worked on the Skylon, one of the landmarks for the 1951 Festival of Britain and the design of Stevenage New Town.

Subsequently he joined the firm of Lyons Israel Ellis (wrongly assuming Eric Lyons was a partner) where he met James Stirling. They formed a practice together in 1956, which lasted until 1964. During this period, they created a number of important and influential buildings, including Langham House Close, Ham Common, Richmond (1957) and the School of Engineering, University of Leicester (1963). Towards the end of their collaboration, they designed Perrygrove, an old people's home in Charlton, now demolished.

After leaving the practice, Gowan worked on smaller but extremely influential projects, such as the Schreiber House in Hampstead and a second house for the same client in Chester in 1982. In the 1990s, he completed projects in Italy, notably a medical clinic on the outskirts of Milan.

Gowan was greatly admired as a teacher at the AA and at the Royal College of Art, where he mentored Richard Rogers and Peter Cook amongst many others.

Local projects	Perrygrove, Rectory Field Crescent, Charlton (demolished)	1964
	Creek Road housing, Greenwich	1967
	Trafalgar Road housing, Greenwich	1968

Other projects	Langham House Close, Ham Common, Richmond	1957
	School of Engineering at the University of Leicester	1963
	Schreiber House, Hampstead	1964

James Gowan and James Stirling, 1962

25	Project	Trafalgar Road Housing
	Architect	James Gowan
	Completed	1968
	Client	GLC

Designed by Gowan after his acrimonious split with James Stirling, this housing scheme, 'within cannonball range of Wren's hospital'[127] and the Queen's House, is now disfigured by oversailing pitched roofs, which were installed by Greenwich Council in the 1990s. When first built, its bold and abstract sculptural form and layout was highly influential among contemporary architects.

The estate consists of four linked blocks, which create a quiet quadrangle, Corvette Square at the centre. The severe massing of dark red brickwork, recessed balconies and corner windows, were in strong contrast to the more utilitarian municipal housing of the time. The sculptural massing and composition have a conceptual connection with the work of the Dutch early modernist masters, J. J. P. Oud and Willem Dudok.[128] The sparse windows and doors on the main elevations were employed to avoid the endless repetitive 'front door and toilet' windows common in deck-access social housing of the time.

The 38-unit scheme is divided into studios and one-bed flats for older people on the ground floor, with larger maisonettes above. Access walkways thread through to staircases at the corners. Gowan resisted the brief to build standalone blocks of flats, preferring the model of an enclosed central square. He regretted Greenwich Council's unwillingness to add more soft landscaping to the communal space.

Gowan explained that 'The idea is of stacking smaller blocks on larger ones… The configuration of the flats has been contrived to give a very large scale, almost like a giant order. This is not characteristic of British terrace housing which tends to be based on the precedent of the flat Georgian façade. However, there are one or two serrated terraces with a giant scale, Leinster Square, W11, the north of Gloucester Terrace and Powis Square, W2 and these were all models for this project.'[129]

A similar scheme, by Gowan on nearby Creek Road, which used the same typology, was completed in 1967. It also suffered later from the same unsightly roof additions.

Following construction of Trafalgar Road, *The Architectural Review* included a snazzy drawing by Gowan of the façade illustrating a speculative kit-of-parts for personalisation that was to be sponsored by a residents' cooperative – the idea being that each tenant could choose a series of clip-on elements. These included balcony covers, porches, screens, trellises and lean-to stairs, all in strong colours. This idea was never put into practice.

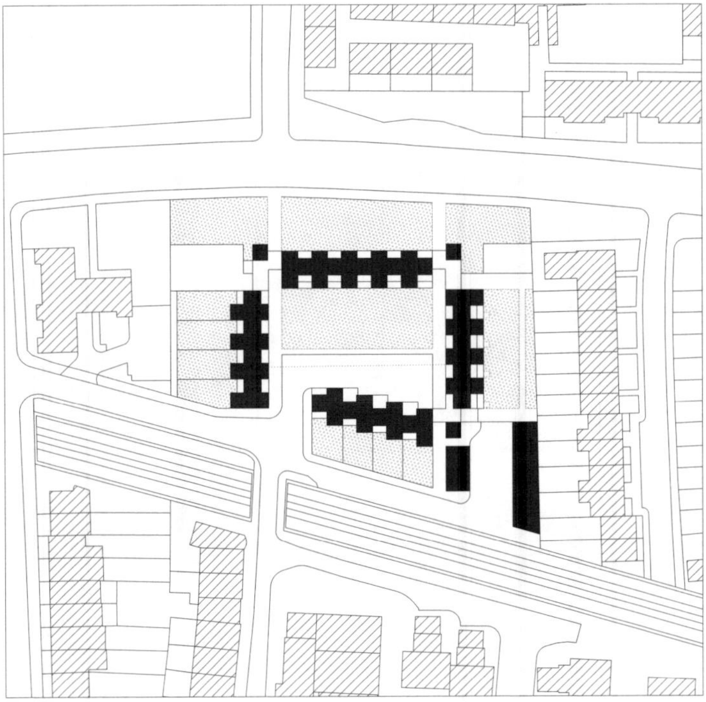

TRAFALGAR ROAD HOUSING

163 Site plan 1:2000 50m

1968

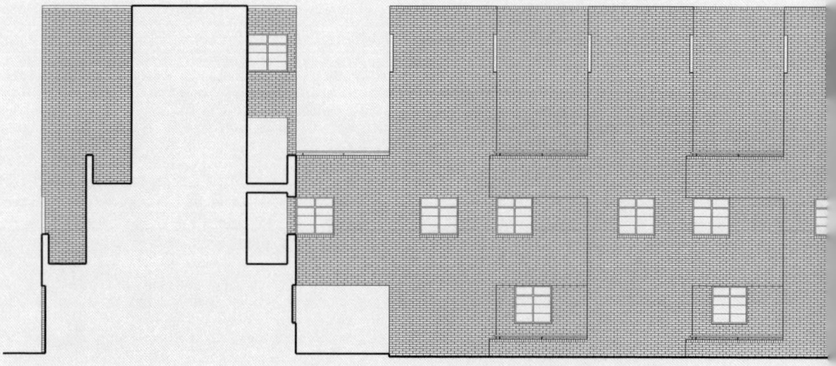

Courtyard elevation, as originally built

TRAFALGAR ROAD HOUSING

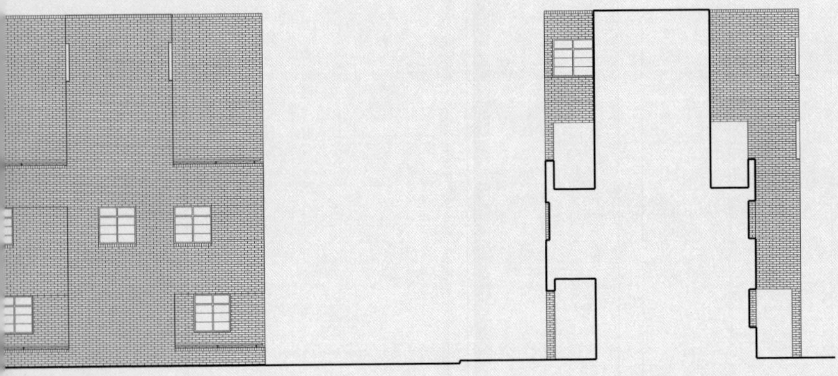

1:300 10m

1968

The north elevation from Trafalgar Road, 1970

TRAFALGAR ROAD HOUSING

1968

John Burden (1924–2005) designed and built his own family home in Blackheath at 14 Brooklands Park in 1952. Later he designed another house, No. 16, to the south on the same plot for his friend Philip Wiggans, a structural engineer. This second house was built perpendicular to his own to retain views towards the shared open gardens. There had been complaints about the asymmetrical pitched roof of 14 Brooklands Park, including an accusation that 'It looks like a factory!'[130] In response, Burden designed the second house with more traditional symmetrical gables.

Burden was born in Pinner, North London. After leaving school during the Second World War, he joined the army. Having embarked for Japan he was diverted to India, where he completed his training in Bangalore and was commissioned to join the Royal Engineers. He was attached to General HQ Intelligence in Delhi and stationed in the Lutyens Old Secretariat Building as head of the map section.

He left India on Independence Day in 1947 and returned to London, where he trained at the AA, then began his professional career in 1958 at Easton and Robertson, Cusdin, Preston and Smith in Bedford Square. In 1965 Cusdin, Burden and Howitt was formed. The practice specialised in the design of university and hospital buildings, including St Bartholomew's, the Middlesex, and Addenbrookes hospitals. In the academic field, work included commissions for the London School of Economics, Bedford College, London School of African and Oriental Studies, the International Hall of Residence in London, and University College Space Science Laboratories.

Burden also worked on ecclesiastical projects, designing several churches, schools, and community buildings – both in Tanzania and in England. These included the local church hall at 1 Pond Road, Blackheath and the Anglican Cathedral in the city of Kasulu. He retired to the village of Hemingford Grey in Cambridgeshire, where he carried out numerous building projects for the local church, St James'.[131]

Local projects

14 Brooklands Park	1952
16 Brooklands Park	1955
St Michael and All Angels Church Hall	1965

John Burden, 1960s

Project	St Michael and All Angels Church Hall
Architect	John Burden
Completed	1963
Client	St Michael and All Angels Church

St Michael and All Angels Church (1828–30) was designed by local architect George Smith. Standing on a prominent crossroads at the heart of the Cator Estate, the church tower and spire have been called 'the Needle of Kent' and 'the Devil's Toothpick'. The church has been Grade II* listed since 1973.

The church hall was built in 1963 to designs by John Burden. It was constructed with help from the church congregation over many weekends, under the supervision of the architect and engineer Philip Wiggans. Both men lived nearby in Brooklands Park and worshipped at the church.

The hall follows a simple square centralised plan with exposed brick piers and glazed doors on four sides. Its main room is a flexible space with a complex geometrical roof and high-level glazing, allowing views of the church and surrounding trees. The ceiling interior is clad in timber slats, creating a warm atmosphere and was inspired by those used in Greenwich University's Avery Hill Library, a beautiful Victorian building with large clerestory windows.[132] The hall was conceived as a flexible space to seat approximately 200 people. Curtains could be drawn to create five smaller spaces and a stage and screen added. There was also a potential plan for future expansion, never carried out, comprising another identical module, to be built towards the lawn.[133]

The new hall was opened by Mervyn Stockwood, the Lord Bishop of Southwark. The vicar at this time was Reverend F. E. Wankling.

In 1992, an extension provided two new halls. This was designed by local architect William Lowe, also a member of the congregation. A new covered walkway connected the extension and hall with the church creating a partly cloistered quadrangle. The landscape for this successful addition is by architect Carol Moller, who had previously worked on projects with Span architect Ivor Cunningham in the 1950s.[134]

Above: view from the central green, with the later pergola addition
Below: a party at the Church Hall in 1965

Above: poster by Bob Godfrey (of 6 Foxes Dale) to recruit volunteers to assist with the building of the church hall
Below: tea break for the volunteers c1963. Left to right: Mrs Wankling, Miss Brookes, Sue Burden, Jean Burden, Miss Brookes; the old corrugated hall in the background

ST MICHAEL AND ALL ANGELS CHURCH HALL

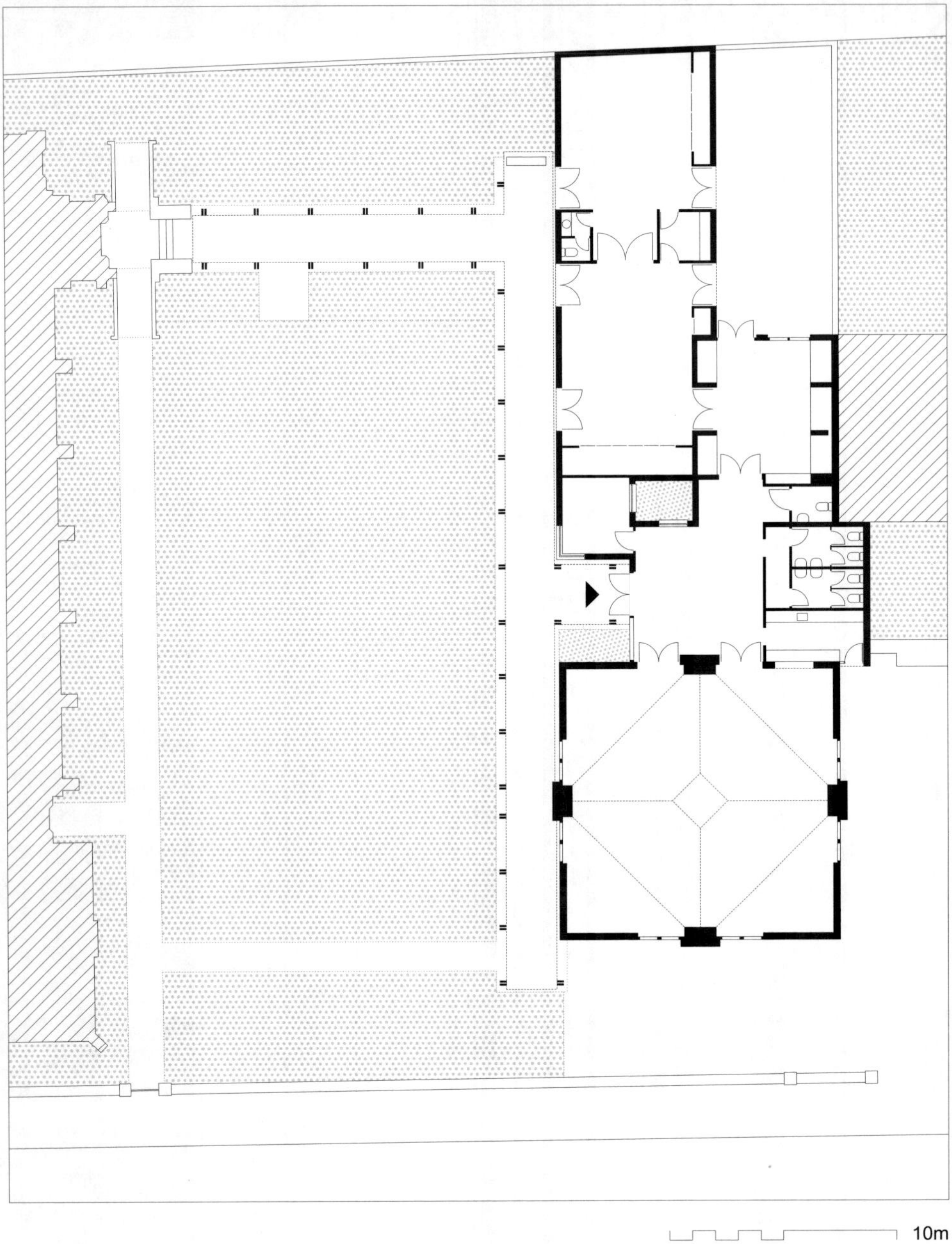

Above: ground floor plan
Below: south elevation

1963

John Newton (1935–2023) was born in Lincoln. He studied architecture at the Lincoln School of Art (1952–56) and the Leicester College of Art School of Architecture (1956–58). After qualification in 1960 he joined the architecture department of London Transport.

In 1965 he joined the practice Austin-Smith Lord whilst also studying town planning at the Regent Street Polytechnic. Subsequently, he was employed by H G Huckle & Partners and Barton Willmore Partnership in Reading as an architect-planner from 1970 to 1978 when he left to set up his own practice.

He was based initially in South Croydon but subsequently moved west to Henley-on-Thames. He continued to work on projects in London and the home counties until the 1990s including a new house in Chertsey (1990) for Vince Clarke, a member of the pop duo Erasure.

His later work included Point Cottage alterations (1991) on an island at Marlow for Andrew Fletcher of Depeche Mode and Ammonite House, Surrey (1993) – a large, spaceship-like home and recording studio with a circular plan and central spiral staircase, again for Vince Clarke. Newton later relocated to Cornwall.[135]

John Newton, 1960s

27

Project	10 and 11 Park Row
Architect	John Newton
Completed	1967
Client	Hayward Underhill

Built as a pair of three-storey houses on Park Row, which runs towards the river from the base of Greenwich Park, they were later extended with a set-back fourth storey, as originally intended by Newton. The houses were designed for fellow student Hayward Underhill at Regent Street Polytechnic where both were studying Town Planning, Newton having already qualified as an architect. Number 11 was built for Underhill's use and number 10 was offered for sale.[136]

The houses contrast and complement the mid-Victorian terrace they adjoin. The street elevation was originally conceived and built as a carefully composed symmetrical composition with a variety of window types and areas of recessed brickwork. Number 10 has since lost its recessed L-shaped ground floor opening and gained a large picture window to the second floor. In plan, the kitchens are on the ground floor with the living rooms at first floor level, enjoying views across the road towards the Queen's House and Maritime Museum gardens.

Over the years, rear extensions have increased the floorspace and a sympathetic full-height side extension to number 11 aligns with the route of the adjacent railway cutting.

Hand-drawn perspective looking towards Trafalgar Road by John Newton

10 AND 11 PARK ROW

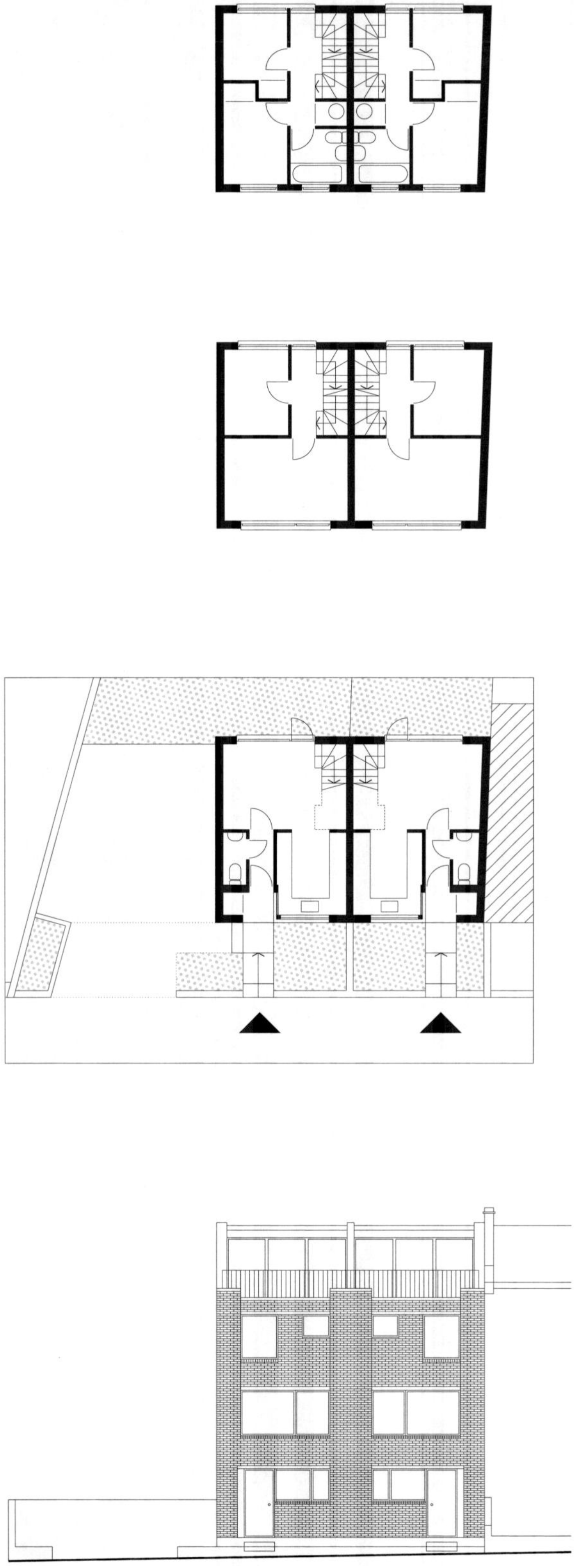

Top to bottom: second, first and ground floor plans; street elevation, as originally built

10m

1967

JOHN ROBERTS

John Roberts (1929–2003) lived in Blackheath for about 25 years. He was a close friend and neighbour of the architects Michael Hook and Peter Moro. At Moro's house he met artist Victor Passmore, who lived in the area.[137]

Born in Dulwich, Roberts's earliest ambition was to be an aircraft designer. However, after service in the army, he decided to focus on architecture. He first studied at the Royal West of England Academy of Architecture and then undertook further studies at the AA in 1952. The 1951 Festival of Britain had a profound impact on Roberts, particularly the Festival Hall. Drawing on a diverse list of influences, including Ruskin, Lutyens, Frank Lloyd Wright and Le Corbusier, he became a fervent supporter of the early Modern Movement.

In 1954, Roberts joined Ernö Goldfinger's practice in Piccadilly, London, as a junior assistant. While there, he produced working drawings for 45–46 Albermarle Street. Although he only stayed with the practice for one year, Roberts enjoyed a good relationship with Goldfinger, who he described as 'a charming bully'. He even lodged at Goldfinger's house at 2 Willow Road, Hampstead for a short while. However, after just one year Roberts resigned and joined Sheppard, Robson and Partners, where he worked on school projects, including Worcester Technical College and the new Churchill College, Cambridge, completed in 1962. He also worked at Lyons, Israel & Ellis.

In 1967, Roberts started his own practice with the commission for 4–7 Rocque Lane – a development of four houses, including one for his family. He collaborated with Leonard Manasseh on several projects including the conversion of Garth Castle in Perthshire, and also assisted Peter Moro on a housing scheme in Southwark.

Later in his career, Roberts served as acting surveyor for the Royal Academy working on Foster and Partners' Sackler Gallery project, as well as being the surveyor of the John Nash house at Llanerchaeron in Ceredigion, West Wales, prior to its opening by the National Trust.

John Roberts

Project	4–7 Rocque Lane
Architect	John Roberts
Completed	1968
Client	Pat King

Built on the site of the demolished coach house of 1 Pond Road, this small development of four houses stands behind a scheme of three houses by Walter Greaves, built at the same time. The two schemes share the use of the lane.

The identical two-storey brick houses have garages to the front and are arranged in an L-shape layout. Number 6 was allocated to the architect and his family and 7 to the developer, Pat King. Roberts then invited architect Michael Hook to join and he acquired number 5.[138] Hook and Roberts had met at Lyons, Israel & Ellis. Hook later became a partner at Castle Park Dean, where he was responsible mainly for their housing projects, as well as for the library building at Hull University. During this project, he and his colleagues enjoyed working with the Poet Laureate Philip Larkin, then the University librarian and the practice's de-facto client.

Originally planned with a unifying pergola, the plain front elevations of carefully composed doors and small windows contrast with the more open garden façades. Roberts had toured Scandinavia and admired its modern residential architecture, which influenced the internal detailing and the design of the timber staircases. All four houses were identical when first built but pitched roofs (designed by Roberts) were later added above the garages forming additional accommodation for the houses.

Michael Hook recalls a meeting he had with John Roberts and Walter Greaves, during which they discussed the name of the newly formed lane. From the many possibilities discussed, Roberts proposed *Rocque Lane* – a name inspired by John Rocque, the eighteenth-century London cartographer. Roberts was also responsible for the bespoke painted concrete nameplate that adorns the entrance to the lane.

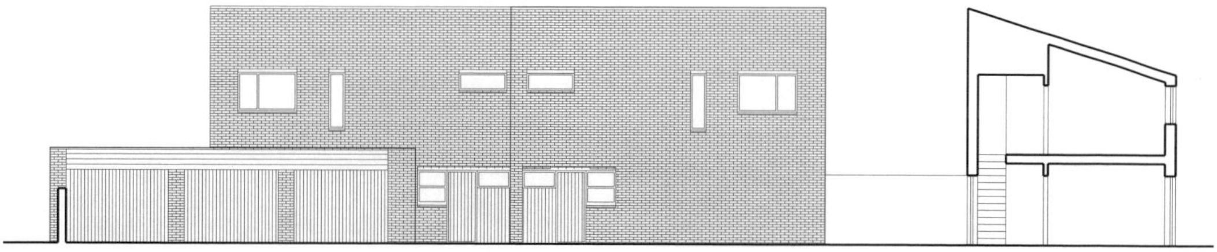

North elevation, as originally built

10m

 Entrance doors seen from the lane

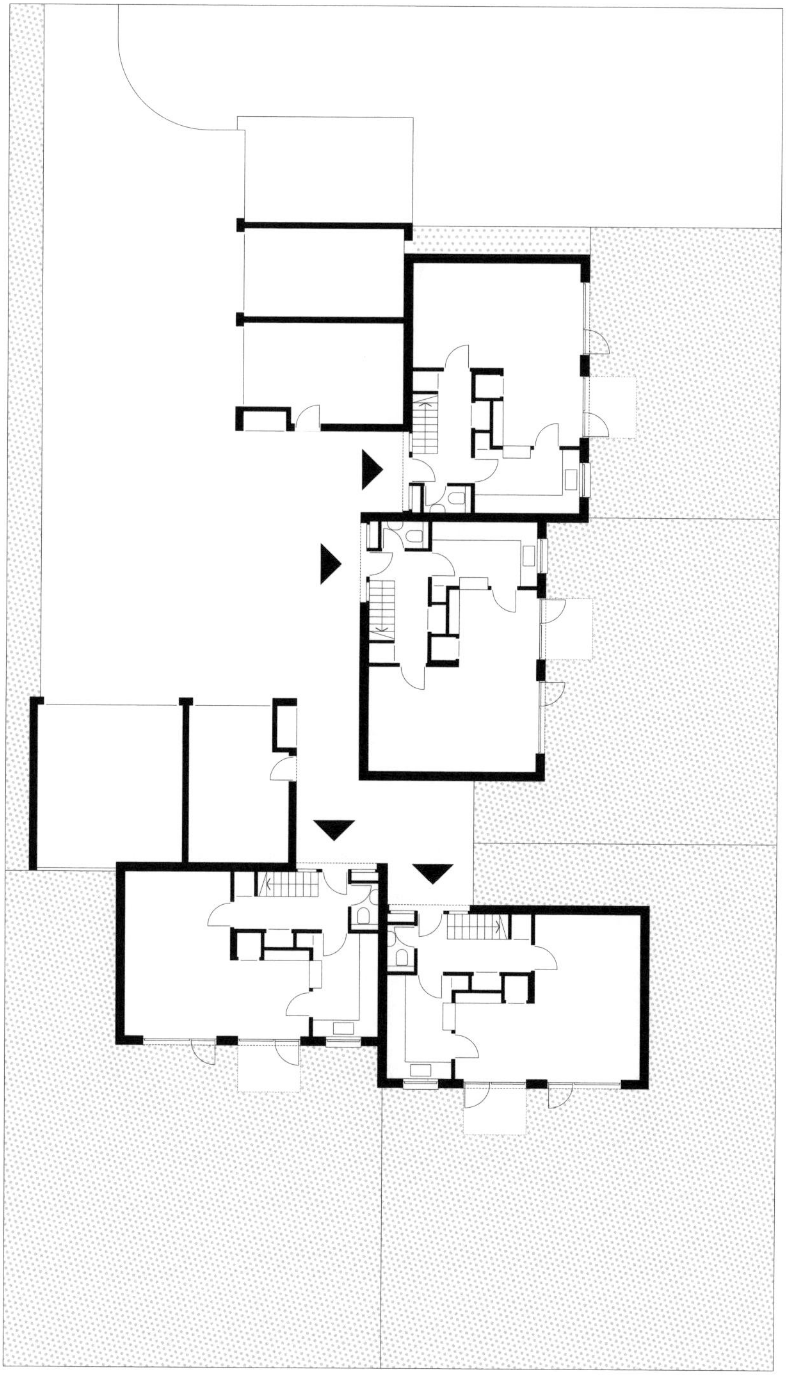

Ground floor plan

10m

4-7 ROCQUE LANE

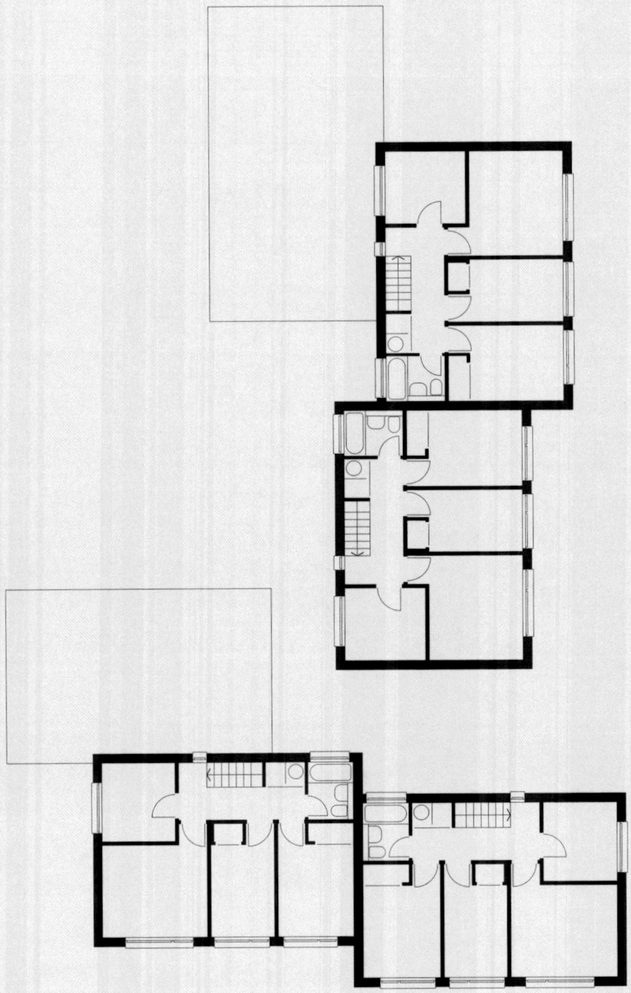

 First floor plan 10m

1968

Site plan

1:2000 50m

 Entrance hall staircase

Julian Sofaer (1924–2017) had few connections to southeast London, but designed one of Greenwich's best modern residences, Meridian West, built in 1963–65.

Sofaer was born in Iraq into Baghdad's Jewish community. During a period of religious prosecution, his widowed mother fled to India with Sofaer and his sister. In Bombay, he attended a Jesuit school and then entered the Architecture Department of the School of Art. Having ambitions to become a violinist, he also studied music to a high level.

In 1945, Sofaer was admitted to the AA and moved to London. From 1949 to 1955 he joined Yorke, Rosenberg and Mardall, where he worked on several projects, including the Susan Lawrence School at Lansbury that was part of the 1951 Festival of Britain 'Live Architecture' exhibition.

He left Yorke, Rosenberg and Mardall to set up his own practice. After a slow start, he won significant commissions from the LCC and the GLC, for which he eventually designed around 60 schools and colleges and more than 1,000 flats and community facilities.[139] He also built offices and homes for older people. In 1961 he won a Civic Trust Award for the extension of the West London Synagogue in Seymour Place near Marble Arch.

Sofaer's modernist style has a natural and integral sense of social purpose. He was a strong advocate for the work of Alvar Aalto.

Local projects	Meridian West, Diamond Terrace	1965
Key London projects	West London Synagogue Youth Centre and Library	1961
	Hugh Myddleton Primary School, Islington	1965
	Edinburgh House, Wembley	
	Canal Club, Wellington Estate, Bethnal Green	1980
	Heckfield Place offices	

Julian Sofaer

29	Project	Meridian West, Diamond Terrace
	Architect	Julian Sofaer
	Completed	1965
	Client	Brant Screeton
	Status	Grade II listed

Entrance view from the drive

Meridian West is a house situated on the twisting lane of Diamond Terrace, sheltered in a beautiful and secluded vale on the northern slopes of Blackheath. It was designed for the businessman and entrepreneur Brant Screeton, who ran a successful paint company in New Cross and was well known in architectural circles as the 'go-to man' for paint specification. Sofaer was a friend of Screeton's daughter.

The house is like a garden pavilion or a piece of sculpture that can be enjoyed from every angle. Partly embedded into the sloping ground, it was built on the orchard land of the adjacent early nineteenth-century villa, Cedar Bank (now grade II listed), owned by the Screeton family. The one-acre garden has mature trees and an extensive system of tunnels that were once used for fine sand mining and later as a bomb shelter for local residents during the Second World War; graffiti from the time is still visible on the walls.[140]

Meridian West is believed to be the only single-family house that Sofaer designed. It demonstrates a fresh, modern approach to the use of traditional materials, high-quality finishes and attention to detail.[141] Sofaer's vision was to create a building, 'with the harmony of proportion equivalent to that found in music'. He prepared 13 designs before finalising his proposals assisted by Miss D. C. Loader, who was responsible for the joinery detailing. In a 2017 interview, he said: 'That building remains representative of what I was about as an architect.'[142]

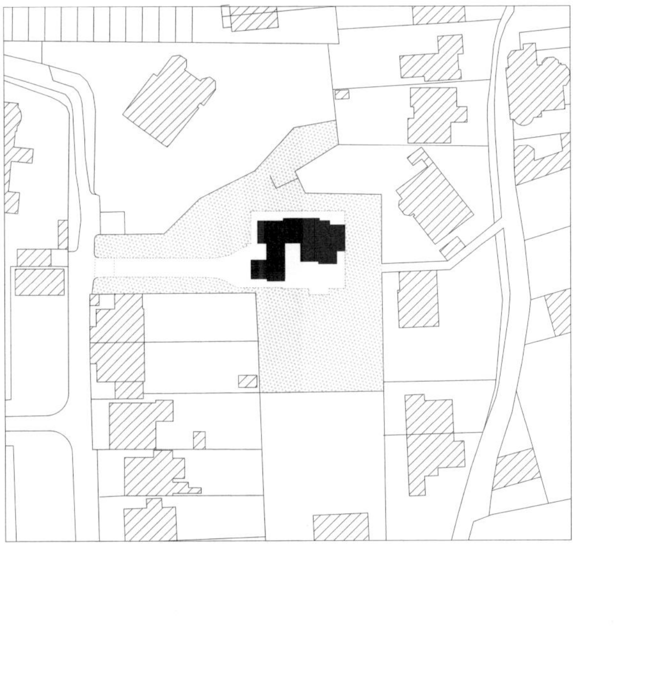

Site plan

With its oversailing flat roof, Meridian West has a strong horizontal emphasis and is constructed in buff brick with fair-faced concrete beams and robust timber detailing. The structure comprises of two blocks linked by a glazed bridge, one L-shaped, the other rectangular. Rooms are arranged around a partially enclosed terrace or courtyard that, as *The Architectural Review* commented in 1968, 'welds the house to the garden in an indivisible whole.'[143] After the house was completed, Screeton asked local architect E Morton Wright to draw up some subsidiary structures including two entrance gates and frontage walls to the property.

In fact, Morton Wright purchased the house in the early 1970s when Screeton and his family decided to move to the country (Mrs Screeton was never entirely happy with the house). The new owner then extended and made alterations in a complementary style including the addition of a new bedroom wing, partly dug into the hillside, enclosure of the main staircase at ground level and a semi-sunken studio beneath the kitchen and bathroom. Morton Wright also added the southern pedestrian gate, linking the site to Westgrove Lane and the Heath beyond, a handy amenity for local people, especially schoolchildren, who use this private route as a shortcut.

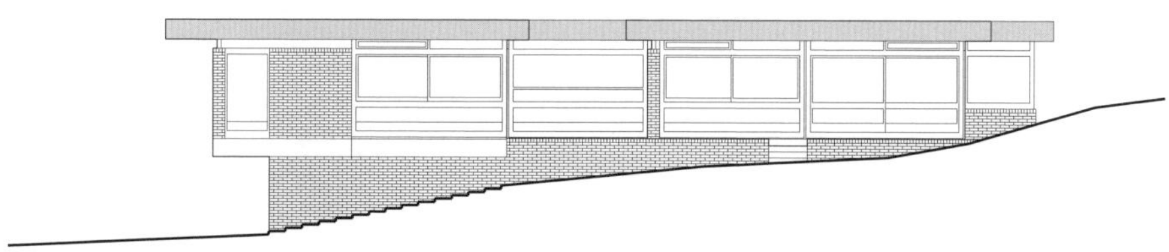

West elevation

10m

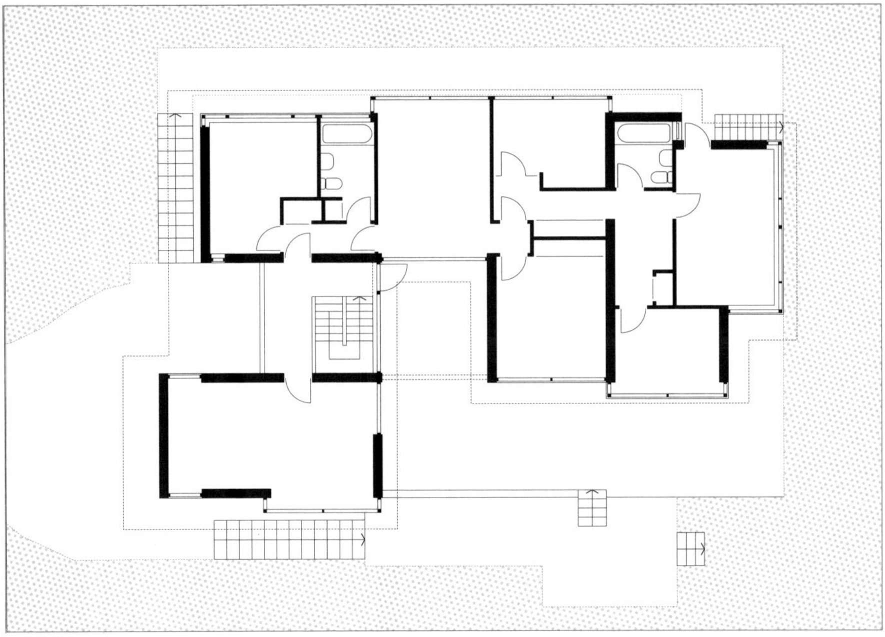

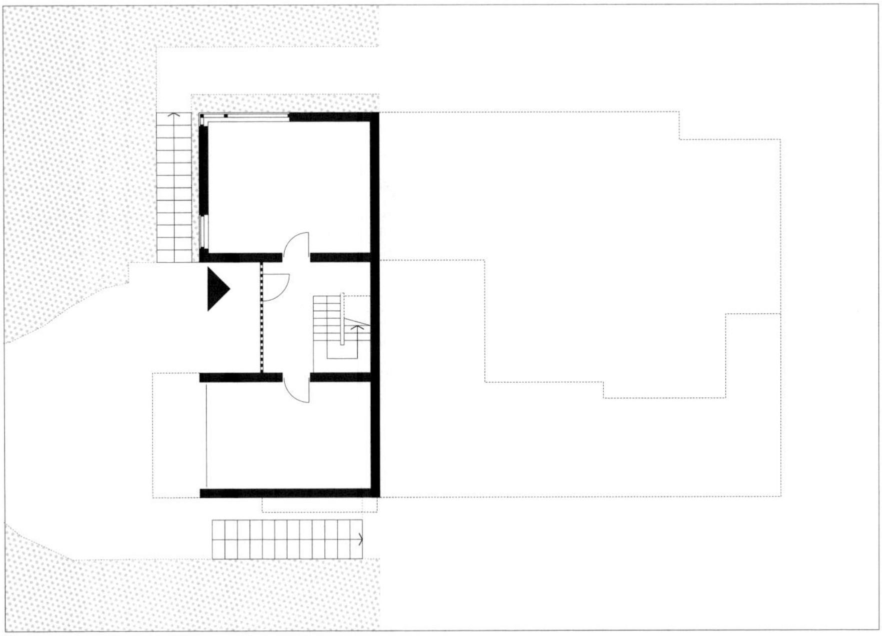

MERIDIAN WEST, DIAMOND TERRACE

Above: upper ground floor plan
Below: lower ground floor plan

10m

1965

Garden elevation

MERIDIAN WEST, DIAMOND TERRACE

1965

The architect Rosemary Owen Stjernstedt (1912–1998) was a local Span resident living at 17 The Hall.[144]

Stjernstedt (née Smith) was born and raised in Birmingham and studied at the Birmingham School of Architecture. She graduated in 1934 and joined the RIBA the following year. After graduating she initially designed furniture before joining architect Robert Atkinson's practice, where she worked on the Barber Institute of Fine Arts in Birmingham.

She then undertook a town planning course in the evenings at the AA in London and moved to Sweden in 1939 where she worked for the local authorities in Uppsala, Stockholm and Gothenburg. There she married lawyer Gunnar Stjernstedt and had a son in 1941.

Returning to England at the end of the Second World War and after her divorce, Stjernstedt worked first in Cambridge and Stevenage, then joined the LCC Housing Division in 1950. As a group leader (of which there were only four) she directed about 12 other architects and later progressed to become the first woman to achieve the civil service's senior ranking of Grade 1. It is important to note the collaborative nature of the design process at the LCC, which brought together several different groups within the Architects Department.[145]

From 1963 to 1967, she worked at Lambeth Borough Council under Chief Architect Ted Hollamby. There she led a number of award-winning social housing projects, including the Central Hill Estate. One of her references for Lambeth came from her friend and neighbour Peter Moro.

She went on to work with Patricia Tindale (1926–2011), another influential civil service female architect, before retiring and establishing a small practice in Wales in 1972. Her projects through this practice included her own home (with partner Frederick Parker, whom she met at the LCC) and a house conversion for Led Zeppelin's lead singer Robert Plant.[146]

Local projects	Brooklands Park Estate	1958
	Pagoda Gardens Estate, off Eliot Vale	

Other projects	Alton East Estate, Roehampton	1955
	Fitzhugh Estate, Wandsworth	1955
	Aboyne Road Estate, Tooting	1950s
	Central Hill Estate, Norwood	1967–74

Rosemary Stjernstedt on a site visit

Project	Brooklands Park Estate
Architect	LCC, Rosemary Stjernstedt
Completed	1958
Client	London County Council

The Brooklands Park Estate and Brooklands Primary School were built on the extensive grounds of Casterbridge House (previously Elmsdale House) and Dacre Court (still standing, now locally listed), which were acquired for development by compulsory purchase order. Casterbridge House was demolished but its lake, conduit house and many mature trees were retained, contributing to the unique quality of the estate. Brooklands Primary School took over most of Dacre Court's grounds. A magnificent cedar tree growing in its central court provides the symbol for the school logo, as well as welcome shade for its pupils.

The lake, part of the Kid Brook stream, contains an island, on which stands a statue, *Ganges*, by Raffaele Monti (1818–1881) that was commissioned for the 1851 Great Exhibition in Hyde Park, London. Part of a set of sculptures, *Ganges* was relocated following the exhibition, first to Crystal Palace Park, then to the Brooklands Park Pond in the early 1950s.[147]

The estate comprises 289 units in total, arranged in seven five-storey point blocks of flats, and a series of two-storey terrace houses, as well as a community hall, two shops and a primary school. It was designed by a LCC architects department team led by Rosemary Stjernstedt, at the time when Hubert Bennett was LCC leader.

Many of the ideas used on the Brooklands estate, including the point blocks, had already been tested by Stjernstedt's team on other estates, for example, Alton East, Roehampton (1955), Fitzhugh Estate, Wandsworth (1955), and the Aboyne Road Estate, in Tooting (late 1950s), which also comprised five-storey blocks. However, Brooklands Park is the only one of these developments with pitched roofs.

The small community hall at the heart of the estate contains a chipboard and coloured resin mural by the celebrated sculptor William Mitchell (1925–2020), a design consultant for the LCC from 1957 to 1965 who created many public sculptures and murals. Stjernstedt was instrumental in securing both the *Ganges* statue and Mitchell's mural for Brooklands Park.

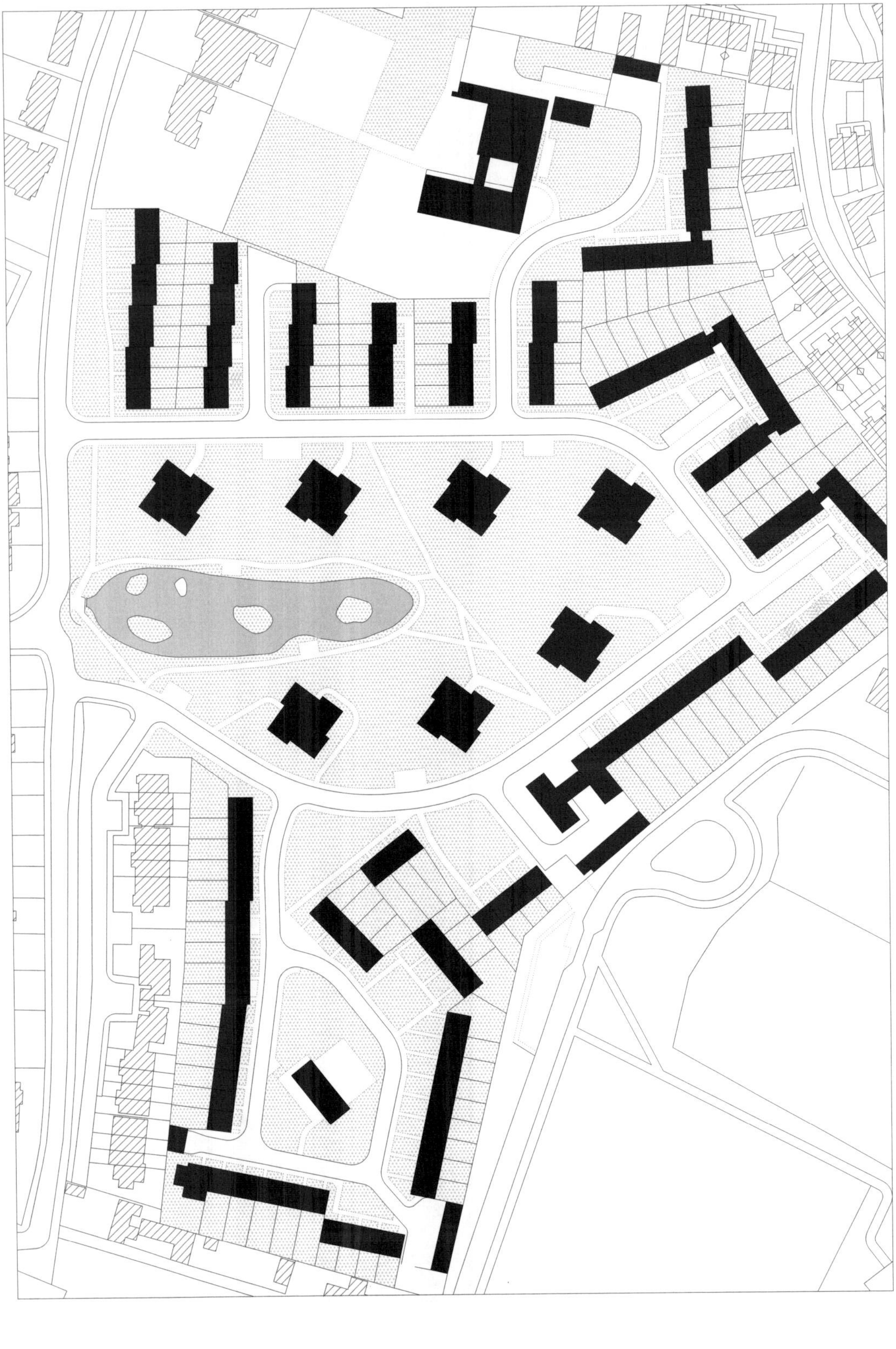

BROOKLANDS PARK ESTATE

 Site plan

50m

1958

Above: View over the pond
Below: Shared open space between the point blocks

Above: Brooklands Primary School entrance
Below: William Mitchell working on the mural for the estate's community hall

BROOKLANDS PARK ESTATE

1958

Henry Leonard Froome Lewis (1929–1999) moved to The Plantation Span estate when it was completed in 1962. He had purchased the show house, so the family was happy to keep the modern furniture already in place. Later Lewis designed and built a new house for his family at 85 Brooklands Park.

After National service in Egypt, Lewis attended the Emanuel School in Battersea and studied architecture at the Thames Polytechnic, graduating in 1955.[148] His colleague there, E Morton Wright, recalls that he was known as *Leonardo* Lewis, in reference to the inventiveness of his designs.[149]

Lewis worked for central government, first in the LCC Schools Division and then in local government with Nottingham County Council. At Nottingham he focused mainly on education projects, often with CLASP, the Consortium of Local Authorities Special Programme. Believing strongly in the role of the public architect, Lewis continued to work for the Ministry of Works and the Property Services Agency (PSA) attaining a senior position, and designing army projects, special hospitals and Crown Courts.[150]

Len Lewis's career was largely devoted to public buildings; his family home at 85 Brooklands Park and a farm restoration project in South-west France during the 1970s, were his only residential designs.

85 Brooklands Park

Len Lewis

31		
	Project	85 Brooklands Park
	Architect	Len Lewis
	Completed	1967
	Client	Architect's own house

85 Brooklands Park sits on a secluded site that was once the cherry orchard of 83 Brooklands Park, a house built in the 1880s, facing the street.

Accessed by a private drive, the design of this one-storey house is beautifully simple and inventive, comprising two squares in plan, each with a shallow pyramidal hipped roof and linked by a smaller flat-roofed volume.

One square accommodates the living room and kitchen with a solid brick core that serves as the flue for a stove and support for the roof. The centre of the other square is open, with a rooflight above. Framing the rooflight, a pinwheel arrangement of structural brick piers creates doorways into three of the four bedrooms, and again supports the roof. The linkway incorporates the hallway, bathroom and utility room. Outside, a carport with a glazed canopy frames the entrance area to the south.

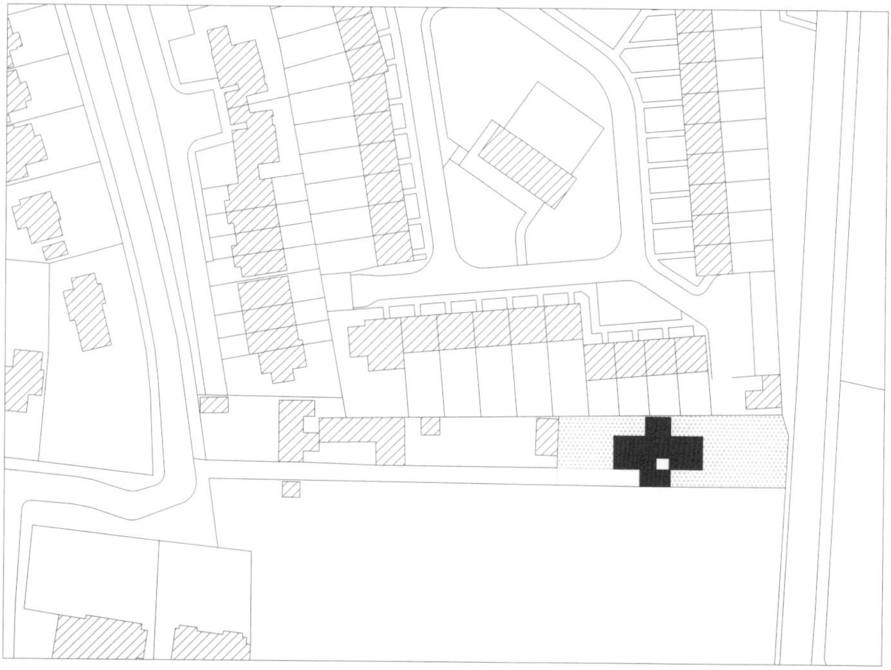

Site plan 1:2000 50m

85 BROOKLANDS PARK

 The living room seen from the front garden

1967

The building is carefully detailed: external brick walls are punctuated by asymmetrical steel-framed windows – hinting at the pinwheel arrangement of the plan within – and capped by a continuous concrete ring beam. Above, a black metal gutter aligns flush with the face of the beam. Internally, the rooms are open to the sloping roofs; their soffits lined in white painted timber boarding. Inventive bespoke joinery contributes to a unique atmosphere – a kitchen hatch on a pulley, integrated shelving, sliding doors and mezzanine sleeping platforms. A simple raised skirting profile creates the illusion of walls floating above the quarry tiled floor.

Although it has been extremely well maintained, with a dedication usually reserved for listed buildings, the house required some rebuilding in 2000, during which, a fourth flat-roofed volume accommodating a study was added to the north. This additional 'square' was shown on earlier plans as a glazed garden room or conservatory. The carport was also enclosed, creating an inner courtyard and completing the symmetry of the floorplan.

85 Brooklands Park has only changed hands once – a testament to its architectural quality and status as an exemplary 'lifetime home'.[151] Its number sign uses the same typeface as Peter Moro's 20 Blackheath Park. Paul Harpin, graphic designer and current owner of the house suggests that 'these are proprietary and presumably both Moro and Lewis simply chose the best sign available at the local architectural ironmongers'.

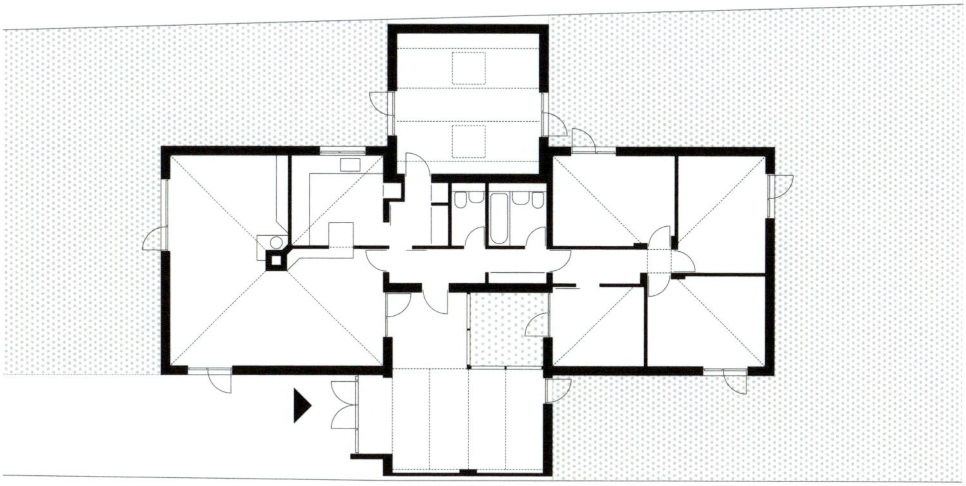

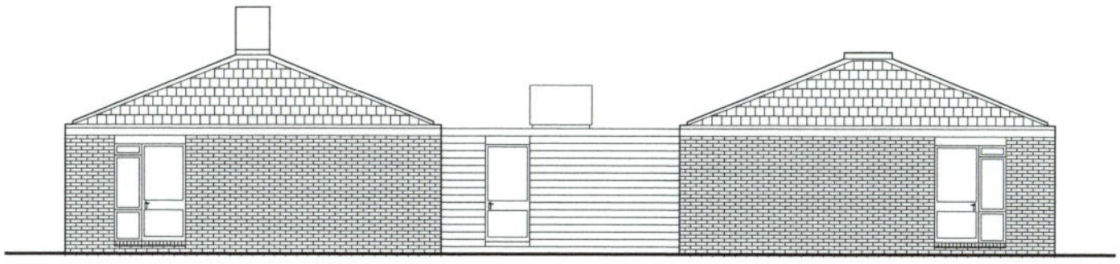

Above: ground floor plan, current
Below: south elevation, as originally built

10m

 The living room and screened kitchen with central brick pier

Leopold or Leo Rubinstein (1929–2012) and his brother Arthur both studied architecture at the Brixton School of Building. The family were Jewish, originally from Germany and had been housed for a time in the Jewish Temporary Shelter in Whitechapel. Leo was born in Stepney.

After qualification, Rubinstein worked for Chamberlin, Powell & Bon, and was a project architect on the Barbican estate project, through which he met Mike Hohmann.

Lothar Michael (Mike) Hohmann (1935–2020) studied architecture at the Karlsruhe Institute of Technology, Germany. In London he worked for Chamberlin, Powell & Bon from 1961 to 1969, where he was in charge of detailed design of residential buildings, especially windows.

Hohmann also worked closely with Twyford to design the iconic Barbican basin[152] in the early 1960s, which won a Design Centre Award in 1966. From 1969 to 1987 he worked for the GLC (including its residual body) and after leaving, set-up in private practice as LMH Design, specialising in sustainability and clean energy.[153]

Hohman and Rubinstein designed 11 Westgrove Lane, Rubinstein's own house in Greenwich, where he lived with his family from 1964 to 1984. He had previously lived nearby with wife Eileen at 8 Maidenstone Hill.

Rubinstein was introduced by his brother Arthur to Bernard Hartley and all three went on to work in practice together for a short period in the 1960s.[154] One of the practices' projects, led by Leo was a terrace of 9 large four-storey houses, with 6 studio flats above garages in Notting Hill.

After Arthur emigrated to the US, Leo remained in practice with Hartley as Bernard Hartley & Partners. The practice prioritised residential work, including projects for housing associations.

After retiring, Leo moved to France in the 1990s, later returning to the UK to live in Pembrokeshire, Wales.

Local projects	11 Westgrove Lane	mid-1960s
Other London projects	3–11 Clarendon Road and 8–13 Ladbroke Mews, Notting Hill	1966

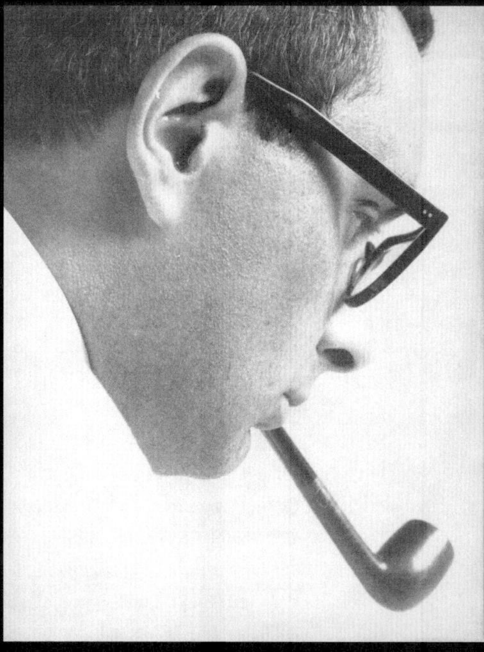

Lothar Michael Hohmann

32

Project	11 Westgrove Lane
Architect	Leo Rubinstein and Michael Hohmann
Completed	mid-1960s
Client	Architect's own house (Leo Rubinstein)

11 Westgrove Lane was designed by Leo Rubinstein for his own use, in collaboration with Mike Hohmann. The two were colleagues at Chamberlin Powell & Bon and worked together on the Barbican estate project. Hohmann took specific responsibility for the window detailing at the Barbican and similar details can be seen at 11 Westgrove Lane. The site on which the house stands was pointed out to Rubinstein by Bernard Hartley, his partner at Rubinstein & Hartley, who lived at 15 Westgrove Lane.[155]

This extraordinary concrete and brick flat-roofed house has a two-storey main frontage on Westgrove Lane. The rear is three-storeys as the site slopes steeply and its garden connects to a lane off Diamond Terrace below. It was designed with double aspect accommodation and enjoys panoramic views across the river Thames, Canary Wharf and central London.

An initial scheme, dated 1963, was even more ambitious. It included a floating glass box supported on four steel columns, in the spirit of Mies Van der Rohe's Farnsworth House. The ground floor was intended to provide a carport and studio space, with all the main accommodation on the first floor and a roof terrace above.[156]

Although the house eventually built is not as architecturally ambitious as this earlier scheme (one wonders how the discussions with the planners went), it is, nonetheless, a striking modern building. Its quality is apparent in the detailing but also in its transparency; the full-height windows and open circular staircase create a sense of light and openness, both from inside looking out but also from the street when facing the house with the city beyond.

The original photographs show an integrated carport and open balcony within the building volume. This has subsequently been filled in to provide a larger kitchen without compromising the overall massing or design. The lower ground was a separate studio, with access only from the outside. At some point, the circular spiral staircase was extended below to connect all three floors.

The accommodation comprises of a study with mezzanine, bedroom, bathroom and laundry room on the lower ground floor; a kitchen, bedroom, study and bathroom on the ground floor; and an open-plan living room and second bedroom with bathroom on the top floor.

The current owners have dealt with several leaks over the years – 'the curse of the flat roof'. A local architect who helped them solve various issues on several occasions, joked 'You can't live in a masterpiece and expect it not to leak!'[157]

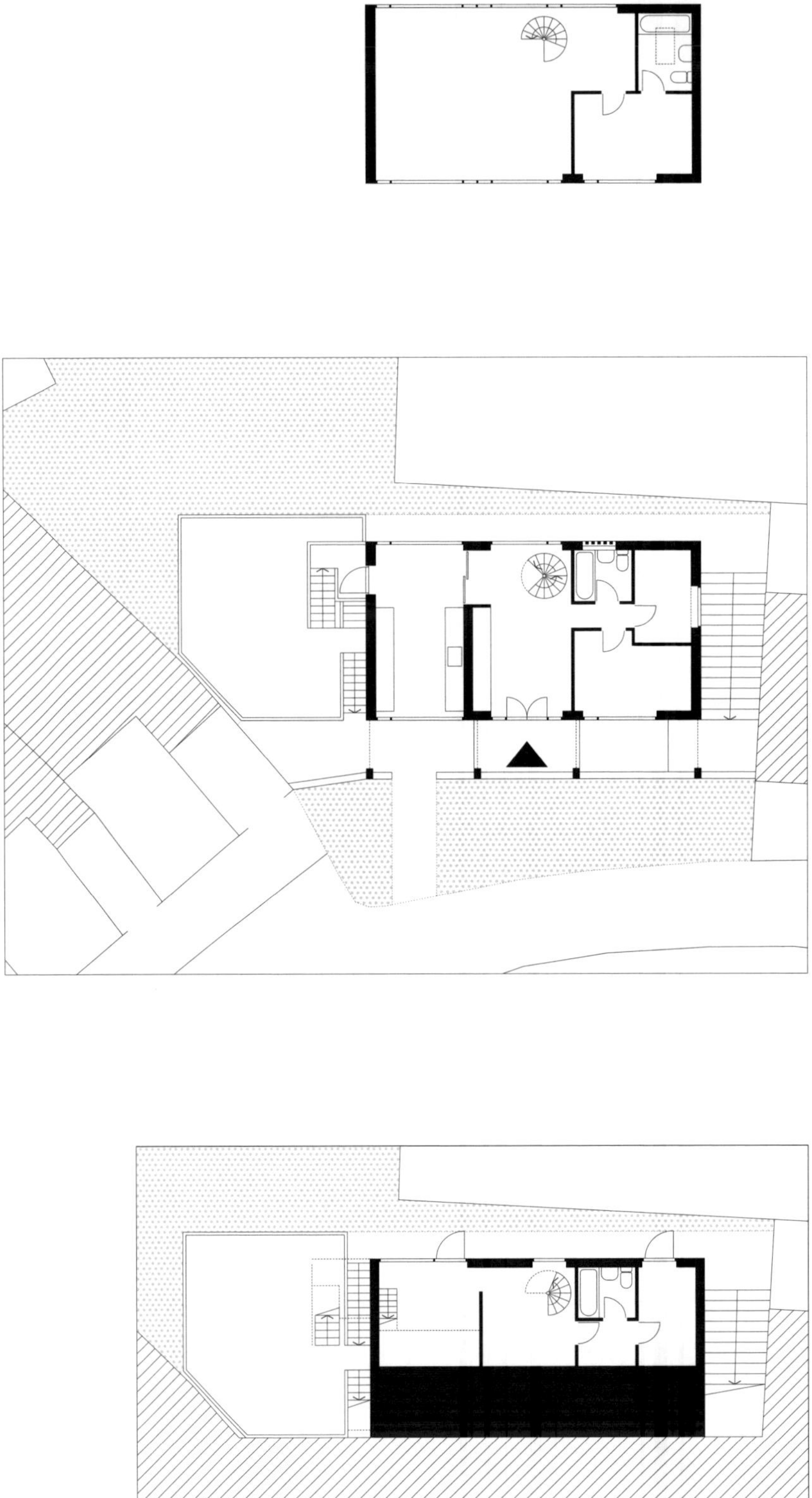

Top to bottom: first, ground and lower ground floor plans

10m

Entrance on Westgrove Lane

11 WESTGROVE LANE

The front elevation from Point Hill, 1960s

View from the lower-level garden showing the three-storey volume and the original open carport

Lorenzo Renato Masini (b.1933) joined the in-house team of architects and designers at Wates Built Homes (developers and housebuilders) in the mid 1960s. His first project there was the design for five terraced houses at St Germans Place, Blackheath.

The project caused controversy within Wates and the local council due to its radical modern design and use of concrete. However, Neil Wates, managing director, went ahead with what he believed was an important departure from the typical 'Wates home'. Masini also worked on a 72-unit housing scheme in Reigate, Surrey for Wates.

Masini was born in Glasgow to Italian parents and raised in Italy. After graduating from the Rome School of Architecture he returned to the UK but had to study for a further three years to requalify. He joined Shepheard and Epstein (later Shepheard Epstein Hunter) where he worked mainly on LCC residential schemes.

He joined Wates because he was attracted by the quality of the company's in-house design team, many of whom were ex-LCC staff. Neil Wates was also an inspirational figure, always on the lookout for innovative design and construction methods. He was personally responsible for commissioning the renowned Swiss practice, Atelier 5, to design Park Hill, Croydon (1969–70).[158]

Masini went on to form the Masini Franklin Partnership with Norman Franklin, where he enjoyed a prolific career in the 1970s and 1980s. The practice worked on housing schemes for the GLC in Croydon, including Forestdale and its community centre, as well as Millside in Dorking. Masini Franklin also completed office and warehousing projects in Croydon and Tonbridge, as well as the St James' Church café in Piccadilly (1983).

In the early 1990s, the Masini Franklin Partnership was absorbed by a larger practice, Rolfe Judd.

Lorenzo Masini

33

Project	5a–5e St Germans Place
Architect	Lorenzo Masini
Completed	1970
Client	Wates

A terrace of five three-storey houses with highly articulated façades of integrated balconies, brickwork piers, white timber cladding and metal balustrades. It was built on the site of the old St Germans Chapel (1923), which had been severely bomb-damaged during the Second World War. A large tree at the rear of the site constrained its design. The front façade is articulated with narrow balconies and recessed entrance areas alongside the private front patios. These extend towards a strip of lawn and mature trees opening directly onto the Heath.

The building utilises a curious plan of interlocking staircases, which give a sense of extra width to the interiors. The project was the first undertaken by the Wates in-house architect, Masini, and was considered a testing ground for the use of pre-cast concrete structures and balconies. As such, it was a forerunner for the development of Wates' prefabricated construction methods, which were being promoted within the company by Neil Wates.[159]

By the 1980s, all five houses had been extended to the rear, at ground floor level, to enlarge the dining rooms; a project carried out by Teresa Forrest. During excavation work, the crypt of the old chapel was uncovered and then sealed up again.[160]

The terrace front elevation with recessed entrances and balconies, 1970s

The kitchens originally had glass louvered windows. However, these were no match for strong winds across the Heath and so at Wates' expense they were replaced soon after completion. One original feature that has survived is a fan assisted hot air system. It avoids the need for radiators and has proved more reliable than most under-floor-heating systems fitted in the 1970s.

 The terrace from the Heath

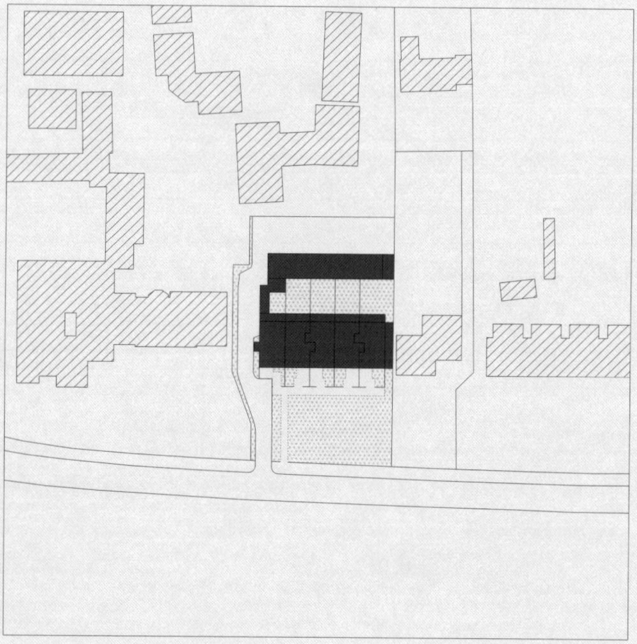

Site plan 1:2000 50m

5A–5E ST GERMANS PLACE

Above, left to right: ground, first and second floor plans
Below: front elevation

1970

Myles (b.1927) and Deirdre Dove (1924–1979) built their family home and practice studio in Maze Hill, Greenwich, in 1968. Two of their children became architects and the third is the composer, Jonathan Dove.

The Doves met while working for Richard Sheppard and Partners and were in practice together as Myles & Deirdre Dove Architects from 1959 until Deirdre's sudden death in 1979. At Richard Sheppard they were colleagues of E Morton Wright, who was a neighbour in Greenwich.

Their work included housing, community buildings and refurbishment of listed buildings. Their 1964 extension to the Ripon Theological College, Oxford (Ripon Hall, Boar's Hill) won a Civic Trust Award for environmental design. Another of their designs won the Peckham Society Award; this was for a scheme comprising the restoration of the Beer and Wine Homes (originally of 1850's) and the associated development of Barton Close with houses and flats. They were also involved in school extensions in the East End of London and in the extension of the Livesey Museum, in the Old Kent Road.[161]

Local projects	Our Ladye Star of the Sea alterations, Crooms Hill[162]	1966
	57a Blackheath Park	1960s
	129 Maze Hill	1968
Other London projects	Livesey Museum extension, Old Kent Road	1974
	Beer and Wine Homes and Barton Close, Nunhead Green	

Deirdre in 1970

Myles in 2023

Project	57a Blackheath Park
Architect	Myles and Deirdre Dove
Completed	1961
Client	Mr and Mrs Hudson

This coach house conversion was designed to create a clear contrast with neighbouring properties along Blackheath Park. Other conversions, such as number 53a, from 1935 by Charles Bernard Brown, aimed at blending in with the adjacent Georgian and Victorian buildings.

Number 57 Blackheath Park was built in 1826 and is Grade II listed. The coach house conversion was designed by Myles and Deirdre Dove for friends and comprises a two-storey, four-bedroom house, which features an impressive central staircase of open teak treads held by stainless-steel rods and a central timber spine. A lower-ground level garage is accessed by a steep ramp and roofed over to create a front patio.[163]

The building has been altered over the years, with the addition of a porch to the front and a small balcony to a bedroom. In 2020 the building was extended to the rear and fully refurbished.

The front elevation from Blackheath Park, 1960s

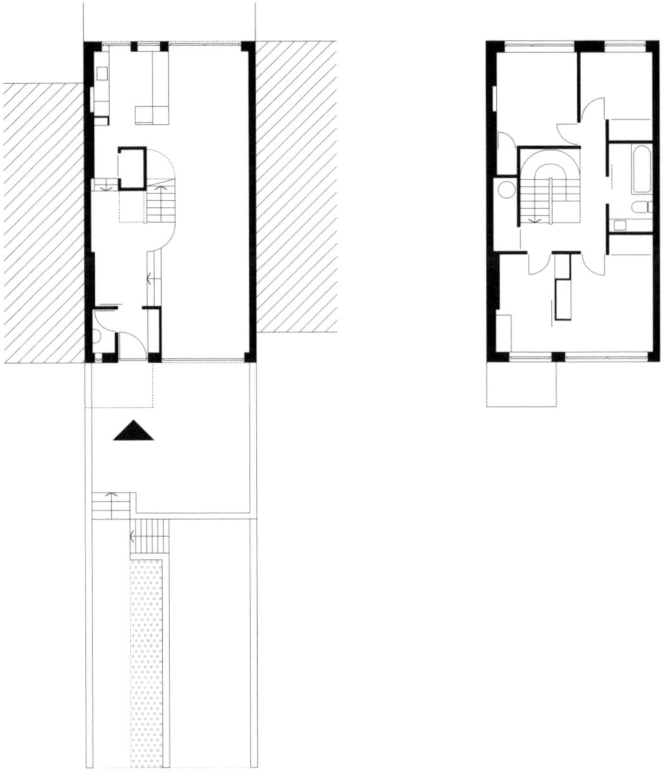

Above, left to right: ground and first floor plans, as originally built
Below: street elevation, as originally built

10m

35

Project	129 Maze Hill
Architect	Myles and Deirdre Dove
Completed	1968
Client	Architect's own house

This two-storey, four- or five-bedroom house was designed as both a home and studio for the Doves' architectural practice. The house is situated at the top of Maze Hill, overlooking Greenwich Park. The Dove family, who previously lived at Montague House, Dartmouth Hill, all helped with the construction. Even the three children were involved in the final stages, painting walls and varnishing woodwork.

Previously a billiard room, garage and air raid shelter, the site has an unusual trapezoidal shape. This, together with the planning constraints, inspired the design of a unique building. Height restrictions to the windowsills, for example, led to long horizontal openings at a high level, which produce good daylight in the rooms and views from inside of the sky. A restriction on the number of habitable rooms was solved through open-plan spaces that can be sub-divided by sliding doors.

The Scandinavian-influenced design of the interior features internal fair-faced brickwork painted white, birch-faced ply panelling and ceilings, and Douglas fir door frames and linings. The rooms are designed to maximise the sense of space and light, particularly the striking double-height living room, open spiral staircase and upper gallery. On the ground floor, all rooms connect directly to the surrounding gardens through full height windows. The many bespoke joinery details include a linen-chute hidden in the apparently solid balustrade, through which laundry can be dropped into the utility room below.[164] Fitted kitchen cupboards cleverly integrated into the design of the windows, blur the distinction between inside and outside.

Front elevation

10m

129 MAZE HILL

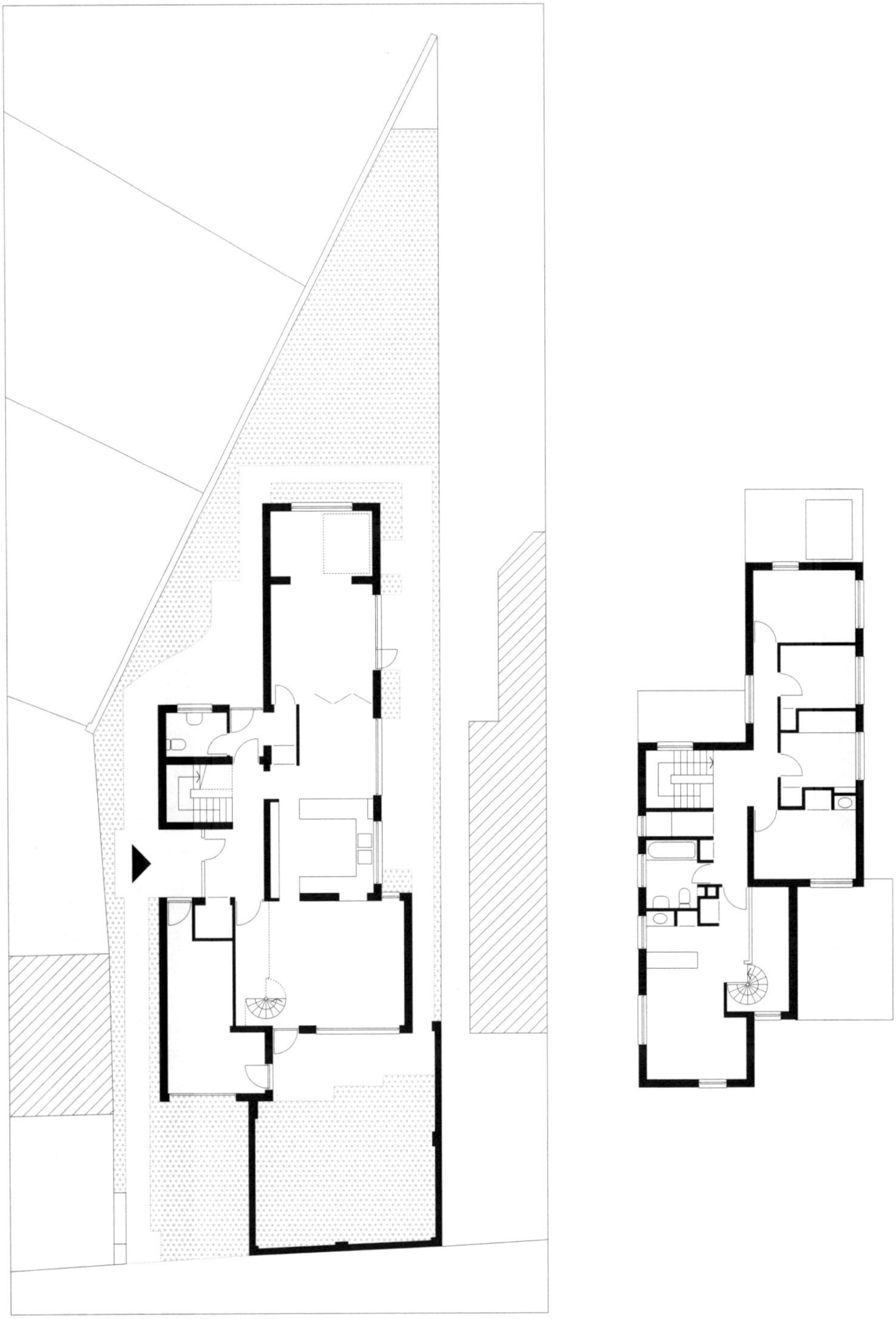

Left to right: ground and first floor plans

10m

1968

The bedroom gallery looking towards the street frontage

The brochure prepared by the Dove family for Open House weekend in 2018 (the house's fiftieth anniversary) explained that 'when the studio was in use up until Myles's retirement, the separate entrance was used for visitors and practice staff. A sliding door and a folding timber partition separated the studio and the kitchen from the dining room, so it could be used for meetings. Children could come and go while work carried on in the studio. Living and working have always been intertwined at Maze Hill.'[165]

 Double-height living room and gallery

Patrick Gwynne (1913–2003) designed four houses on the Cator Estate between 1949 and 1979. All were family homes for the Span director Leslie Bilsby. One was demolished and one never built; two still stand – the extraordinary 10 Blackheath Park (1969) and the secluded 22 Parkgate (1979).

Gwynne was born in Porchester, Hampshire, the son of a naval officer from a family with Welsh roots. He attended Harrow School, where he discovered English Modernism on day trips to the countryside. A particular highlight was a visit to High & Over, an exemplary early modernist country house designed by Amyas Connell, in Amersham, Buckinghamshire.[166]

Between 1934 and 1937, Gwynne worked in Wells Coates's practice where he met and became good friends with Denys Lasdun. Gwynne left the practice in 1937 to set up on his own. He won a competition to design a large restaurant at the 1951 Festival of Britain and two more restaurants in Hyde Park, including the grade II listed Dell and the Serpentine, now demolished.

In 1937, still only 24 years old, Gwynne designed The Homewood in Esher, Surrey, for his parents. They both died during the Second World War, but Gwynne continued to live and work at The Homewood for almost 60 years, until his death.

The house became a favourite haunt for Gwynne's friends and clients. It contained many bespoke pieces of furniture and ingenious features, including an integrated bar and sound system in the living room wall and a circular meeting table with pull-out shelves for drinks. Some of these were fitted out by Leslie Bilsby who was both a friend and client. The Homewood is now owned by the National Trust.

Gwynne worked mainly in the UK but also in Dubai and Malta. He specialised in one-off private homes, hotels and restaurants.[167]

Local projects	115 Blackheath Park (demolished)	1949
	House in Blackheath (unbuilt project)	1960
	10 Blackheath Park	1969
	22 Parkgate	1979
Other London projects	24 Spaniards End, Hampstead	1959
	Four Houses, Combe Hill Road, Kingston (part demolished)	1959
	3 & 4 Beechworth Close, Hampstead	1961 + 1963
	The Serpentine Restaurant, Hyde Park (demolished 1999)	1964
	The Dell Restaurant, Hyde Park	1965

Patrick Gwynne outside The Homewood, Esher, Surrey

36

Project	115 Blackheath Park
Architect	Patrick Gwynne
Completed	1949 (demolished 1966)[168]
Client	Leslie Bilsby

The elevation facing the front garden

Patrick Gwynne's design for 115 Blackheath Park was an extensive remodelling of a large early Victorian villa that suffered severe bomb damage during the Second World War. Built in 1836–37, the original house was first known as Kidbrooke Lodge then from 1882, as Park End House.

Gwynne's clever design was thoroughly modern and completely obscured the original building, although to meet government rules constraining new-build projects after the war, he retained much of the original structure as well as the structural window openings.[169] He removed the top storey and built a new roof in metal that curved down, creating a deep overhang supported by tall leaning posts. Balconies were added to the first-floor rooms.[170] The roof material had been developed for the post-war temporary housing programme by Arcon, who built the prefabs on the Heath using the same curved roof profile.

The new entrance door, set within a tiled surround, overhanging canopy and cantilevered seat, announced the modern nature of Gwynne's design. This modernity continued into the interior, with an open tread staircase and a bespoke room-divider cum servery to separate the kitchen from the dining room.[171]

In 1966, the house was demolished as part of the project to build Parkend – a Span estate of 19 houses completed in 1967. After the demolition of number 115 and before moving into 10 Blackheath Park, Bilsby lived at 21 Morden Road, a unique modular home designed by Walter Greaves. Gwynne subsequently designed two more houses for Bilsby on the Cator Estate: 10 Blackheath Park (1969, Grade II listed) and 22 Parkgate (1979).

Park End House, 115 Blackheath Park, circa 1938 before war damage

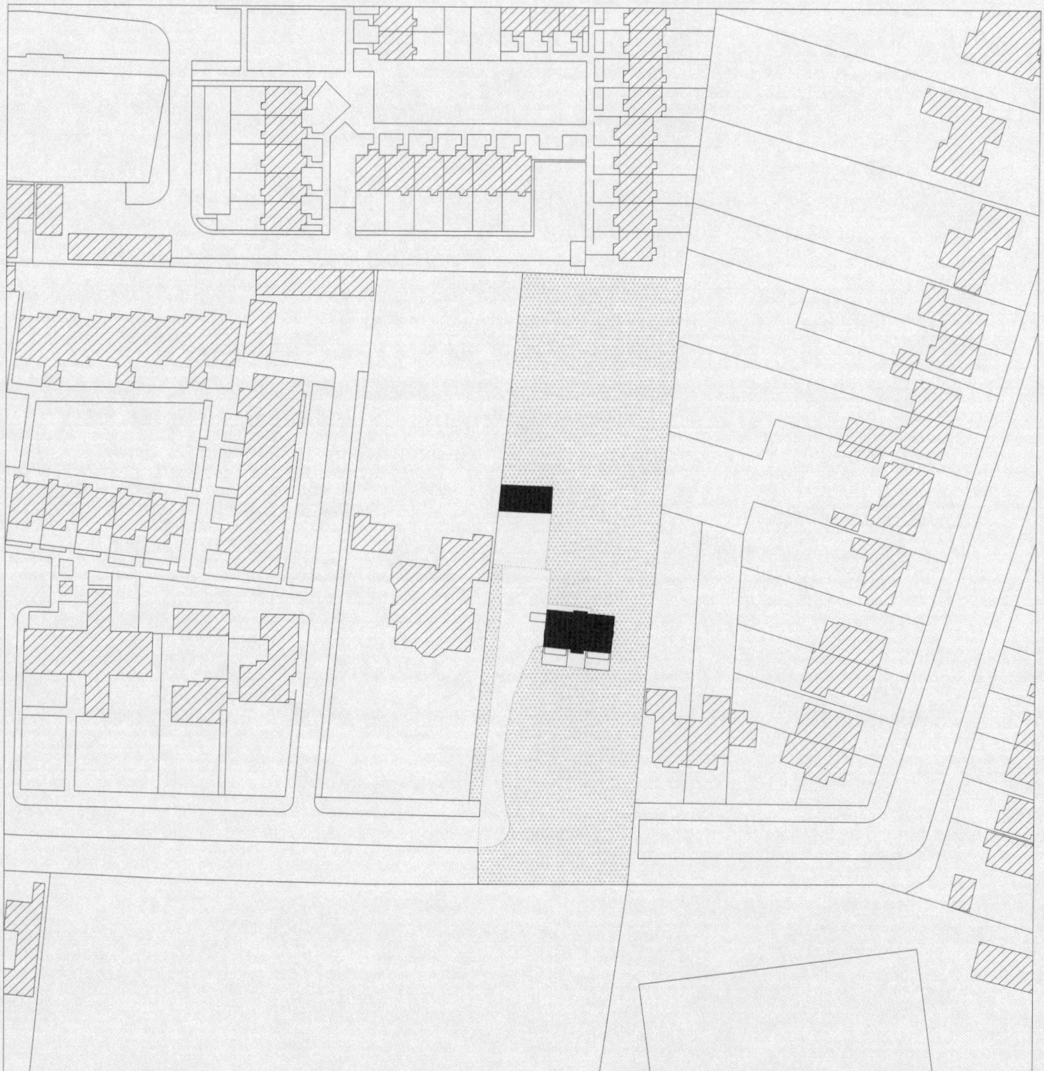

Site plan 1:2000 50m

115 BLACKHEATH PARK

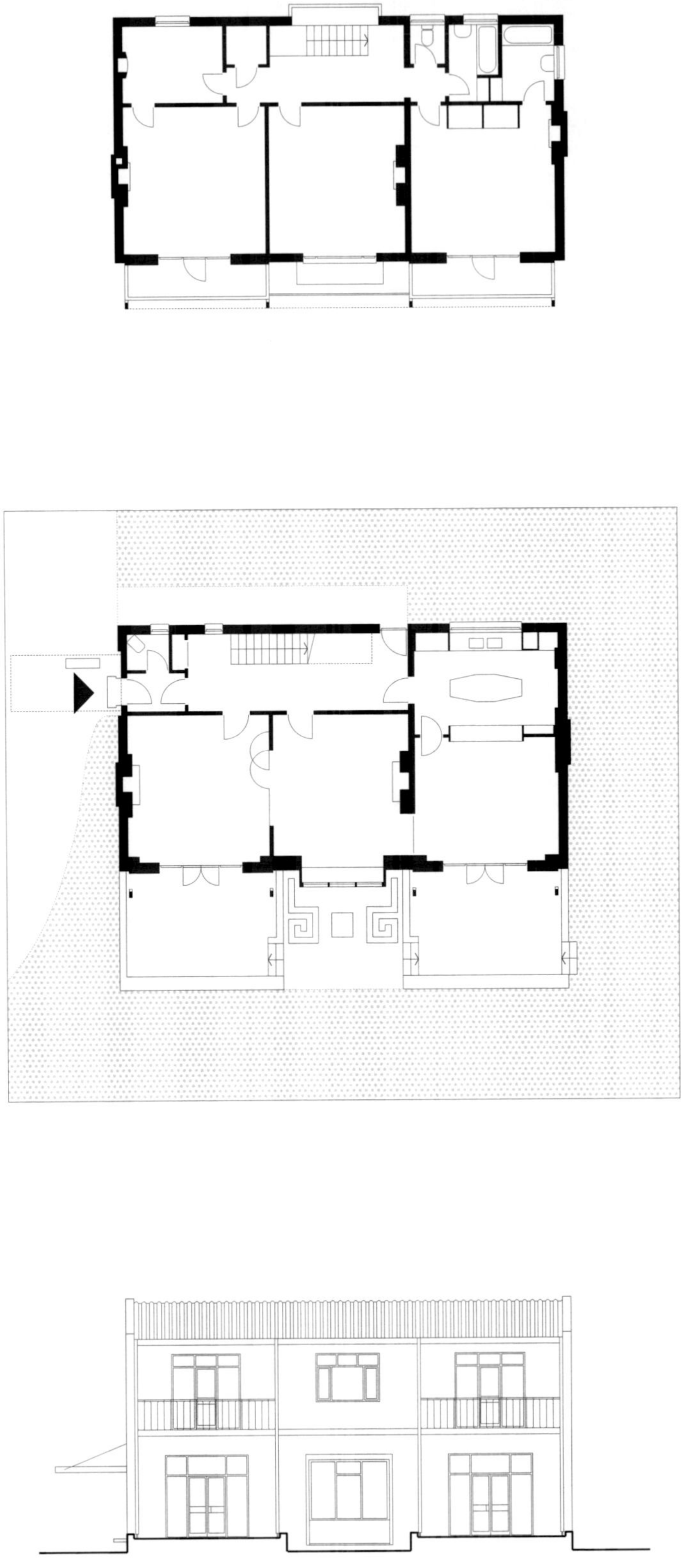

Top to bottom: first and ground floor plans; south elevation

10m

1949

37	Project	House in Blackheath (unbuilt project)
	Architect	Patrick Gwynne
	Designed	1960
	Client	Leslie Bilsby

Possibly designed for the empty plot at 21 Morden Road, which was acquired by Leslie Bilsby as part of the Plantation development, Gwynne's plan was for three separate circular pavilion-like structures, set within a walled garden.[172]

One volume housed the garage, the second, larger volume contained the social spaces and a third, the bedrooms and bathrooms. The garden was a mix of edge planting, extensive patio areas and a shallow pond. With large expanses of glass, the social block, placed in the centre of the composition, was intended to be integral with the garden. An internal 'snuggery' with curved walls and fitted sofa was provided to counter the exposure of the glazed walls. A small, enclosed toilet 'pod' was provided adjacent to the entrance area.[173]

Construction was to be of light steel with timber studwork and lining, with most components fabricated off-site. The design was commissioned by Leslie Bilsby, who subsequently abandoned it, but went on to build another experimental modular house, also with a pond, to a design by Walter Greaves at 21 Morden Road (now demolished).

A charming mechanical architectural model of this proposal, made by Gwynne, is in the collection of the RIBA.

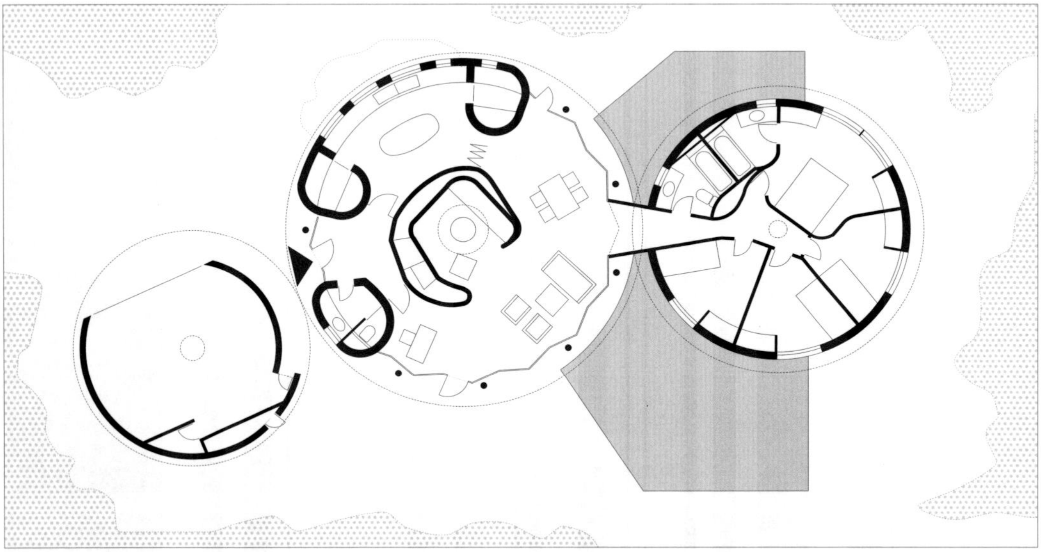

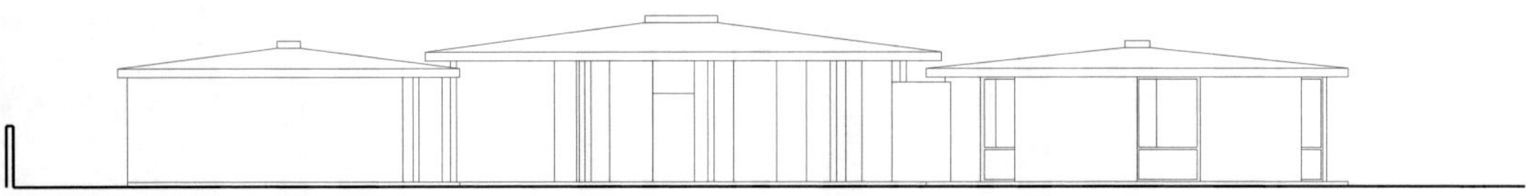

Above: ground floor plan
Below: side elevation

10m

1960

38

Project	10 Blackheath Park
Architect	Patrick Gwynne
Completed	1969
Client	Leslie Bilsby
Status	Grade II listed

The front entrance from Blackheath Park

Described by Nikolaus Pevsner as 'a design which sets out to shock',[174] this is undoubtedly an extraordinary house that cannot be ignored. Patrick Gwynne explained that 'the elevational treatment was intended to result in a frankly contrasting infill between the two period houses on either side but in such a manner that it would complement the neighbours rather than appear as a separate unrelated building.'[175]

The front and rear elevations are designed as curtain walls, with projecting bays of seamless dark tinted glass windows and vertical slate cladding, creating a recessive central entrance. These sit on top of a white rendered base containing the garage. The symmetrical façade, with its bay windows and raised first-floor, refers to the double-fronted Victorian architecture of the neighbours, but is reimagined in a modern language. The eaves heights align, as does the street frontage, but the unrelieved smooth black material is in stark contrast to the traditional stucco and brick walls.[176]

The floorplan is symmetrically arranged into four equal pentagons, which contain the main living spaces and the kitchen with a sensual curved staircase in the centre illuminated by circular rooflights. Externally a sculptural stair and precarious unguarded ramp wrap around a water feature and provide access across a metal bridge to the entrance hall. This leads to a chain of rooms, with the kitchen and study at the front and the dining and sitting rooms to the back. These main rooms are interconnected by red lacquered sliding doors and separated by intermediate spaces, including a hall, lobbies and servery. This flexibility enables the living rooms to open up to each other for entertaining.[177] At the back, a metal terrace and stairs provide access to the garden, designed by Ivor Cunningham. The top floor accommodates four bedrooms, one in each pentagon, duplicating the rooms below. The interconnecting spaces are a dressing room, bathrooms and stores.

The structure is of concrete slabs on load-bearing block walls. Internally the walls are lined in plywood faced with 'plastic cloth' – a textured Formica-like material more commonly used in aeroplane interiors. The central staircase has rendered walls and a black leather-wrapped handrail; the doors' hardwood full-height architraves are framed in chrome with a black trim.

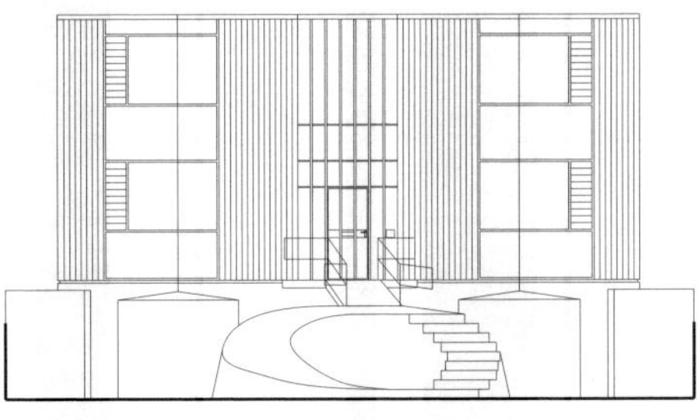

Front elevation

38 The house provides a key example of Gwynne's use of pure geometrical shapes in plan. These can also be seen in several of his other buildings, including the York Theatre Royal extension, for which the same vertical slate cladding is used. The theatre was completed in 1968, around the same time as 10 Blackheath Park. The project architect Bob King recalls that the slates chosen were usually installed horizontally as a damp-proof course in brick walls but are here repurposed as cladding.[178]

Built for Leslie Bilsby, the house was a grand statement that predictably 'appalled' the Blackheath Society. For a few years after its completion, Number 10 was referred to as 'the ogre's castle'.[179] Other nicknames used by local people have been rather more affectionate. They include 'the elephant's head', 'Darth Vader's house', and the 'Thunderbirds base'.

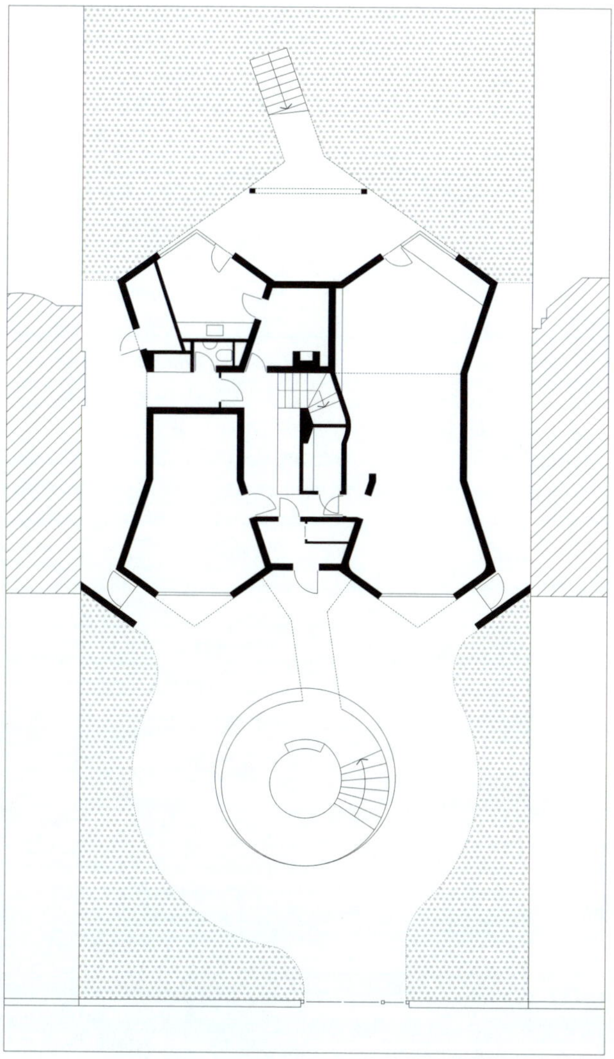

Lower ground floor plan

10m

The dining room from the living area, with the garden lobby between, 1977

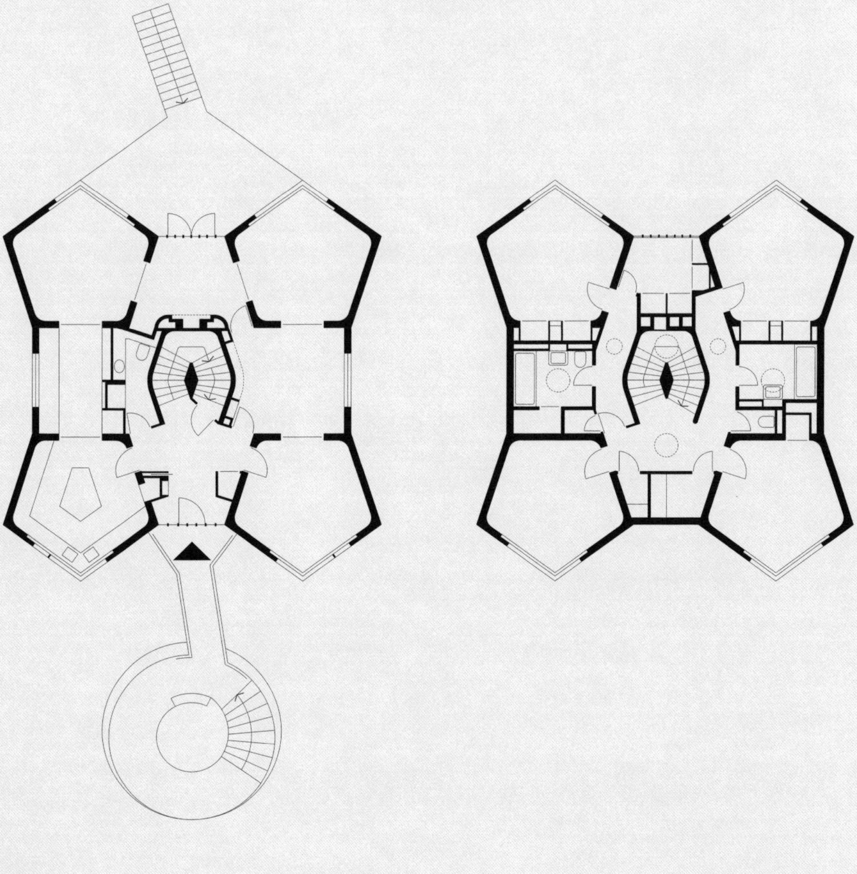

Left to right: upper ground and first floor plan

10m

Above: central staircase with rooflight
Below: rear garden terrace in 1977

39

Project	22 Parkgate
Architect	Patrick Gwynne
Completed	1979
Client	Leslie Bilsby

Entrance from Parkgate

Ten years after the completion of 10 Blackheath Park, Patrick Gwynne was commissioned to design another house for Leslie Bilsby, on the unmade section of Parkgate. It benefits from mature trees, a long garden and the Kid Brook stream, which runs along its southern boundary. It lies adjacent to The Priory Span estate, which Bilsby had developed back in 1956.

The plan is of three connected octagons, each built of dark brown brick with sloping felt roofs in a similar colour. The geometry and form recall Gwynne's previous work for the Crescent Restaurant at the Festival of Britain and his two M62 motorway service buildings in Cheshire, both built in the early 1970s.

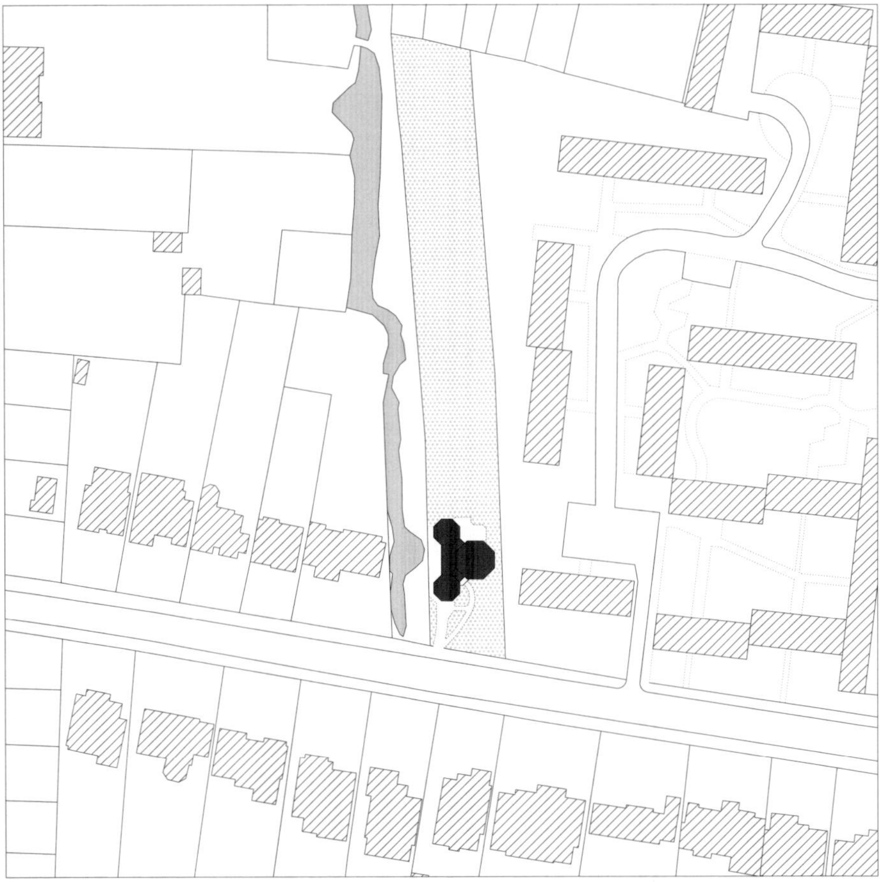

 Site location 1:2000 50m 1979

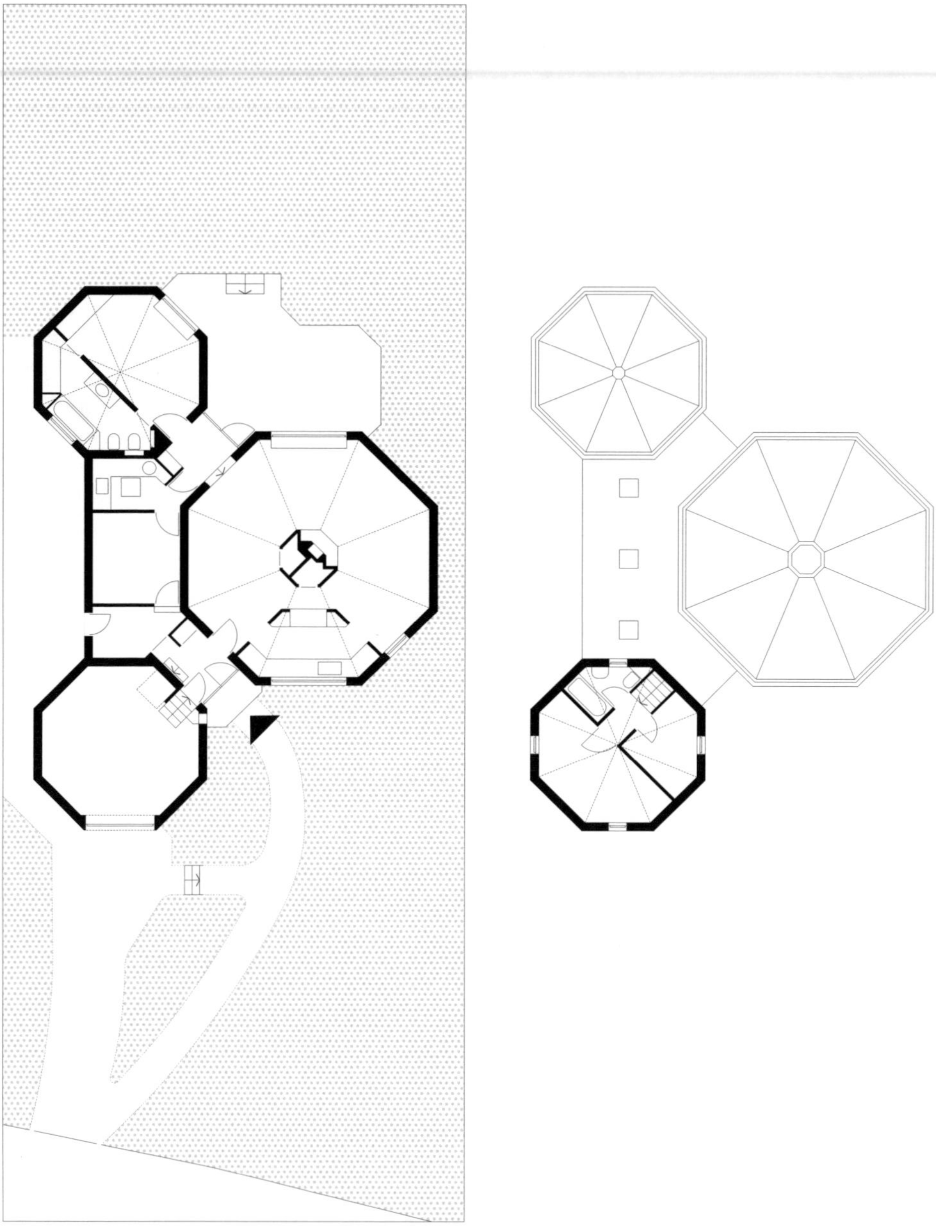

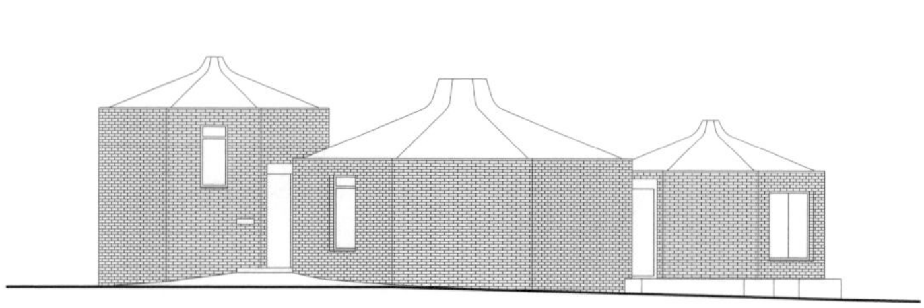

Above, left to right: ground and first floor plans
Below: north elevation, as originally built

10m

In an arrangement similar to 10 Blackheath Park, the octagonal forms are designed to link together, creating secondary spaces in between, which are used for a workshop, storeroom, laundry and to access the garden. The three main volumes accommodate a living space and kitchen in the larger octagon; the smaller octagons contain the master bedroom and a garage, with a guest bedroom over. The living room's timber roof structure is left exposed so that it can be enjoyed internally, together with the central supporting brick chimney.[180]

An earlier scheme, developed in 1976, was for four cubes of timber structure and aluminium cladding. In 1987, Gwynne made changes to the layout for its then owners, Colin and Jacqui Hawkins, creating a more family-friendly home. The changes included a new storey to one of the smaller octagons, for the master bedroom and a relocation of the kitchen from the main octagon to the service area.

The house number is displayed on a unique pierced metal plate, similar to the one at 10 Blackheath Park.[181]

 The living area in 1983

Paul Tvrtkovic (1927–2010) must be the only architect to ever receive planning permission for a riverside Dolphinarium in Greenwich – a feat he achieved in 1900. An émigré from the former Yugoslavia, he built a house for his family in Blackheath in 1963 and set up his practice there in 1965, after a few years living in a Span house.

Tvrtkovic was born in Sarajevo and the city's Ottoman, Austro-Hungarian and European traditions all had a profound influence on his personal aesthetic. The same is true of his experiences at a boarding school run by Franciscan monks in Rome and the time he spent in Padua and at the Sorbonne.

In 1945, while serving in the Croatian army, Tvrtkovic was taken prisoner of war. On his release, he studied architecture in Zagreb (1946–52) under tutors who were inspired by the British Arts and Crafts movement and had connections to Adolf Loos and Otto Wagner.

Tvrtkovic left his home country in 1955 and did not return for 30 years. Despite his initially poor spoken English, he obtained work with architectural practices in London. By 1960, tired of working for others, he decided to venture into speculative development by forming a company with investors. Until 1965, this venture mainly involved the development of residential blocks in Hampstead, London.

Subsequently, he continued to initiate his own projects, with the most important being the New London Theatre complex, Drury Lane (now the Gillian Lynne Theatre), which took 10 years to complete (1962–1972), with Tvrtkovic responsible for the whole process, from feasibility studies to land acquisition, planning permission and construction.[182]

Working together with the scenic designer Sean Kenny, the auditorium was modelled after Walter Gropius's Total-Theatre concept. The building opened in 1973 and was the home of Andrew Lloyd Weber's musical Cats for 22 years. Its more recent productions include *War Horse* and *School of Rock*.

Tvrtkovic taught part-time at Kingston Polytechnic from 1974 to 1981. He designed houses and flat conversions in central London, along with several projects that were never built – including his proposed Dolphinarium for the Greenwich riverfront. He chose not to exploit his many contacts and advantages, believing that architecture should be a personal and solitary art form.[183]

From 1974 to 1984, Tvrtkovic designed the Croatian stall at the annual International Book Fair in Frankfurt, Germany. After the fall of the communist regime in 1990, he returned to the Balkans to work on the restoration of war-damaged churches in Bosnia-Herzegovina and a church and monastery in Shkodra, Albania.

Local projects	14 Baizdon Road	1963
Other London projects	Daynor House, Quex Road, Kilburn	1962
	Romney Court, Haverstock Hill, Belsize Park	1963
	Golders Park Close, Golders Green	1963
	New London Theatre (now The Gillian Lynne Theatre)	1968

Paul Tvrtkovic

40	Project	14 Baizdon Road
	Architect	Paul Tvrtkovic
	Completed	1964
	Client	Architect's own house

Hidden away from view, Tvrtkovic's introverted building is arguably, one of the most underrated of the local modern houses. It was built on part of the gardens of a large house, 9 Eliot Vale (1805, Grade II listed).

Tvrtkovic explained that the house was designed 'for cosmopolitan elegant living, with plenty of space and light, rejecting all the pastiche of bygone styles, yet it sits happily among its period neighbours as part of an enclave of some ten large private houses varying in style from Regency to Georgian and Modern'.[184] This enclave includes 16 Baizdon Road and 40 Heath Lane.

This long, narrow house is positioned so that its narrow side faces the road, while its long side has an open southerly aspect over gardens. Enclosed by mature trees and 2.4m high walls, the site is a secluded garden. To quote Tvrtkovic: 'the principle adopted is that the house is for privacy and not a status symbol. The opposite of the extroverted nature of the Regency and Georgian street façades.'

The building's layout is similar to Peter Moro's house at 20 Blackheath Park, with the two-storey flat-roofed building designed as a floating volume, in part lifted on pilotis above a recessed ground floor. The first floor is timber clad with carefully composed windows.

The ground floor accommodates the architect's studio, utility room and guest bedroom. The footprint is relatively small leaving most of the site free for gardens, the carport or covered patios which are animated by two monumental sculptures by Croatian sculptor Ivan Klapez. On the first floor, the main living room, kitchen and three bedrooms benefit from open views.

Referring to the building process, Tvrtkovic explained that 'it took only three days to erect the steel frame. The structure was made up from six steel portal frames with cantilevers on both sides, to achieve the most economical structure.' Light trusses and diagonal bracing stabilise the frames.

Internally, the central core (bathrooms and kitchen) is enclosed by concrete and brick walls, painted white. The walls of the staircase (a sculptural mahogany structure) and living space are covered in natural linen. The upstairs rooms are arranged *au enfilade*, allowing sight lines along the entire 16m length of the house. The floors and ceilings are lined in maple wood and the steel columns encased in wood. The southern wall of the living room is fully glazed with floor to ceiling double-glazed windows; a raised bench at the base accommodates the warm-air ducting and helps to protect the glazing.

14 BAIZDON ROAD

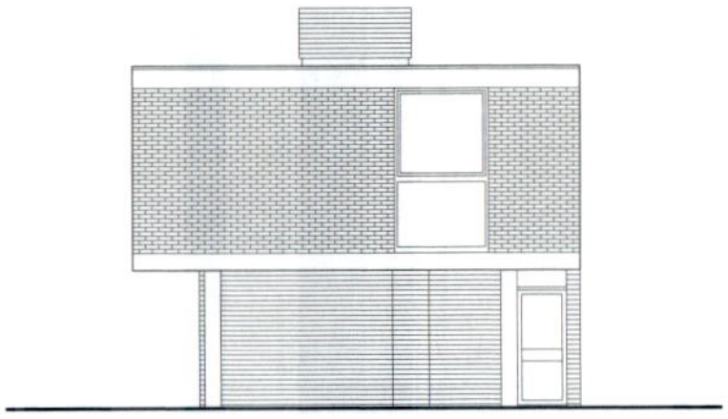

Above: entrance on Baizdon Road
Below: east elevation

10m

1964

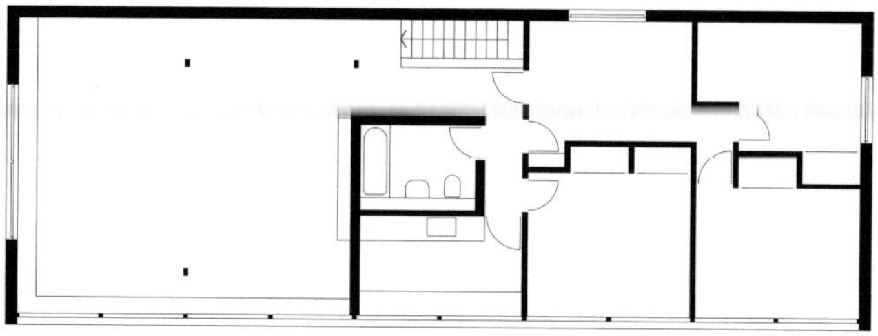

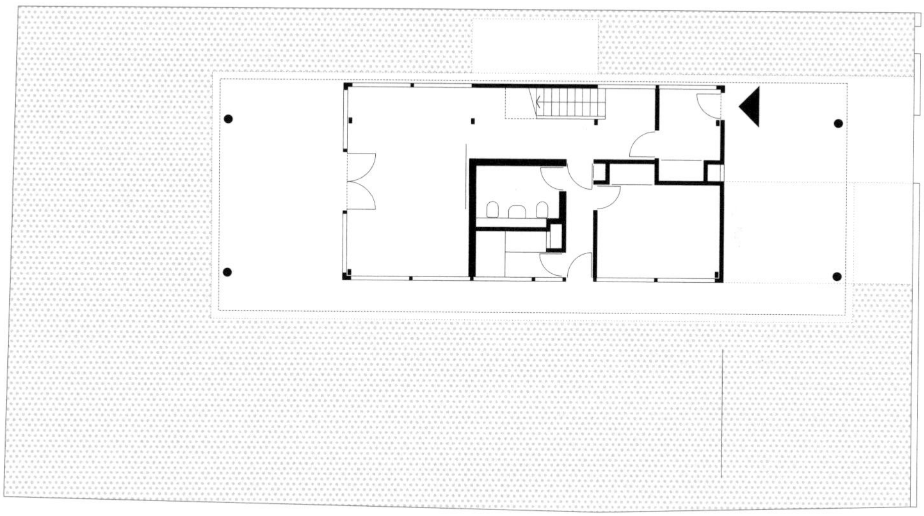

PAUL TVRTKOVIC

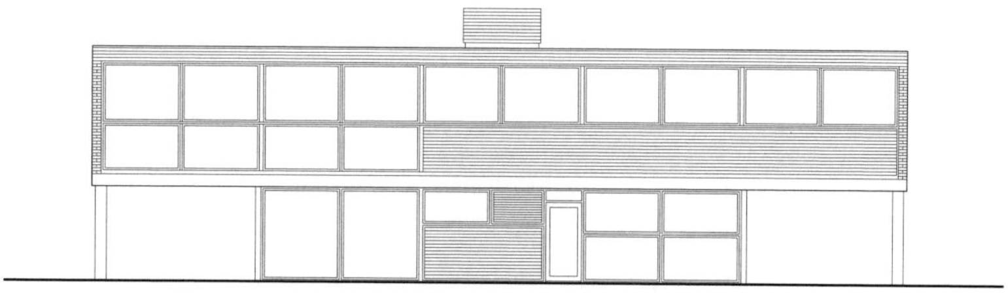

Top to bottom: first and ground floor plans;
garden elevation

 The south-facing living room windows

1964

Peatfield, Mayo and Bodgener formed their practice in 1952. They were based in 3 Lloyds Place, Blackheath. In the same year they entered the Golden Lane Estate competition, which was won by Chamberlin, Powell & Bon. In the mid-1950s the practice moved to offices at 39 Blackheath Hill, near Brian Meeking's studio, and was later based at 11 Gray's Inn Square WC1.

Thomas (Tommy) Alexander Peatfield (1921–1978) and Geoffrey Bodgener (1920–1991) were schoolmates, studied architecture together and served in the Royal Air Force during the Second World War. Joseph (Joe) Leslie Mayo (1920–2014) studied at the Polytechnic and served in the army with the Royal Engineers. After resuming his studies in 1946, he qualified as a RIBA associate in 1948.

Mayo had great drawing ability and joined the LCC Festival of Britain team, working on the Royal Festival Hall, assisting Leslie Martin in creating visuals for each day's ideas. Mayo bought and shared 3 Lloyds Place with Peatfield from 1948. Bodgener lived just around the corner at 11 Eliot Place.

Mayo left the partnership in 1953 and went on to teach at the Polytechnic until his retirement in the 1980s. There he taught Nick Mason, who went on to form Pink Floyd. Peatfield also taught at the Polytechnic and later at the Brixton School of Building. Alongside teaching, Mayo also worked on mosaics, paintings and murals, including the ceramic mural at Bradford University.

Like many of their peers, Peatfield and Bodgener looked for potential projects in the emerging independent nations of the Commonwealth. In 1953 they won second prize in the competition to design the head office of the Uganda Electricity Board in Kampala. Their big break came in 1956 when they won the competition for a National Assembly Building in Kampala. From that date on, Bodgener stayed in Kampala and Peatfield was based in London. Mayo secured two assignments for the Parliament building: the bas-reliefs on either side of the entrance door and the large internal wooden screen – it features in the film *The Last King of Scotland*.[185]

The London office closed in the late 1980s but the firm Peatfield and Bodgener continues to practice in Kampala, led by director Philip Curtin who joined in 1987. Curtin was instrumental in setting up the first school of architecture in Kampala.[186]

Local projects	81–89 Blackheath Park	1950s
	81–88 Ashburnham Grove	1962
	Cedar Mount, Mottingham	

Projects in Kampala, Uganda	National Assembly Building	1956
	National Theatre	1959
	Mary Stuart Hall, extension	1965
	Bank of Uganda	1966
	12 district hospitals	1960s–70s
	Uganda Commercial Bank	1976

Peatfield and Bodgener with telegram—2nd prize in architectural competition,1952. Tommy's Rolls Royce.

41	Project	81–88 Ashburnham Grove
	Architect	Peatfield, Mayo and Bodgener
	Completed	1962

This terrace of eight three-storey houses was built on the site of a bomb-damaged Victorian terrace.

The building work started in 1958 but the building company went bankrupt and the houses were left roofless until their eventual completion in 1962.

The original layout comprised a garage, entrance and utility room on the ground floor, living room and kitchen on the first floor and two bedrooms and a bathroom on the top floor. The garage is recessed from the front face of the building to create a sheltered porch. Most of the houses have now converted the garages into accommodation (there is off-street parking in a driveway) and some residents have also extended the compact houses into the rear gardens, which back onto St Paul's Church. The end-of-terrace house has been extended to its full height and width, with matching brick walls and details.

The light brick elevations have two bands of exposed concrete, one capping the top of the brick façade, the other expressing the living room slab at first-floor level. Carefully placed window openings and the recessed entrance area complete the composition.

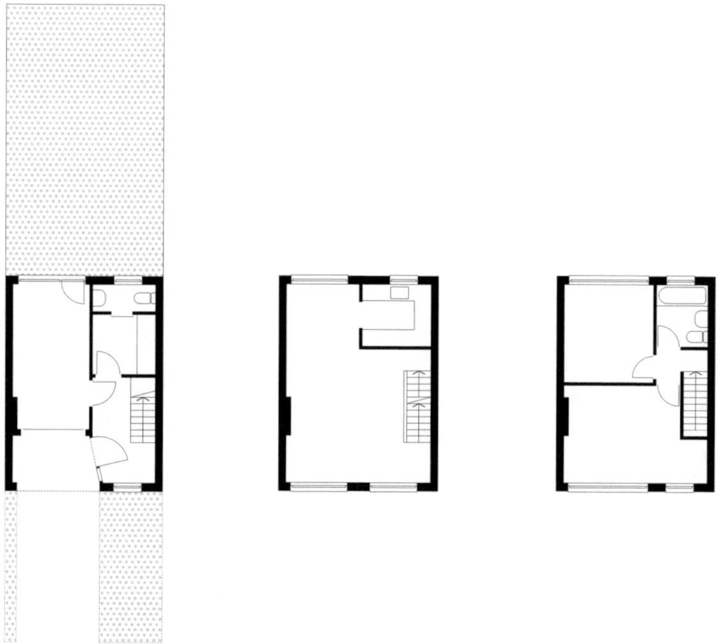

Left to right: ground, first and second floor plans

1:300 10m

81–88 ASHBURNHAM GROVE

Above: street view
Below: street elevation, as originally built 1:500 15m

1962

Inspired by the celebrated Case-study houses built in California by Richard Neutra, Craig Ellwood and Ray and Charles Eames, Peter Foggo (1930–1993) and David Thomas (1931–2010) designed 12 private houses in partnership between 1959 and 1965. The projects were conceived as prototypes for future speculative developments. All the houses were organised on a strict structural geometry and all were built with single-storey steel or timber frames and extensive use of glass and wood with the exception of their own houses at Cambridge Street.

Foggo was born in Liverpool and worked as a bank clerk before studying architecture. He set up in practice with David Thomas in 1959. They shared a passion for the work of Mies van der Rohe and once persuaded the legendary architect to travel to Merseyside to give a talk to students.

Foggo and Thomas were workaholics. With minimal secretarial support, they practiced outside standard office hours while still working full-time at other practices. Their first completed house (Sorrell House, near Chichester, Grade II* listed) was commissioned in 1959 through Kenneth Capon at Architects' Co-Partnership, where Foggo worked at the time.

Thomas was born in Sydenham, London. After working for several practices and in partnership with Foggo, he joined the multi-disciplinary Ove Arup Building Group in 1957. On his recommendation, Foggo also joined two years later. At Ove Arup, Foggo and Thomas produced some ground-breaking work together. However, Thomas was then appointed to lead a separate design group. Their joint projects included a major development for IBM at Cosham, Portsmouth, buildings at Stockley Park, Heathrow, and the masterplan for the Central Airport Station, Hong Kong.

The Ove Arup Building Group became Arup Associates in 1963, led by Philip Dowson and two engineering partners. Foggo became a partner in 1973 and Thomas a director in 1977. Together, they designed the masterplan for Loughborough University. Later Foggo designed Gateway 1 and 2 (now listed) in Basingstoke, 123–150 Buckingham Palace Road and the renovation of the celebrated Liver Building on Liverpool's waterfront. Foggo's work at Broadgate completed a string of influential projects that he led during the 1980s, with 1 Finsbury Avenue regarded as one of his finest achievements. Foggo set up Peter Foggo Associates in 1989 which continues to operate today.

Local projects	31 Langton Way	1960
Other London projects	Forrester House, Murray Road, Wimbledon	c.1963
	St Mary's Road, Wimbledon	1965
	76–78 Cambridge Street, Pimlico	1969

David Thomas

Peter Foggo

42

Project	31 Langton Way
Architect	Peter Foggo and David Thomas
Completed	1960
Client	Norman Hurst

One of the earliest of Foggo and Thomas's experimental houses, 31 Langton Way is one of the more modest but also one of the most provocative.

Inspired by Mies van der Rohe and exploring his concepts, construction methods and details, a quote in the Peter Foggo Memorial Exhibition catalogue (1994) explained that: 'Change is the essence of twentieth-century living. The traditional approach to house designing is inhibiting. The resulting houses are ill-equipped to cater for growth, change and the renewal of parts. Our aim, therefore, has been to design a unit of space which alone or in combination provides a structural shell within which the mechanical services, the partitions and the spaces for living can be so arranged that they are independent of the structure and each other, thereby allowing for maximum response to pressure for change.'[187]

This single-storey house is set between garden walls, on a plot formed from part of the rear garden of 4 St Johns Park, a large villa. Two houses were actually built there: number 29 Langton Way was designed by Norman Plastow and built in 1964 by Parsons, the same contractor for number 31.[188]

Concealed from the road by a high wall, the house is accessed through a front courtyard. It is divided into two with the double-aspect living room and kitchen on one side, and the three bedrooms and study on the other. The external structure is a regular series of laminated timber beams, supported by twinned posts, and from which the roof is suspended. Above the central core, kitchen and bathroom, a raised roof provides clerestory light to the spaces below.[189]

With the structure independent, the front and rear elevations are good examples of Le Corbusier's 'free façade' put into practice: large areas of glass allow the living room to connect with the garden whilst the bedrooms are screened for privacy. The interiors have a natural warm feel with ceilings clad in pine, walls and partitions of cedar and floors in maple.

In 2006, the house was featured in the film *Our Kind of Traitor* (directed by Susanna White), a John Le Carre thriller starring Ewan MacGregor and Damian Lewis.[190]

31 LANGTON WAY

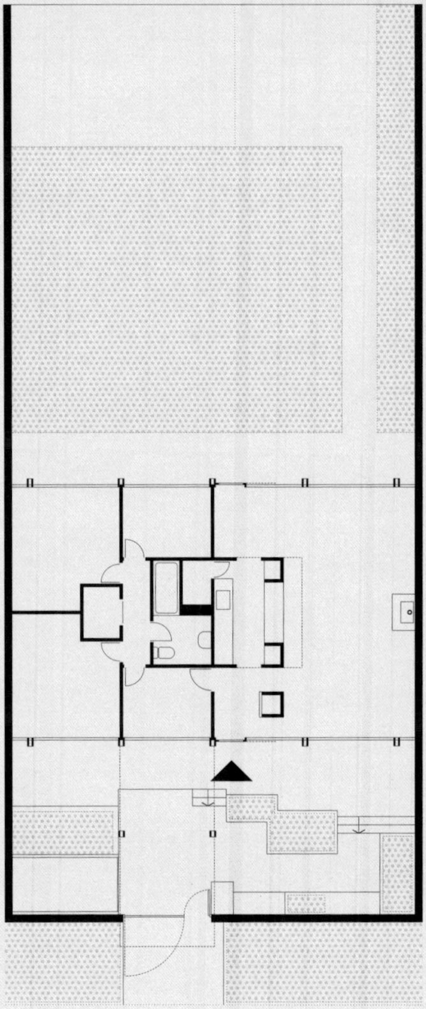

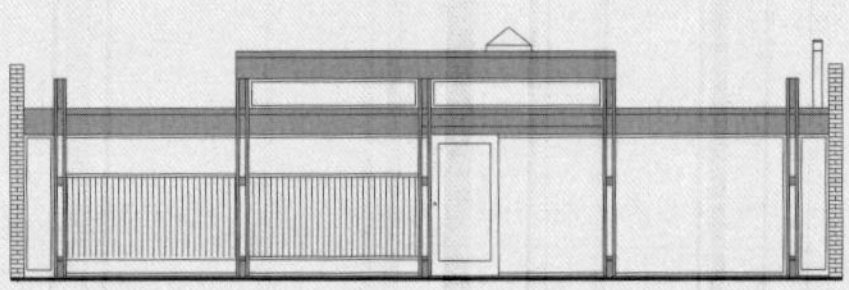

Above: ground floor plan
Below: front elevation

10m

1960

The house from the rear garden

The living room with the central skylight above the kitchen block

Peter Moro (1911 – 1998) lived in Blackheath for more than 40 years, in the house he designed at 20 Blackheath Park. He was an influential teacher and the focal point for a flourishing network of local architects.

Moro was born and raised in Germany but advised to study in Zurich as he had a Jewish grandmother. After graduating in 1936, he moved to London. Despite his limited spoken English, he soon settled and worked with Berthold Lubetkin at Tecton, where he stayed for two years. In 1938, Moro and his friend Richard Llewelyn-Davies designed Harbour Meadow at Birdham, Sussex – one of the most original modern houses of the 1930s and now Grade II listed.

At the start of the Second World War, Moro was interned as an enemy-alien, first in Liverpool and then on the Isle of Man. He later wrote of that time: 'I shared the house with a number of interesting people. A journalist, an historian, an engineer and three musicians. Artists painted portraits of the officers or fellow prisoners or female nudes – the later, alas, entirely from memory. Nikolas Pevsner gave lectures on French Impressionists. [...] there were enough 'academics' to start our own mini university.'[191]

On his release, he taught at the Regent Street Polytechnic from 1941 to 1947. Several students in his class, including Trevor Dannatt (who introduced Moro to the local area), Walter Greaves, Ursula and Gordon Bowyer, were drafted into the design team for the Royal Festival Hall in London. He also met fellow teacher Robin Day there and they often collaborated on projects.

From 1952 to 1984 he led Peter Moro and Partners, working mainly on public sector projects, including schools, council housing and theatres. The partners over the years were Michael Mellish, Andrzeg Blonski, Michael Heard, Frank Linden, Michael Merritt and Charles Peel.[192] The theatre designs included many notable and influential projects, for example the Nottingham Playhouse, 1963, Theatre Royal Plymouth, 1982 and the Gulbenkian Centre at Hull University, 1969.[193] Moro retired in the mid-1980s and Peter Moro and Partners was subsequently wound up.

Local projects	20 Blackheath Park	1958
	11 Manor Way, with Walter Greaves	1960
Other London projects	Fairlawn School, Honor Oak Road	1957
	Camberwell housing, Comber Grove	1970
	Borough housing, Hamilton Square	1973
	Peckham housing, Montpelier Road	1974

Peter Moro, 1948

Project	20 Blackheath Park
Architect	Peter Moro
Completed	1958
Renovations	Architect's own house
Status	Grade II* listed

20 Blackheath Park was built on the site of Hurst Lodge, a three-storey villa dating from 1826.[194] By 1956, the site belonged to Leslie Bilsby who demolished the villa, making way for Moro's project. The project architect was Michael Mellish who lived nearby at 17 Montpelier Row. 20a Blackheath Park, Hurst Lodge's coach house, was converted into a home also in the late 1950s with a modern interior added in 1962 designed by Walter Greaves.

Peter Moro lived at No. 20 from its completion in 1958. The building was one of the first post-war houses to be listed, in 1988. In a 1996 interview he said: 'To live in anything else would be a terrible come down from a house which is tailored to your wishes.'[195]

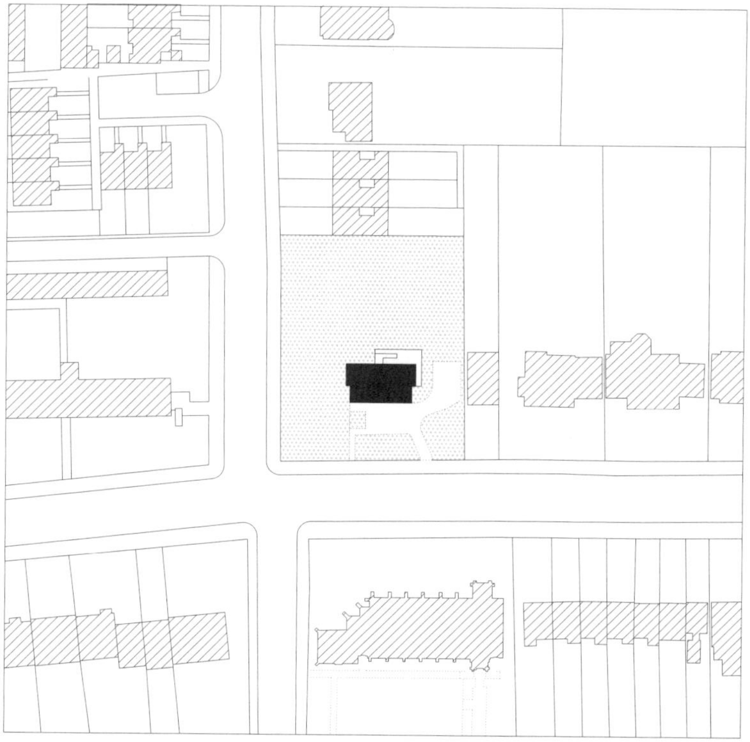

Site plan 1:2000 50m

Above: street elevation
Below: front door, 1960s

10m

1958

The first-floor volume cantilevers over the lower brick block

20 BLACKHEATH PARK

1958

43 Described by architect and author June Park as a 'bungalow upstairs', all the main living and bedroom accommodation is on the first floor, with ancillary rooms, workshop and garage on the ground floor.[196] The façades have irregular but carefully composed fenestration. Each elevation tells a different story: the sides express the internal split level; the front maintains privacy towards the street; and the rear is open, addressing the broad sloping garden. The relatively small scale of the house and its setting within the garden allow it to be read as a pavilion and appreciated from all four sides.

The two-storey rectangular building features a cantilevered first floor, positioned over a partly sunken ground floor. With the ground floor faced in dark brick and the first floor clad in white timber boarding, the effect is of a floating volume. As you move around the building, the side elevations show that the house has a more complex section, with the rear dropping into the garden to create a half-level internally that adds dynamism, and a row of clerestory windows that bring light into the centre of the plan. At the rear, a steel balcony and open stair evoke the deck of an ocean liner, looking onto the 'sea' of the lawn. This structure was wrapped in chicken wire when Moro's children were small, to prevent falls.[197]

Behind the beautifully detailed front door, next to the black steel column (which doubles as a rainwater pipe) visitors are welcomed by a recessed entrance mat of wavy rubber (brand name 'Mat-a-door') and post-shelf. The stairs between the half-levels have open treads, visually linking the garden with the house interior.

The internal fittings were designed, sometimes even made, by Moro himself. These include flush doors with Tecton-style handles and toggle light switches, timber balustrades to the staircase, sliding doors and fitted cupboards, wardrobes and shelves throughout the house. The fireplace is framed by two brick piers and topped by a brass 'boiler' – a design identical to the one used in Moro's earlier project for his brother-in-law, the White Lodge in Waldringfield, Suffolk (1953).[198]

Artists Glenys Johnson and Tony Bevan are only the second owners and residents of Number 20 and they have cared for and nurtured it.[199] As they were during Moro's time, the house's informal and yet clear spaces are used for displaying and appreciating art.[200] In 2010, a summer house was built in the garden designed by Fraser Brown MacKenna Architects.

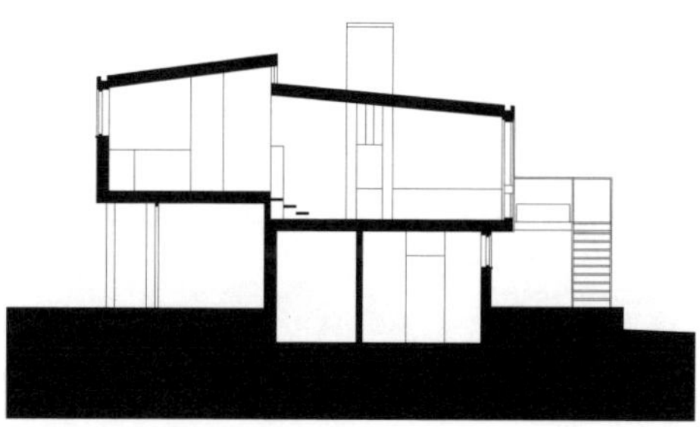

Section

10m

20 BLACKHEATH PARK

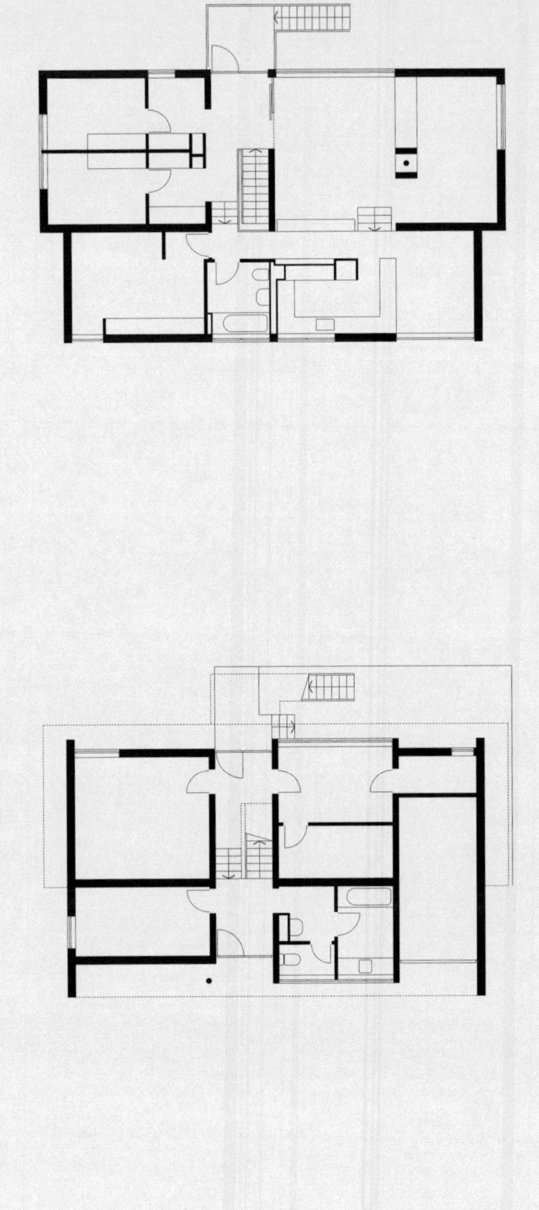

Top to bottom: first and ground floor plans; garden elevation

10m

1958

The entrance hall with open-tread staircase

 The open-plan split-level living spaces

View from the lower wooded area of the garden

20 BLACKHEATH PARK

1958

Pierre d'Avoine (b. 1951) substantially redesigned and extended a 1960s house at 21 Westgrove Lane.

D'Avoine was born in Bombay, India. His father, of French and Indian descent, worked as an architect in Bombay. Following his father's death, the d'Avoine family moved to the UK, where their maternal relatives already lived.

He studied at the Birmingham School of Architecture during the 1970s and worked with the Peter Bond Partnership and Fitzroy Robinson before establishing Pierre d'Avoine Architects in 1979. In 2017, he set up studio DA with his daughter, Pereen d'Avoine, and Nilesh Shah.

He taught at several different institutions, including the Cass School of Architecture, Bath School of Architecture, the AA, the Welsh School of Architecture and the Bartlett (UCL).

D'Avoine still practices internationally, with work completed or still ongoing in Japan, India, Italy, Ghana, the West Indies and Iran. These projects include individual homes, larger housing projects, mixed-use developments, urban design, interiors and public art. His books include *Housey Housey, A Pattern of Ideal Homes* with Clare Melhuish (2005) and *San Salvatore* (2021).

Local projects	Chatfield House, 21 Westgrove Lane	2009
Other London projects	White House, Barnes	1992
	Tapestry court, Mortlake	2003

Pierre d'Avoine

44

Project	Chatfield House, 21 Westgrove Lane
Architect	Unknown
Completed	1965 altered in 2009[201]
Alterations	Pierre d'Avoine

PIERRE D'AVOINE

The tree-storey volume from Westgrove Lane

Chatfield House is located along the unpaved Westgrove Lane, on a site which drops dramatically towards Greenwich and the River Thames to the north. Originally, a detached two-storey 1960s building of brick and timber cladding, rather like a detached Span house, it was adapted and transformed vertically, rather than laterally, into a three-storey brick cube by d'Avoine. The original owners were artists John (1921–1996) and Anne Christopherson (1921–2013). The new owners, Ben and Pusia Chatfield, wished to create a contemporary family home but retain the richly planted garden and open vistas from Westgrove Lane. Client and architect had worked together before, when Ben's design agency produced d'Avoine and Melhuish's book *Housey Housey, A Pattern of Ideal Homes* in 2005.

The decision was made to reuse the original house, add an extra storey and completely re-plan the internal layout and external openings. The ground floor now accommodates the living rooms and kitchen in a series of interconnected spaces; the first and second floors contain the bedrooms and bathrooms, which benefit from magnificent panoramic views over Greenwich, the river and beyond. This was a radical change, as in the original house the bedrooms and studios were at ground level with the living rooms on the first floor.

 Site plan 1:2000 50m 1965, 2009

44

Chatfield House is notable for its fine joinery in utile hardwood, including large pivot doors to the garden and sliding windows that were inspired by the detailing of Meridian West, the adjacent listed building designed by Julian Sofaer in 1965. The connection between these two houses involves more than just the windows; E Morton Wright, living at Meridian West, was one of only two neighbours who supported the Chatfield House project.[202] He was also the local resident most affected by the planned transformation but he saw the value of the proposals and even allowed access to the site through his garden. He invited the architects, joiners and architecture students to visit and study the woodwork and detailing in Meridian West. The two houses can now be read as a pair – one horizontal, one vertical – and the gardens are connected visually into one space.

On the external elevations, where the original timber cladding was removed, a brick-slip infill in herringbone pattern was used; the pattern reappearing internally on the maple herringbone floor. Minimalist marble detailing in the kitchen and master bathrooms creates an interior of understated luxury. Vertical circulation is by a dramatic staircase that turns into a large light filled landing at first floor level, where there was once an open terrace above the entrance. The children's bedrooms and the top floor master bedroom and bathroom suite are designed as flexible spaces, with folding and sliding doors used to vary the privacy. A new balcony on the top floor affords magnificent views across London.

This 2009 project exemplifies the sympathetic reuse of a 1960s building. The client and architect worked genially and 'with the spirit of the existing house and its physical fabric.'[203]

Chatfield House seen from the garden of Meridian West

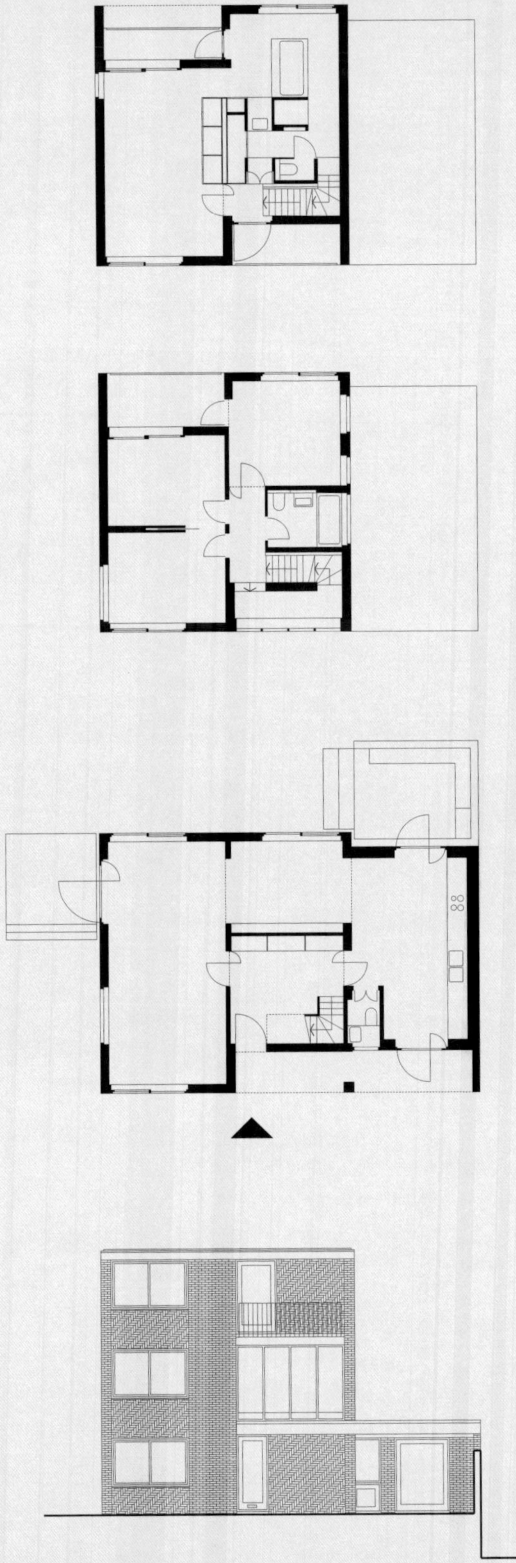

Top to bottom: second, first and ground floor plans; south elevation

10m

1965, 2009

Raymond Smith (1930–2001) was first attracted to Blackheath by the Span housing estates. However, the limited availability and cost of land prompted Smith and his family to build their own house on a bomb-damaged site at Park Vista, Greenwich. This house was followed by a second split-level extraordinary home almost opposite, standing at the base of Greenwich Park.

Smith studied architecture at the Northern Polytechnic and gained his Diploma from the AA. After qualifying, he worked briefly with E. Vincent Harris on the Neo-Georgian style Kensington Central Library project. Smith became a RIBA associate in 1954 and founded RSP Architects in 1961. He had previously worked for Donald H. McMorran – a modern-classicist who had nevertheless supported Chamberlin, Powell & Bon on their winning entry for the Golden Lane Estate competition. Smith also taught architecture and surveying at the North-East London Polytechnic.

During his time with McMorran, Smith gained experience in Police Station projects. MacMorran had completed Hammersmith Police Station in 1939 and Smith's practice subsequently undertook further extensions and refurbishments to the original building in 1993 and 2016. Another Police Station project was for South Norwood, which was exhibited at the Royal Academy during the mid-1970s. This project led to further refurbishment work on several other police stations.[204]

Smith designed a series of interesting houses for his own family. The two Park Vista houses were followed by a cottage in Frant, Kent, four apartments in a converted Baptist Chapel in Lewes, and finally a home and office in a converted derelict barn near Alfriston, East Sussex. His last family project was a derelict coach house in Eastbourne, which he transformed into a smaller version of 37 Park Vista.

In the late 1980s, Smith designed a house in a chalk quarry at Piddinghoe, near Newhaven – cleverly using the building to link two parts of the quarry that were separated by 15 meters high chalk faces. His design was inspired by Frank Lloyd Wright. As a student, Smith had written to Lloyd Wright and kept his letter of reply framed in his office. Smith's wife Eileen helped to fund his AA studies and worked as the practice's office manager until his death. The Raymond Smith Partnership is still operating in Eastbourne, led by Roy's son, Peter, and Simon Whitmill.[205]

Local projects

21 Park Vista	1959
37 Park Vista	1967
33 Park Vista, St Alfege's Vicarage refurbishment	1960s
2 Hassendean Road and 1 Furzefield Road, Charlton	

Ray Smith on a site visit

45	Project	21 Park Vista
	Architect	Ray Smith
	Completed	1959
	Client	Architect's own house

Situated next to the Plume of Feathers, the oldest pub in Greenwich, this three-storey house was built on the site of two demolished workmen's cottages in a street of mixed Georgian and Victorian terraced houses. The opposite side of the street is enclosed by the historic brick wall that forms the northern boundary of Greenwich Park.

The house enjoys views over the park through floor-to-ceiling glazing on the upper floors.

The open-plan living room is located on the first floor to maximise the views and to give the occupants some privacy from passers-by, with the three bedrooms on the level above.

The ground floor originally had a study, WC, integrated garage and utility room with access to a paved garden at the rear. Situated immediately next to the pavement it lacked privacy; this problem was solved by recessing the entrance door to create a porch or internal courtyard screened by a low timber fence, with a gate and a coal store.

Internally, the house originally featured sapele wood flooring and timber panelling with an oak-lined ceiling in the living room. An open steel and timber spiral staircase connected all floors – a space-saving solution for such a restricted site.[206]

The floor slabs are represented externally with horizontal bands (originally painted white), which conceal planting boxes and give a more complex horizontal expression to what would otherwise be a simple vertically proportioned façade.[207]

The Smiths' son, Peter, remembers that his mother was quite stressed about having a toddler in the house, with its full height staircase and widely spaced balusters. The family subsequently moved across the road to a single-storey house, also designed by Smith. Ironically, Peter fell off a ladder while inspecting the roof of this new building with his father during construction. Thankfully, no harm was done.[208]

The building was much altered in 2021, with replacement windows, doors and plant boxes in grey metal, and the loss of the recessed entrance porch.

21 PARK VISTA

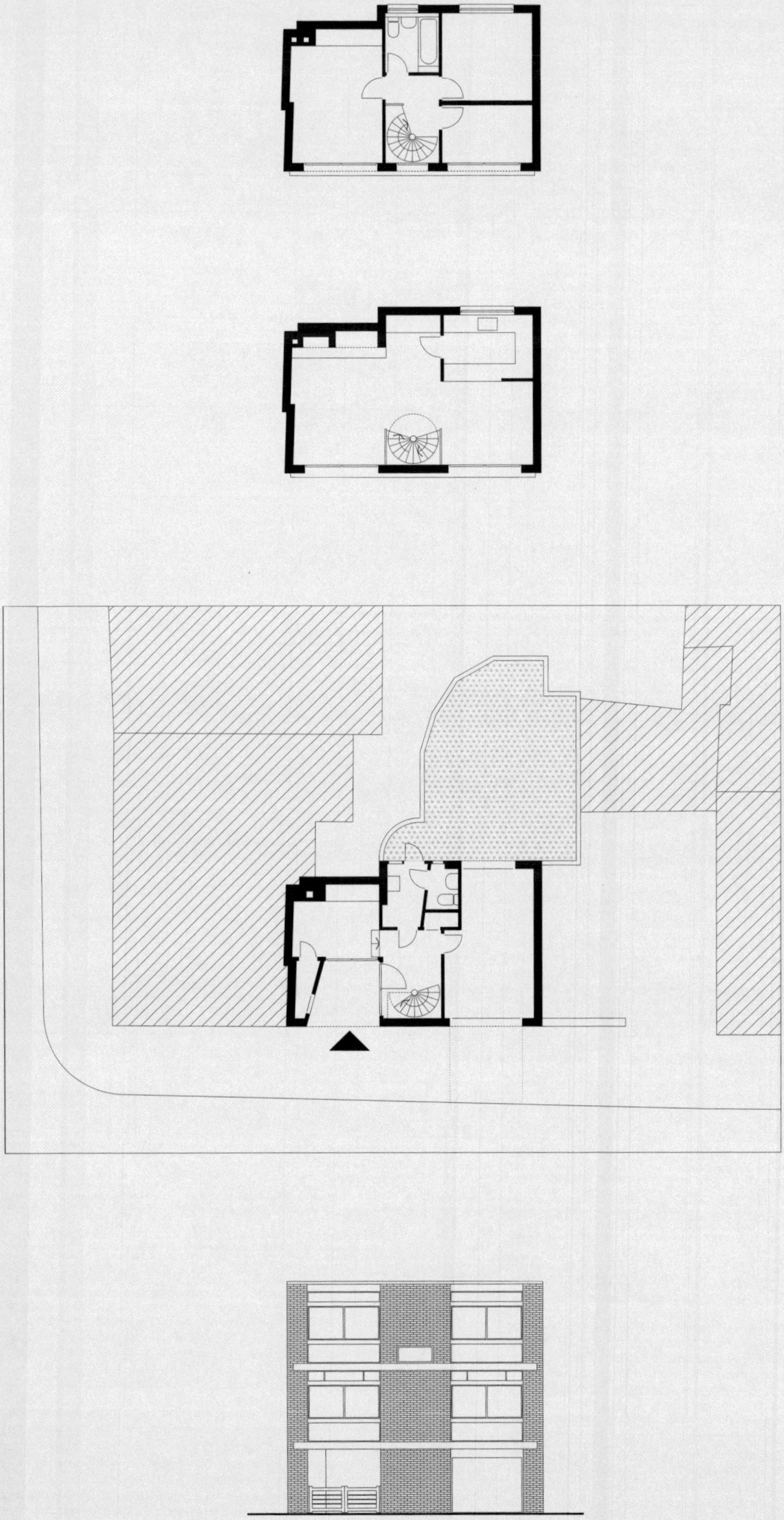

Top to bottom: second, first and ground floor plans; street elevation, as originally built

10m

1959

Above: street view
Below: semi-enclosed kitchen and service hatch

 Open-plan living space at first floor

Project	37 Park Vista
Architect	Ray Smith
Completed	1967
Client	Architect's own house

At the base of Greenwich Park, along Park Vista, there are two parallel park walls, enclosing land historically belonging to the Church. While living at 21 Park Vista, and employed as surveyor to the Diocese of Southwark, Smith was able to purchase a remarkable plot opposite his house, between the walls. The disused allotment garden was linked to the Grade II listed St Alfege's Vicarage, at 33 Park Vista, which Smith was working on at the time. The only clue that there is a house behind the walls are a pair of gates: one for people and one for cars. The larger one has a green man keystone salvaged by Smith from another site.[209]

Located next to the park but yet constrained by high brick walls, the house is naturally introverted but employs an ingenious section to bring in light and allow views out. A spine of sloped rooflights illuminates the centre of the plan, while the sitting room, placed at the farthest end from the park, is raised by a half level to allow glimpses of treetops.

The entrance to the house is through a patio. There is a self-contained annex to the left (originally planned for an elderly relative, it was eventually used as Smith's studio).[210] To the right, the main dining area and kitchen are at garden level; this central space is open to the raised sitting room, six steps above.

The internal finishes and fittings include pine clad doors and fitted cupboards, with flush detailing. Highly glazed Swedish tiles line the fireplace wall (the internal face of the historic brick wall) and the bathrooms. The living room floors and ceilings are finished in maple strip. Integrated bookshelves are framed by exposed concrete beams.[211]

The house has changed hands only once, in 1973, when the Clarke family moved in. A sympathetic conservatory and garden room have been added since then.

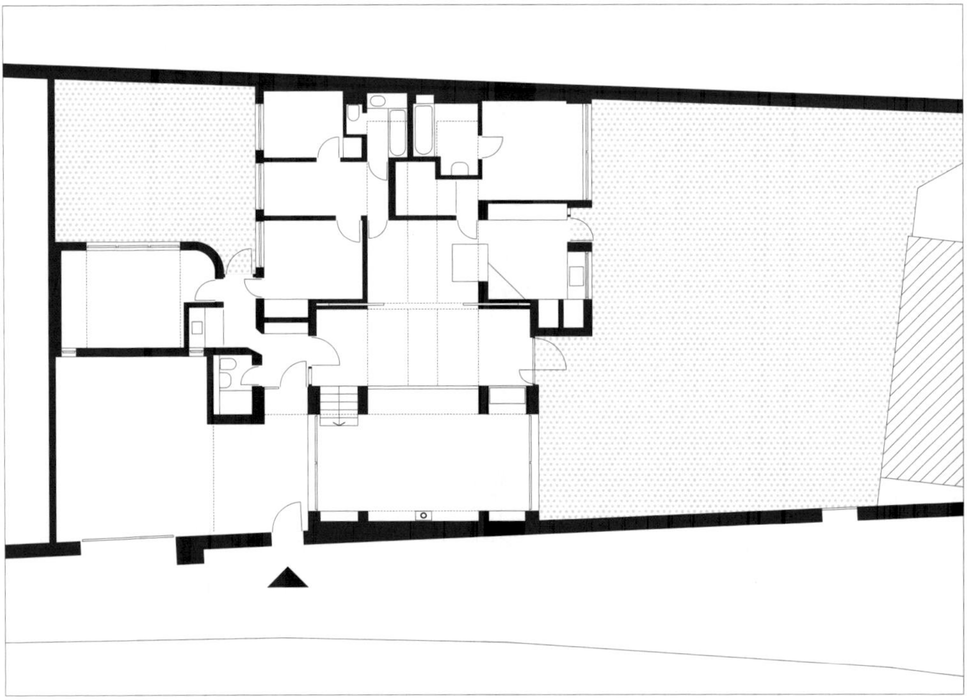

37 PARK VISTA

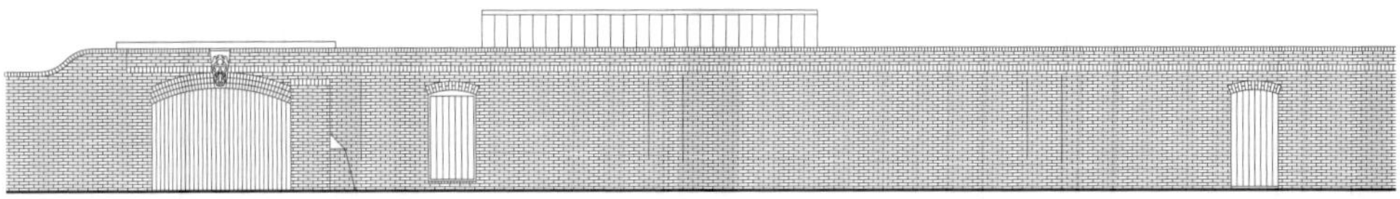

Opposite: upper level sitting room
with butterfly roof to the left, 1973
Above: ground floor plan, as originally built
Below: street elevation

10m

Richard MacCormac (1938–2014) and Peter Bell (b.1938) were working together on social housing schemes for Merton Council when they met their client Michael Burton, who had acquired a site in Blackheath for a new house. The three became lifelong friends.

MacCormac was born in Marylebone, London, into a medical family with roots in Northern Ireland. He attended Trinity College, Cambridge, before enrolling at the Bartlett. He later taught at Cambridge, from the late 1960s to the early 1980s. He started his architectural career at Powell and Moya in 1963, joined Lyons Israel and Ellis in 1965 and then moved on to Merton Council in 1967. In 1972, he established MacCormac Jamieson Prichard, with Peter Jamieson and David Prichard.

MacCormac worked on many projects and considered his finest work to be the Burrell's Field accommodation blocks for Trinity College, Cambridge (1996). His other significant projects included the Sainsbury student accommodation building for Worcester College, Oxford (1982); the Bowra Building, Wadham College (1993); the Garden Quadrangle at St John's College, Oxford (1994); the Ruskin Library at Lancaster University (1996); and Southwark Tube Station (1999). His architecture owes much to the work of Frank Lloyd Wright and the Arts and Crafts movement. The incorporation of artwork and coloured glass in his buildings is a recurring theme.

From 1981, MacCormac lived in Spitalfields with his partner Jocasta Innes, a well-known designer and author. In June 2014, he published Two Houses in Spitalfields, a book about a pair of joined houses near Brick Lane that the pair lived in, separately yet together, for 30 years. He was President of the RIBA from 1991 to 1993 and knighted in 2001. In 2008, his practice was renamed MJP Architects and closed down in 2023.

Peter Bell set up in private practice and completed projects in many areas, including one-off homes, low-cost housing schemes and commercial buildings (amongst them, a small art gallery and a major radio station). As a sub-committee member of the MCC, he also advised on new buildings at Lords Cricket Ground, including the Stirling Prize-winning Media Stand, designed by Future Systems. In the 1990s Bell was involved in the retrofitting and over-cladding projects, most notably Parsons House in Edgware Road, W9, for the City of Westminster.

Local projects	4 and 4a Langton Way	1974
Other London projects (Richard MacCormac)	Shadwell Basin housing, Docklands	1987
	Vining Street flats, Brixton	1989
	Southwark Tube station	1999
	The Wellcome Wing, Science Museum	2000
	Wellcome Wolfson Building, Science Museum	2003
	John Watkins Plaza, London School of Economics	2003
	Warwick Court, Paternoster Square	2003
	10 Crown Place, City of London	2003

Richard MacCormac

Peter Bell

47

Project	4 and 4a Langton Way
Architect	Richard MacCormac and Peter Bell
Completed	1974
Client	Michael Burton
Awards	RIBA Architecture Award Commendation 1976 for number 4a

The inner central circulation spine towards the entrance hall

A pair of single-storey four-bedroom courtyard houses, discreetly located in Langton Way, an unpaved mews lane accessed directly from the Heath. The houses are sited on a plot divided from the rear gardens of numbers 3 and 5 Shooters Hill Road, owned by Greenwich Council. This plot is further sub-divided into two plots of 25m x 11m each, separated by a central access route to the gardens of the Shooters Hill houses.[212]

The plots are constrained by boundary walls on each side, so the rooms receive natural daylight thanks to the clever use of internal courtyards and gardens of various shapes and sizes; the large central courtyard also serving to separate the children's rooms from the parents' area. This zoning and modular arrangement is essentially the same concept used in MacCormac's Huddersfield Building Society winning competition entry of 1972, which answered a brief for fresh thinking about privately owned housing models.

The houses are accessed directly from the mews; in the case of number 4a, through a large double garage that has also been used as a children's play space, parents' entertaining room and teenagers' disco. An inner circulation spine penetrates the length of each house. The client used a wheelchair and required good accessibility throughout. This route, finished in smooth quarry tiles (a practical surface for the owner's often muddy wheelchair) opens out on the left and right to the family rooms. Internal separation is achieved with deep timber storage units in the zone of the structural brick piers.[213]

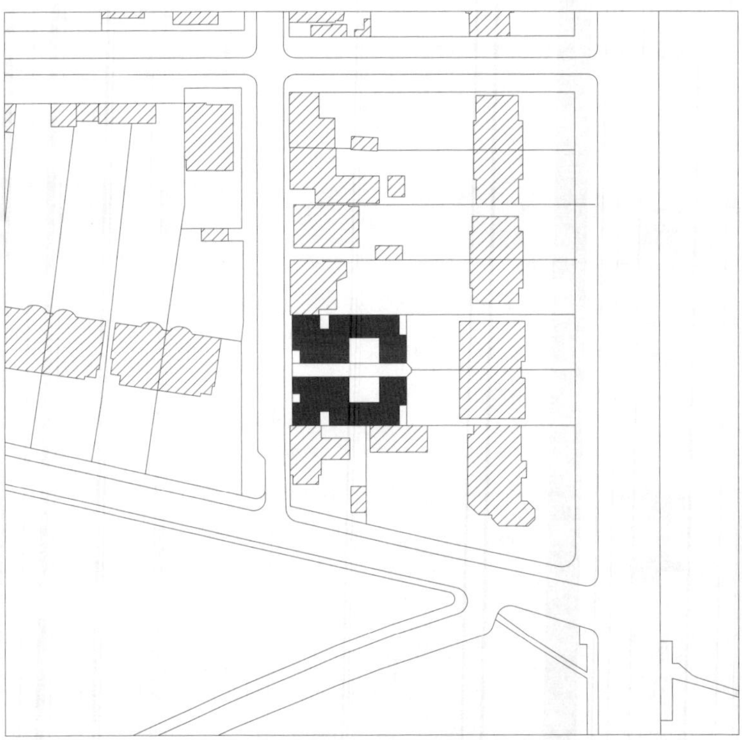

Site location 1:2000 50m

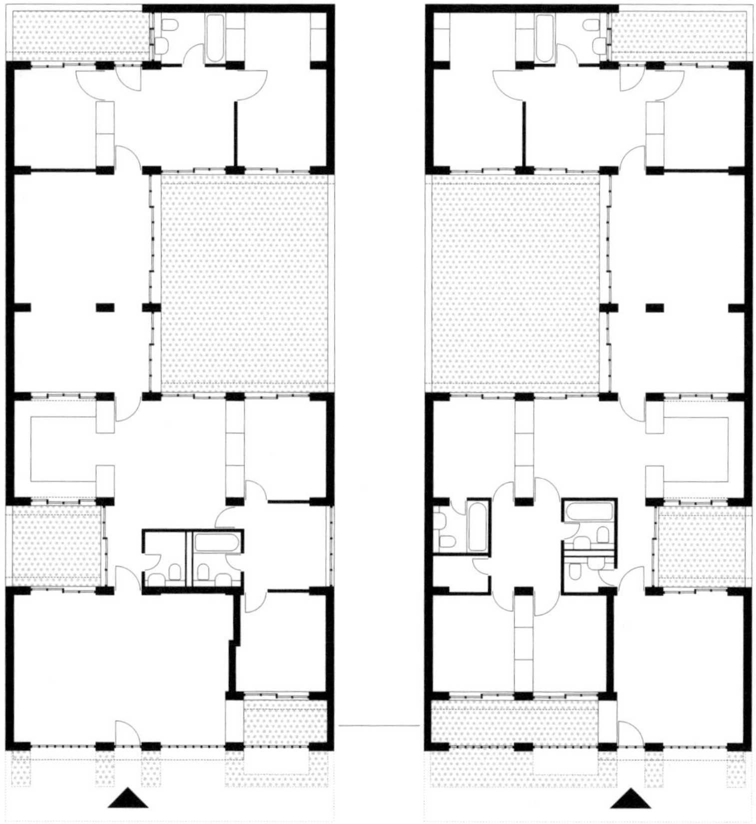

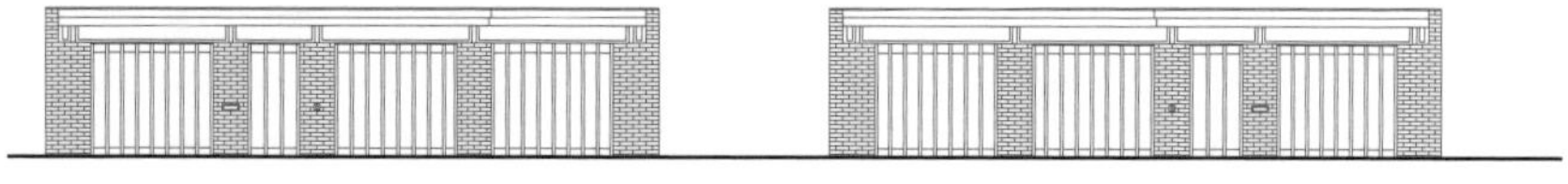

Above, left to right: no. 4a
and no. 4 ground floor plan
Below: street elevation

10m

The plan is structured by a tartan grid of columns in reclaimed London stock bricks supporting exposed Douglas fir beams, with secondary softwood joists and a boarded ceiling. Full-height glazed screens enclose the different spaces.[214] The screens are designed with regular vertical mullions; the spacing varies to provide more privacy to the street or more openness to the courtyards.

The atmosphere evokes both Scandinavian and Japanese architecture and number 4 has indeed been the home of the Urasenke Foundation of Kyoto since the mid-1980s. Urasenke is one of the main schools of the Japanese tea ceremony, which takes place in rooms furnished with tatami mats that overlook a Japanese garden.

It is interesting to note that the high-level windows in the building use blue glass, which was to become something of a signature material in many subsequent MacCormac projects.[215] Another unusual detail is the omission of frames around doors and windows, giving a clearer definition between structure and infill. The heating was by means of warm air supply from a furnace in the garage through ceramic drains and outlet gratings in the floor – a system devised by young engineer Max Fordham.[216]

This was the only private house project undertaken by MacCormac. In an interview with *The Telegraph* in 1991, he said: 'I would like to see an end to the British passion for period houses. It wasn't always this way. The Georgians and the Victorians choose to live in contemporary buildings… The taste of the British in housing is like the taste of the British in food in the fifties. We lag behind the continent, and ours is not a very visual culture anyway.'[217] 4a Langton Way received a RIBA commendation in 1976 signed by Eric Lyons, who was President of the RIBA at the time.

Living room; hand drawing by Peter Bell

Langton Way looking towards the Heath

4 AND 4A LANGTON WAY

1974

Robin Goodman Simpson (1934 – 1991) lived locally for many years, in homes he designed for himself at 80 Langton Way and 112 Hervey Road. Simpson and architect Brian Meeking were neighbours on Langton Way.

Simpson was born in Sussex and studied at Regent Street Polytechnic from 1951 to 1956. Between 1956 and 1961 he worked as an architectural assistant at several practices, including Ove Arup and Partners. By 1963, he was established in practice with Stanley Ivatts at Simpson & Ivatts (later Robin Simpson and Associates) in Hervey Road, Greenwich. He became a RIBA associate in 1963.

Simpson worked on several house and flat conversions, mainly around Shooters Hill and the Westcombe Park area. These included two houses in Westbrook Road – both with arched windows, exposed concrete and expressive external stairs in brick. A conversion at 25 St Johns Park includes a glassy modern extension with a metal mansard roof to the side of a Victorian house. Simpson also designed a strikingly modern block of flats at 35a Hyde Vale.

Simpson created the home interiors for the couple Sandie Shaw and Jeff Banks. Shaw was an international pop singer (her 'Puppet on a String' was the British entry in the 1967 Eurovision Song Contest) and her husband a fashion designer who owned the *Clobber Boutique* (now *The Age Exchange*), which opened in Blackheath Village in 1964.

Simpson's work spanned brutalism and modernism. His designs made particular use of double-height spaces, exposed concrete and large, often arched windows. The house he designed at 112 Hervey Road incorporates striking pyramidal dormer rooflights.

Simpson's other projects included Little-Boxes, in Marlow, Buckinghamshire – a house comprised of two stacked box volumes, built for his brother-in-law Mike Ellis in collaboration with Ronald Coleman.[218] Later in his career, he worked on several projects for Saudi Arabian clients in Lancaster Gate, London and in Saudi Arabia.[219]

Local projects

2, 2a and 3 Westbrook Road

80 Langton Way

112 Hervey Road

35a Hyde Vale 1960s

25 St Johns Park

Robin Simpson, 1960s

48		
	Project	35a Hyde Vale
	Architect	Robin Simpson
	Completed	Mid-1960s

A slender and striking five-storey block of flats with garaging on the ground floor. The building accommodates a two-bedroom flat on each floor, with the living rooms facing Hyde Vale and the bedrooms looking onto the rear communal garden. It was built on an empty fan-shaped site by the owners of the adjacent number 35 to provide a flat for each of their four sons and a large garage for vintage cars.[220]

This dark grey brick building forms a strongly contrasting 'bookend' to a complete row of terraced houses dating from c.1840 – including the grade II listed Glen-Mohr Terrace. The brick walls form dramatic vertical slabs containing the flats. The right-hand wall is set away from the neighbouring terrace, creating a slot that forms a deeply recessed entrance, in which an unusual steel sculpture of an eagle welcomes visitors. The building is accessed via a narrow staircase, set between white-painted concrete walls that project towards the street and terminate the stucco garden walls of the Victorian terrace. Between the brick walls the four flats are expressed by horizontal plant boxes, alternating with full-width glazing.

35A HYDE VALE

Front elevation with entrance gap

The modern block 'bookending' the Victorian terrace

35A HYDE VALE

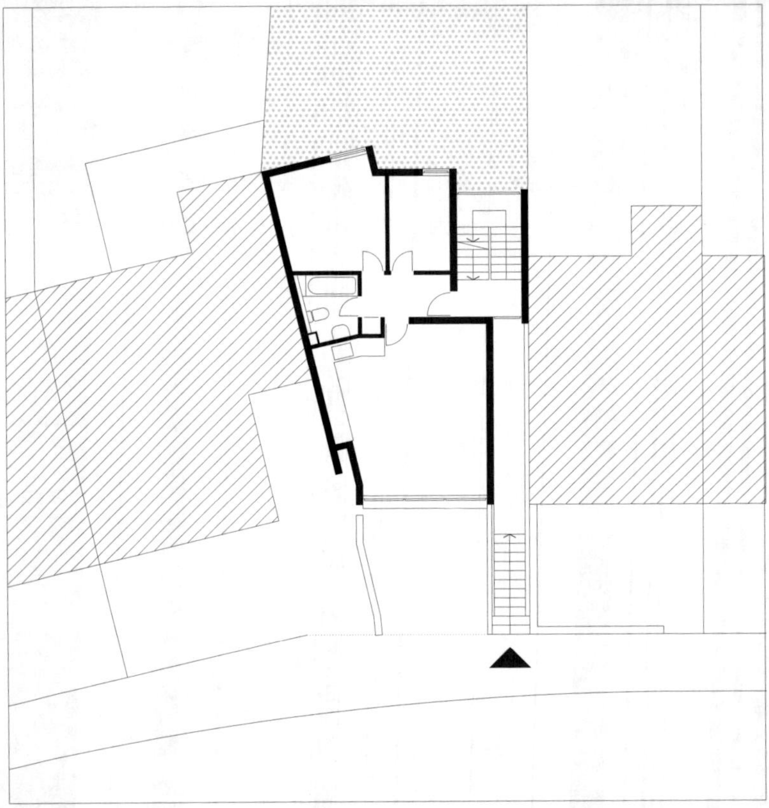

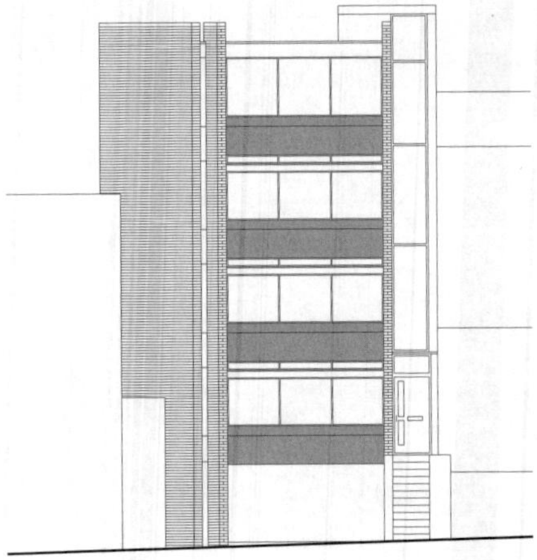

Above: typical floor plan
Below: street elevation

10m

1960s

Ronald Coleman (b.1948) designed and built his family house in Heathway. He completed it in 1976 and has lived there ever since. The scheme was for two connected houses, the other being for the builder A. Dunsford.

Coleman studied structural engineering at the Woolwich Polytechnic but always knew he was an architect at heart. Without wanting to take two diplomas he forged a career in which he could use his drawing and technical skills, first with the surveying arm of Atkins Engineers, then at architects Stone Toms and Partners where he worked on the Churchill Hotel in central London.

Most of his career was spent at International Broadcasting Consultants, a company that designed and built TV and radio stations, mainly in the Middle and Far East. This resulted in Coleman working in Dubai from 1976 to 1978, where he was responsible for fit-outs and detailing, working closely with acoustic engineers and other specialists. This was followed by his work at architects John Clarke Associates, where he contributed to projects in Scotland for Debenhams and finally to the fit-out of the Formula One offices at Biggin Hill, Kent.

Locally, Coleman collaborated for a short period with Robin Simpson on designs for a farmhouse in Surrey owned by Simpson's brother-in-law, and on proposals to develop a mill site in Horsham that belonged to Simpson's father.[221]

Ronald Coleman self-portrait 1978

49

Project	28 and 30 Heathway
Architect	Ronald Coleman
Completed	1976
Client	Architect's own house

The plot for 28 and 30 Heathway was divided from the rear garden of a large house at 25 St Johns Park. Numbers 28 and 30 were the first houses to be granted planning permission on this unpaved lane, which serves the rear gardens of the villas along St Johns Park and Vanbrugh Park and also connects Stratheden Road to the Heath. Before 28 and 30 were added, the mews lane was almost completely unbuilt save for a couple of old cottages.

Coleman designed one house for himself and the other for the builder A. Dunsford and his family. Number 28 was almost entirely self-built over two years. Coleman outsourced the brickwork, but completed all joinery, plumbing and electrics himself. The internal walls were built from blockwork and painted to minimise additional trades and cost.

Number 28 was originally conceived as a compact two-bedroom 'bachelor' house, on a smaller scale than number 30, which had five bedrooms for the Dunsfords and their four sons. However, Coleman later started a family himself and had two daughters, so his mezzanine studio was converted into the children's bedroom.

The houses are linked by a concrete and brick beam, level with the lintels of the windows and forming a large portal between the houses. This emphasises the horizontal proportions of the two and connects them so they read as one. A shared driveway that runs through the portal, provides access to a garage and six parking places, which were intended to serve the flats at 25 St Johns Park.[222]

In 2014, number 30 was sympathetically extended, with the addition of a second floor by architects Foster Lomas.

305 The two houses from Heathway showing the later additions to no. 30

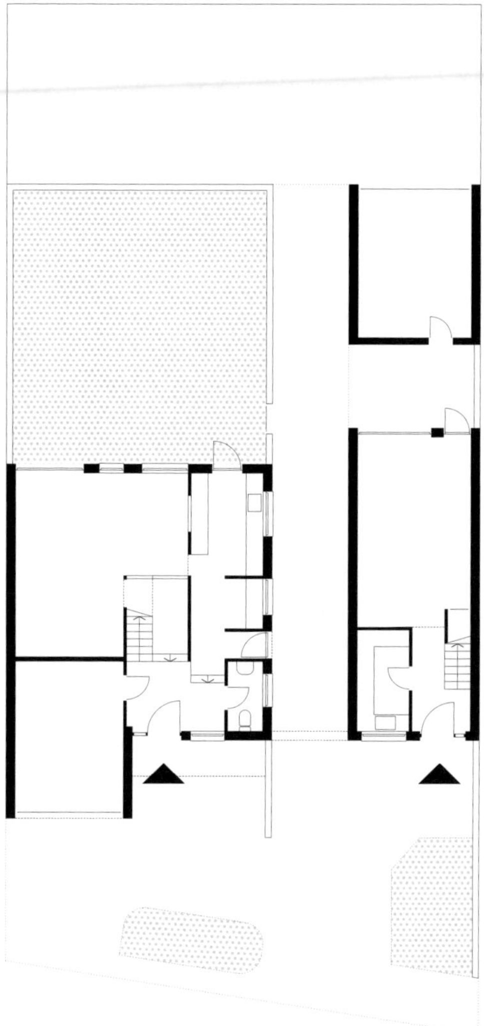

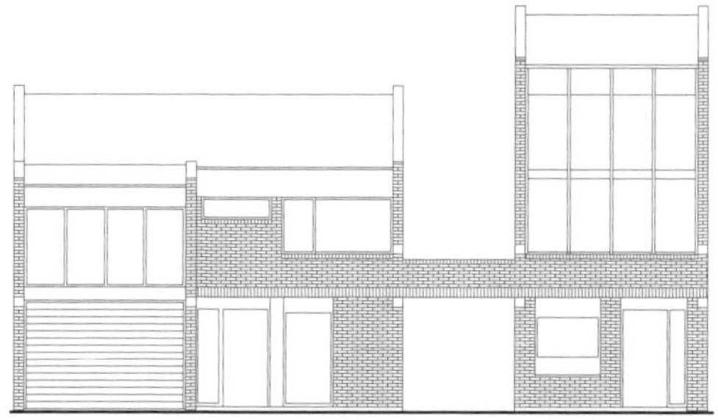

Above: ground floor plan, as originally built
Below: street elevation, as originally built

10m

28 AND 30 HEATHWAY

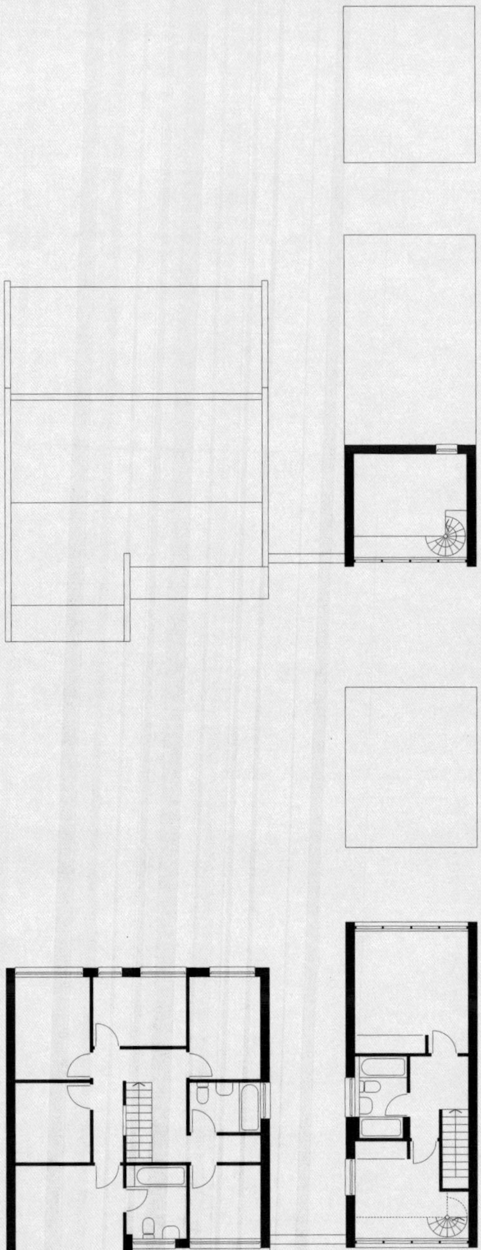

Above: second floor plan, as originally built
Below: first floor plan, as originally built

10m

Ronald Edmund Cuddon (1926–1985) and Ursula Mayer (later Bowyer) studied architecture together at the Regent Street Polytechnic. There they met Gordon Bowyer (who was a few years ahead of them). The three remained close friends until Ronald's death.

Cuddon was born in Camberwell, London. He studied architecture, interrupted by military war service, from 1942 to 1950, completing his thesis in 1954, the year he also became a RIBA Associate. Peter Moro, who had a strong influence on Cuddon and was a close friend, undersigned his application. Cuddon worked on the 1951 Festival of Britain's Sport Pavilion, under the direction of Gordon and Ursula Bowyer, providing illustrative World maps and exhibits. An excellent draughtsman, in the early 1950s he provided garden planting illustrations for *House & Garden* magazine in collaboration with his wife, Margaret; and graphics for other companies and publications. From 1954 until the late 1950s he was employed at R D Russell & Partners, led by Gordon Russell. By 1960, Cuddon had set up in private practice, working on residential, exhibition and commercial fit-out projects. Exhibition design projects came through Henri Kay Henrion of Henrion Design Associates and included work for Wates and Redland. The project for Redlands, was a particularly large exhibition featuring precast building components.

Together with Denys Lasdun & Partners, in 1962–63 Cuddon designed the boardroom suite's fit-out for ESSO House in Victoria Street. From the mid-1960s onwards, he also wrote product design reviews for *The Architectural Review* as guest writer. His office and retail fit-out projects were initially carried out in collaboration with the design practice THM. This work led to a direct commission to design the offices and factory premises for TCK in Dundee, Scotland. The project received a Civic Trust Commendation in 1972. Cuddon also completed the fit-out of Jardine Matheson's headquarters at King William Street, City of London, in 1973.

Cuddon's wife, Margaret, worked at the Council of Industrial Design where she met Geoffrey and Vita Dunn, who owned Dunns of Bromley. The Dunns shop, which opened in 1957, was a rare champion of modern furniture and design. The Cuddons had two children, Lucy and Nick, who went on to become architects.[223]

Ronald Cuddon

50

Project	47a Blackheath Park
Architect	Ronald Cuddon
Completed	1962
Client	Ruari McLean

Street elevation from Blackheath Park, with the main house to the right, 1960s

The client for this project was Ruari McLean (1917–2006), a leading typographer and book designer who was responsible for the Puffin series at Penguin. He was also an educator and the author of several reference books, including *Modern Book Design*, 1958.

McLean, who lived at 47 Blackheath Park, wanted to make better use of the adjacent plot, then occupied by a coach house. He commissioned Ronald Cuddon to design a new structure – a side infill to the main house.

This 'delightfully minute structure'[224] was conceived as a studio flat, suspended above a garage and carport. The street elevation was clad in timber with a full-width horizontal strip window; the rear was a more blank, abstract composition, with high-level slot windows for the sleeping area and bathroom. The carport was originally open, allowing views through to the rear garden; the front garden contained mature sycamores and a copper birch, which were all retained.

The living space from the sleeping area, 1960s

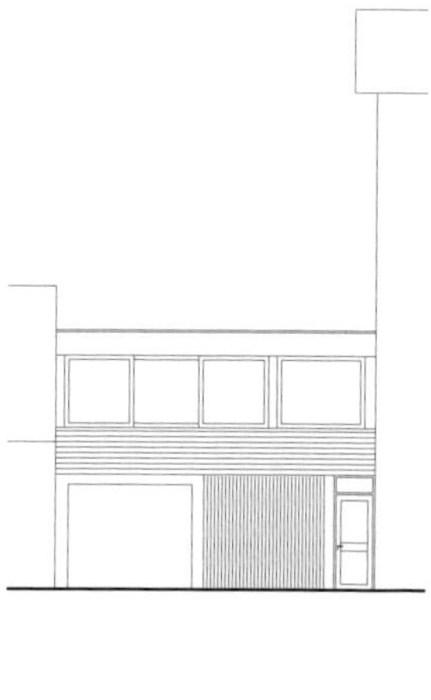

Above: from left to right: ground and first floor plans, as originally built
Below: street elevation, as originally built

10m

The project was perceived as a prototype for the addition of a small dwelling to a large London house – providing flexible rental accommodation for young professionals and extra income for the owner of the main building. The first tenants, both suitably 'modern', were James Currie, a journalist, and Catherine Currie who worked in the modern furniture department of Wollands in Knightsbridge and furnished the flat with the latest trendy furniture. Catherine was subsequently a member of the Habitat management team when the store first opened in 1964.[225] The project for 47a was especially dear to Cuddon and was praised by his friend Peter Moro who lived nearby.[226]

More recently the flat has been connected to number 47, in line with Cudden's original intention, and the carport enclosed for extra garaging.

313 Garden elevation with carport to the right, 1960s

Roy Latham (1927 – 2014) lived at 5 The Plantation and at 1 Sweyn Place.

Latham grew up in Lancashire and gained his Diploma from the University of Manchester School of Architecture in 1953. He first worked at the City of Manchester Architect's Department and then at the Harlow Development Corporation.

In 1955 Latham joined Mathews Ryan & Simpson. In 1966 he became an associate partner and remained in the practice for most of his career. He was responsible for a wide range of projects, including research laboratories, housing, hotels and town centre developments. The practice's founder, E. D. Jefferies Mathews, was Vice President of the RIBA from 1953 to 1955. Latham became a RIBA Associate in 1954 and a Fellow in 1969.

He had a flair for perspective drawing and for vividly presenting projects to clients. Several of his drawings were exhibited at the Royal Academy.

Local projects	40 Heath Lane	1971
Other projects	Ward Royal Estate (project architect), Windsor	1970
	IBM masterplan, Greenock	1971

51

Project	40 Heath Lane
Architect	Roy Latham
Completed	1971
Client	Dr and Mrs Sandy Fife

40 Heath Lane is a single-storey courtyard house. It sits on a plot that was once part of the garden of Eliot Vale House. In the early 1970s, the owners of Eliot Vale House, possibly driven by the need to raise funds to maintain their castle in Scotland, sold a portion of their garden to local surgeon, Dr Sandy Fife.[227] Fife instructed his friend and neighbour at The Plantation, Roy Latham to carry out the project.

The layout is organised on a regular grid, with the bedrooms and bathrooms to the front and the living room, study and dining room in another block to the rear. The two blocks are separated by an internal courtyard, a passageway and the kitchen. The garage, separated from the main house, is linked through the glazed entrance hall that connects front and rear gardens.

The living room spaces are subdivided by an articulated brick core and steps leading down to the sitting room. This core serves as fireplace, storage, shelving and cupboard for the heating unit. Pine-clad ceilings bring warmth to the interiors. The brickwork application is of vertical flush joints and horizontal raked recessed joints – this pointing type was used by architects such as Frank Lloyd Wright to emphasise the horizontality of a building. The patio brick wall is continued internally and the timber ceilings project to form the soffit of the external roof overhang, further connecting the interior and exterior.

Together with 14 and 16 Baizdon Road, this introverted house forms a small cluster of modern buildings – two of them single-storey courtyard houses; the other a two-storey house raised up on pilotis.
As is often the case with well-designed buildings, 40 Heath Lane has only changed hands once since it was built.

The raised dining area from the living room

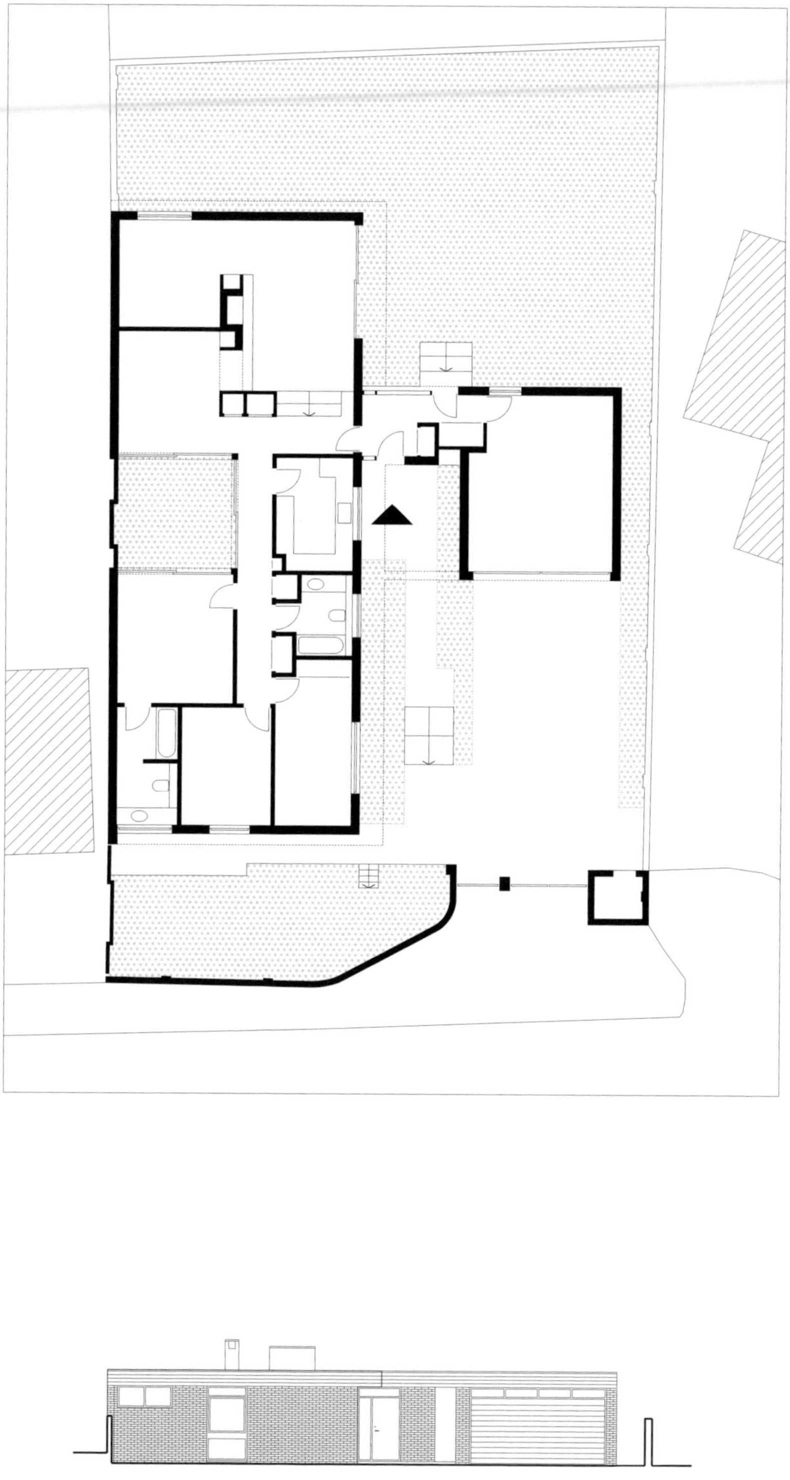

Above: ground floor plan
Below: front elevation

10m

 The sunken living area

Royston Summers (1931 – 2012) was the moving spirit behind North Several, one of the most fascinating local self-build initiatives.

Summers was born in Wolverhampton. After serving with the Intelligence Corps in Germany, he went to Downing College, Cambridge, where he initially read Classics before switching to English, graduating in 1954. Summers then studied at the AA in London and later joined the Architectural Department of Cornwall County Council where he was involved in the project for the New County Hall in Truro. His first solo project was a library in Saltash, completed in 1963 and now Grade II listed.

In 1964, he set up his practice in Blackheath. Whilst living in South Row he designed North Several situated on the edge of the Heath. Summers shared details of the problems he faced while working in the public sector with his friend, the writer Michael Frayn, who also lived in South Row, who used them as the basis for his 1984 play, *Benefactors*. Frayn was also a fellow North Several self-build pioneer.[228]

'In 1969 Royston Summers went to the RIBA to collect his medal for Good Design in Housing from the Minister of Housing, Tony Benn. After the function he returned home and changed into jeans to go to collect his dole money. Meanwhile his wife was having trouble persuading the milkman that anyone living in such a spanking new house was entitled to free milk. Such are the vagaries of life in a small architectural practice.'[229]

In 1977, Summers completed a scheme in Esher, Surrey – the low-density Lakeside Drive estate, now a Conservation Area, which won both a RIBA Architecture Award in 1976 and the Department of Education Diploma for Good Design in 1980. The 16 Lakeside Drive houses were a development of the North Several designs.

While working for Lambeth Council, Summers was part of a team working on the scheme (which did not come to fruition) for 52-storey tower blocks to tackle Brixton's housing problems. For the Lewisham Council, in 1979 he designed Brownhill Road Housing, the first solar-heated council flats. This project won a CIBS commendation for energy use in 1982. Summers also worked on numerous refurbishment projects, including the Bishop's Palace at Winchester, two Grade II Diocesan houses and the restoration and conversion of Redlynch Park.

Local projects	North Several, Orchard Drive	1968
	Brandam Road Community Centre	
Other key projects	Saltash Library, Cornwall	1963
	9 to 15 Tressillian Crescent, Brockley	1970s
	Lakeside Drive estate, Esher	1977
	Brownhill Road Housing[230]	1979

Royston Summers in North Several

52	Project	North Several, Orchard Drive
	Architect	Royston Summers
	Completed	1968
	Client	Tyler's Yard Ltd[231]
	Awards	Ministry of Housing Design Award and Diploma for Good Design, 1969

Seven three-storey houses, arranged in two blocks: five in a terrace overlooking the Heath; two located at the shared entrance from Orchard Drive. They have a strong vertical rhythm thanks to their closely spaced window mullions and projecting party walls. Each house is about 140sq m and can accommodate two to five bedrooms, which are formed using modular wardrobes as room dividers.

The development is the result of seven families' shared desire to move from their smaller houses or flats, many in South Row, the Span estate further east across the Heath. They wanted more living space, but also to stay in the Blackheath area and retain the sense of community they had shared at South Row.[232]

The project was instigated by architect Royston Summers and writer Michael Frayn, who joined forces with Pace Developments' director Peter Dobbs and a solicitor, James Dolman. Ian Forrest, a geologist assisted with soil analysis and Frayn came up with the name. His first choice was South Several, but the Post Office objected and insisted upon 'North'.[233] The word 'several', in this instance, refers to privately owned land adjacent to a common.

Affordability and future energy costs were important factors in the choice of site and building design. The families bought the site of a Victorian house with Edwardian additions that had a narrow wedge-shaped garden, for a reasonable £14,000. Planning permission was only granted on appeal with understandable opposition from the neighbours on Orchard Drive, who lost their open views towards the Heath and gained a block of five houses overlooking their gardens.

The total building costs were held to £9,000 by making the three-storey houses identical and minimising the variety of materials used.[234] However, financing the project was troublesome due to the high interest rate and the bank's reluctance to release funds, resulting in delays on site. Dobbs, the builder, ended up advancing funds and progressing the works at his own risk.[235]

NORTH SEVERAL, ORCHARD DRIVE

323 Site location 1:2000 50m 1968

The entrance block from the Heath

Summers incorporated a number of innovative features to reduce heating costs and also wrote extensively about them. He noted that the party walls and floors are made from materials with high thermal mass (brick, block and concrete), which store heat and cool slowly, helping to maintain a constant temperature.[236] The floor-to-ceiling windows, which maximize the open views of the Heath, were intended to be double glazed in order to reduce heat loss and admit solar energy for winter warmth. However, single glazing was actually used in the build, so the end result is not as energy efficient as it should have been. Summers instructed the residents about when to close or open their curtains in order to avoid overheating in summer and retain warmth in winter.[237]

The internal surfaces were also selected to provide ideal conditions for the occupants. Finnish birch-veneered plywood on battens, which has low thermal capacity and was then relatively inexpensive, was used to line the internal walls. The panels are approximately 2.4m high by 60 cm wide, avoiding wastage, as typical sheets are 2.4 × 1.2m. The private patios for each front door also form an external 'thermal trap' by using dark brickwork to retain the sun's warmth. The rooflight at the top of the stairs can be opened for natural ventilation and the underfloor heating for each house was originally activated by computerised heat sensors on the roofs. These were eventually abandoned, having never worked effectively.

 The original seven families soon after completion

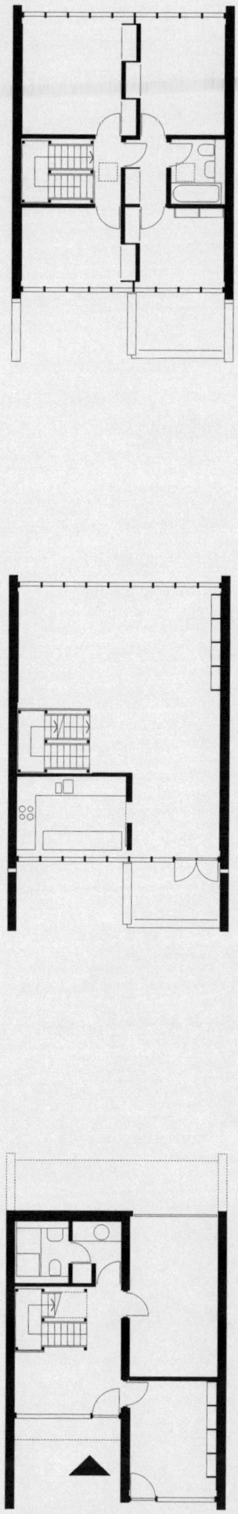

Top to bottom: second, first
and ground floor plans

10m

The maple stairs are open tread. The concrete slabs (exposed on the staircase) were originally carpeted or covered in quarry tiles (fired five times to match the tones of the dark exposed brickwork). Moveable floor-to-ceiling wardrobe units were supplied as dividers, allowing the owners to vary the number of bedrooms.[238] These were meant to be soundproofed, but with the open-plan layout and open stairway connecting three floors, some residents complained that they could not get away from the sound of young children playing, or indeed, from adults arguing.

The plan draws on the typology of a classic college quadrangle, mixed with the modernism of South Row, although the external appearance is heavily influenced by St Catherine's College, Oxford (1962) – the work of Danish architect, Arne Jacobsen. This is evident in both the vertical rhythms of the windows and party walls, and the sectional arrangement of double-storey upper block above a recessive ground floor, something which can also be seen in the South Row houses.

The quad at St Catherine's College, incorporates yew hedges to define the outside space – a feature which Jacobsen felt was integral to his design. Summers, less grandly perhaps, was adamant that each house in North Several should plant the same lavender bushes in its flowerbeds to complement the grey windowsills. The communal garden (which originally included a sandpit and climbing frame), was devised by a pioneering young female architect, Georgina 'Georgie' Wolton. It is home to *Party Girl*, a bronze sculpture by Gerda Rubinstein (1931–2022).

A glimpse inside a local dental surgery at 19 Montpelier Vale, provides a sample of North Several's interiors, thanks to Jo Eisenberg. A dentist by profession, he was one of the initial residents at North Several (replacing the Dolman family, which was not able to secure funding) and so admired its style and materials that he installed similar stairs, quarry tiles and birch panelling at his practice.

'The most striking irony, it seems now, was the paradox between the spirit of openness that the vast glass windows seemed to suggest about the lives of its inhabitants, and the number of marital infidelities that begun to emerge. For behind the public façade all manner of emotional complexity was festering. Marriages broke down, and the families fragmented, and with them the founding Utopian ideals. […] From the original residents, only the architect remained. He and his wife retired to Cornwall in the late 1990s.'[239]

327 South elevation 1:500 15m

Above:Michael Frayn's family at no. 1
Below: Summers' family house at no. 3

NORTH SEVERAL, ORCHARD DRIVE

329 Communal garden looking towards the entrance block

1968

Stephen Gardiner (1924–2007) was commissioned by artist Norman Jenkinson and designer Christine Risley to create their home in Baizdon Road, Blackheath.

Gardiner was born and raised in Chelsea, London. He attended Dulwich College and served in the Royal Navy from 1942, before studying at the AA and qualifying in 1948. He then worked for Wells Coates, and various other practices including Richard Sheppard, Robson & Partners from 1951 to 1957, mainly on school projects. In 1958 he published a thriller, *Death is an Artist*, written mainly while travelling on the train to and from a project for Churchfields Secondary School in West Bromwich, Birmingham.

He founded his own practice in 1957 and formed a partnership with Christopher Knight during the 1960s. His most notable scheme was for banker Sir John Baring who demolished a fine Greek Revival country house, Stratton Park in Hampshire by George Dance the Younger. He then commissioned Gardner to build a largely glass and steel house within the dramatic retained Tuscan portico. Gardiner and Joan Scotson, later his wife, became business partners in 1970. In the 1970s Gardiner and Scotson worked on two large housing schemes in Milton Keynes and on three adventure playgrounds for HAPA (Handicapped Adventure Playgrounds Association), founded and run by Lady Allen of Hurtwood, a pioneering landscape architect.

Gardiner taught at different institutions: the AA from 1955 to 1956; the Oxford School of Architecture from 1957 to 1968; the University of Westminster from 1970 to 1974; Washington University in St Louis in 1978; Cheltenham College from 1979 to 1981; and the University of London from 1981 to 1986.

From the early 1990s Gardiner focused on teaching, feature writing and criticism. He contributed to the London Magazine from 1964 to 2001 and as an architectural correspondent for *The Observer*, writing a weekly column from 1970 to 1993. He also wrote for *The Spectator*, *The Times*, *The Architectural Review* and the *RIBA Journal*. Several of Gardiner's books addressed architectural subjects. They included *Evolution of the House* (1974), a monograph on Le Corbusier; *Kuwait: The Making of a City* (1984); and *The House: Its Origins and Evolution* (2002), and two biographies: *Epstein: Artist Against the Establishment* (1992), and *Frink* (1997), a life of the sculptor Elisabeth Frink.

Stephen Gardiner at Holly Court School, Highgate, 1960

53

Project	16 Baizdon Road
Architect	Stephen Gardiner
Completed	1958
Client	Artists Norman Jenkinson and Christine Risley

Stephen Gardiner met his clients, artist Norman 'Jenks' Jenkinson and designer Christine Risley, through his father Clive Gardiner, painter and head of Goldsmiths' College School of Art where Jenkinson and Risley studied in the 1940s.[240] Risley became an influential designer, author and textile artist, specialising in machine embroidery and serving as Head of the Textile Department at Goldsmiths College, University of London.

The site was part of the garden of Eliot Vale Cottage (now demolished) and originally accessed from Heath Lane. The single storey house that Gardiner designed is a broken L-shape on plan, with a garage and studio in a small block facing the street. The living rooms and bedrooms are grouped in a larger block looking on to the secluded south facing garden. The street elevation is set back behind mature trees and designed to resemble a blank garden wall, with minimal windows.[241] A recessed courtyard forms the entrance, which leads to the living room and a small kitchen at the heart of the house. Three bedrooms complete the main volume.

Several protruding concrete details are built into the walls to provide a shelf for sculpture in the garden and a small canopy over the main living room door. Inside, recessed shelves, areas of timber board panelling and carefully positioned roof lights, all create a simple yet carefully designed interior.[242] Jenks was an avid vinyl record collector and one of the walls was designated for his collection, which eventually expanded to take over much more space.

The house has been much altered, without loss of character. A single storey extension provides an additional bedroom, a conservatory has been added and the kitchen relocated to the studio space.[243]

16 BAIZDON ROAD

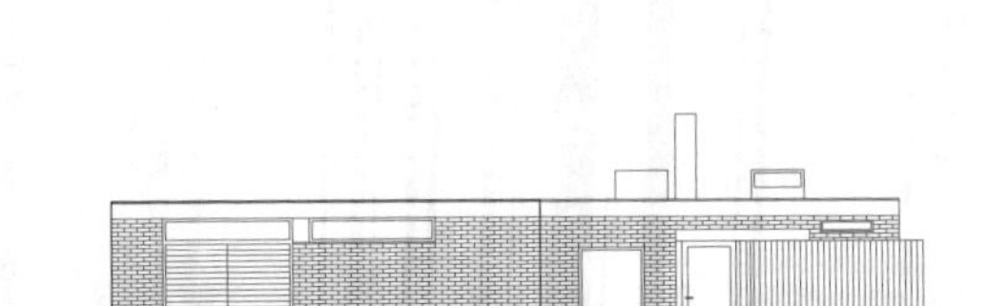

Opposite: living room, late 1950s
Top: ground floor plan
Bottom: street elevation

10m

1958

Teresa Forrest (nee Whitmarsh-Everiss b. 1933) lived in the Blackheath area for more than 20 years – first at 9 The Lane and then at 22 Belmont Hill. She and her husband, Jack Forrest, first set up home together in Camden, North London, but were attracted to Blackheath by the Span housing.[244]

At first sight they thought the Span houses were too small, but eventually settled on a type T15 in The Lane. Their house, number 9, had been used as the site store during construction and they were the last of the early occupants to arrive. They soon acquired two allotment plots adjacent to their back garden, where Streetfield Mews now stands.

Forrest was born in Leicester to an architect and surveyor father. She studied architecture at college in Bristol during the early 1950s, while also working for the City Architects Department. She was the only woman student on her course.

Later, she moved to London where she worked for Sir Frederick Gibberd on Hull College's Queen's Gardens building and the Metropolitan Cathedral project in Liverpool. She met her husband at Gibberd's practice, where they both worked until their daughter was born and Teresa left the practice. Her husband worked as a senior partner at Gibberd until his retirement. Forrest set up her practice in a home studio and enjoyed a long and successful career. She focused primarily on new-build homes and refurbishments in the southeast of England.

In Blackheath, Forrest designed 17 Langton Way, 13 Pond Road and an extension to 17 The Lane. She did not supervise construction of 13 Pond Road but nevertheless ensured that it contained a beautifully detailed staircase, a feature she believed to be one of the most important elements in any house.[245]

The Forrest family owned a weekend cottage in Aldeburgh and later moved permanently to Sherborne, Dorset. From 2000 onwards, Forrest became a prolific embroiderer and exhibited work at the Royal Academy. Her embroidery, heavily influenced by her architectural background, consists largely of streetscapes and cityscapes.

Local projects	13 Pond Road	1973
	17 The Lane, double-storey side extension	
	5a to 5e St Germans Place extension	1980s
	17 Langton Way	1986

Teresa Forrest at Gibberd's office, late 1950s

54

Project	17 Langton Way
Architect	Teresa Forrest
Completed	1986
Client	Brian and Ann Wolf

Teresa Forrest, Brian and Ann Wolf were friends and neighbours in the Span estate, The Lane, when the commission for a new house on a local site came about.

17 Langton Way is a corner site, at the rear of 2 St Johns Park, a large mansion that functioned as a hotel from 1938 to 1983. The site was designated by Greenwich Council for a block of six flats but an agreement was reached and permission was granted for two single-storey houses. 17 Langton Way was built at the corner with Angerstein Lane and the other half of the site was left to be enjoyed as a large garden, until a new planning consent in 2004 led to the second home to be built on the plot, as originally planned.

The single-storey brick building consists of two cubic volumes linked by a dramatic glazed barrel-vaulted linkway. The contractor was Jim Watson, who worked with Forrest for over 20 years. The house was designed on one level with open, spacious rooms, many of which had sliding doors. This arrangement worked for Brian Wolf who was to become increasingly dependent on a wheelchair due to illness.

The front block contains the social spaces; the rear block comprises the bedrooms and a study. The glazed linkway or 'conservatory', as Teresa Forrest prefers to describe it, creates two courtyards or outdoor rooms to either side and in the centre of the plan. Part of the tall linkway contains a small mezzanine space, used as a children's playroom or office. The arch of the linkway is echoed in the arched brickwork window openings to the main rooms and the bespoke fitted joinery (both now lost). The original flooring was of reclaimed handmade terracotta tiles.

17 LANGTON WAY

Entrance from Langton Way

1986

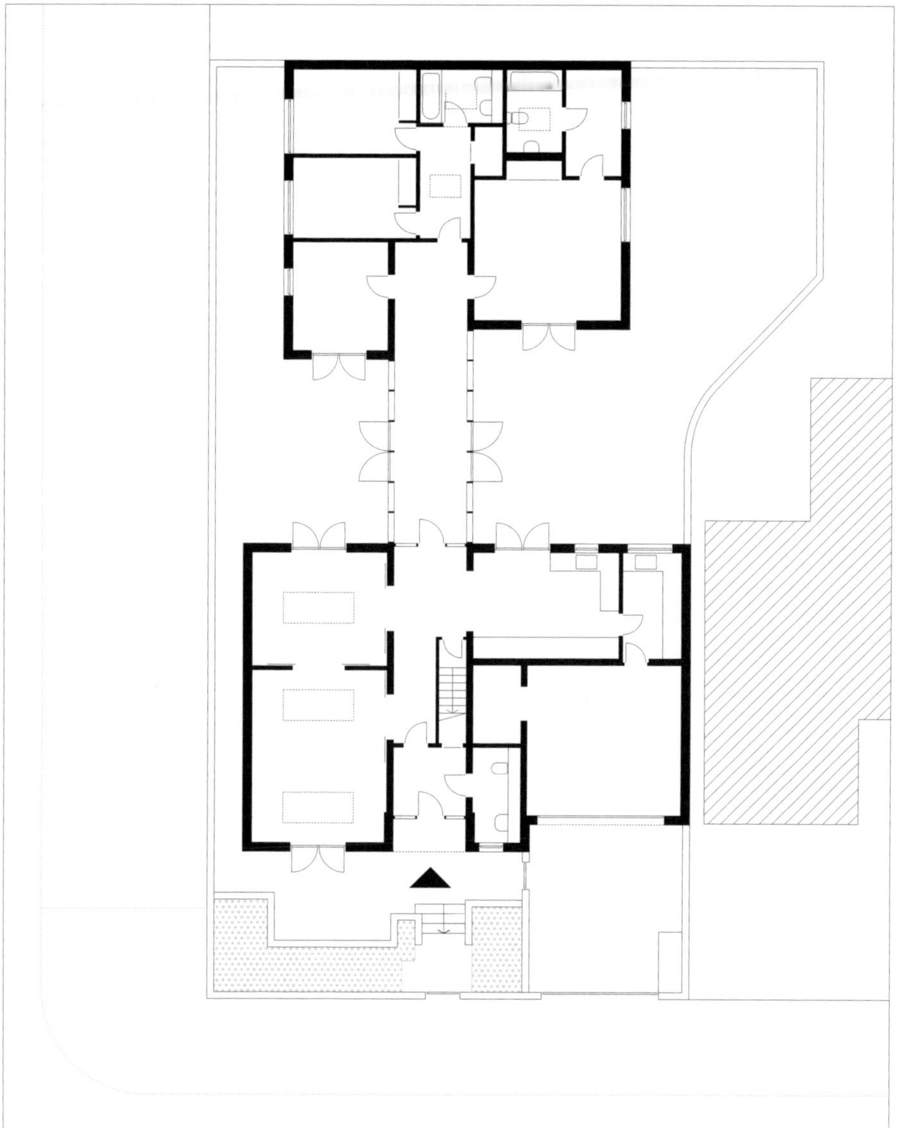

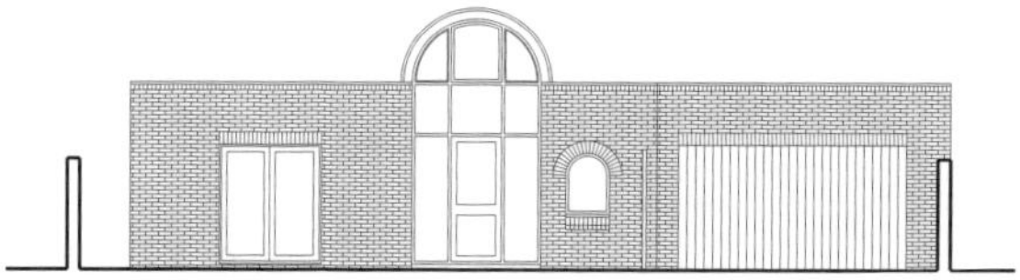

Above: ground floor plan
Below: street elevation

10m

17 LANGTON WAY

Barrel-vaulted glazed conservatory, connecting the two blocks

1986

TREVOR DANNATT

Trevor Dannatt (1920–2021) was born into a Greenwich family of surveyors, estate managers and shopkeepers. His uncle, architect Percy Boothroyd Dannatt, lived in the Westcombe Park area and in the late 1920s was assistant to Sir Banister Fletcher during the design and construction of the John Roan School, which fronts Greenwich Park. Dannatt's father was the third-generation owner of the Village Stores in Blackheath.

Dannatt introduced Peter Moro, his teacher at the time, to Greenwich and Blackheath. He was also a life-long friend of Gordon and Ursula Bowyer. In 1946, he visited Sweden with Gordon Bowyer to look at new architecture and admire the work of Alvar Aalto. Dannatt and Bowyer were best men at each other's weddings.

Dannatt attended Colfe's School (then in Granville Park) and returned many years later to design its Arts and Preparatory buildings, in Lee. After leaving school in 1938, he studied architecture at the Regent Street Polytechnic, where he later taught.

Dannatt's first job was at Fry, Drew & Partners. He subsequently worked with Peter Moro and Leslie Martin on the Royal Festival Hall and the Tea Bar for the 1951 Festival of Britain. He set up in private practice in 1952 and formed Trevor Dannatt and Partners in 1970, together with Collin Dollimore and Ronald Paxton. In 1978, the practice became Dannatt, Johnson Architects, when David Johnson joined as a partner, and it remains active today.

From 1949 to 1962, Dannatt was the sole editor of the *Architects' Yearbook* – a publication he had previously worked for in 1945 as an editorial assistant to Jane Drew. As editor he became widely recognized as a champion for modern buildings. The role also allowed him to travel extensively and meet well known international architects. In 1959, he published a book, *Modern Architecture in Britain*.

During a long, prolific and varied career, Dannatt worked across many different building types, including private houses, social housing developments, offices, schools and places of worship. He undertook projects in England, Scotland and Saudi Arabia. He was particularly proud of his work for the University of Greenwich and his role in helping to secure its right to use historic buildings for public and educational purposes.[246]

Local projects	Congregational Church temporary chapel, Maze Hill	1954
	Blackheath Congregational Church refurbishment, Independents Road	1957
	Greenwich Building Society offices, Greenwich High Street	1958 and 1974
	15 Langton Way (much altered)	
	Eltham Hill School extension	1969
	2 Lawn Terrace, Blackheath Quaker Meeting House	1972
	Old Peoples' Home, 133 Langton Way	1978
	Colfe's School, Arts building, 1984 and Preparatory School building	1989
	The University of Greenwich, Maritime Greenwich Campus[247]	1995–2018

Trevor Dannatt

55

Project	Blackheath Congregational Church
Architect	Trevor Dannatt
Completed	1957
Client	Congregational Union

The new double-height stone piers and looking towards the entrance court

The original church on this site was built in 1853 for the Blackheath Independent Dissenters (Congregational) Church.[248] It flourished until the mid-1930s but following severe bomb-damage during the Second World War and a steady fall in attendance, a decision was made to use what remained of the original building as part of new church with a smaller footprint. Three stone walls were retained, with two deep columns and a pitched roof added to enclose the double height space of the new hall.

Approached through a courtyard, where the footprint of the earlier church is still visible, a striking modern glass façade contrasts with the retained stone walls and reconstructed stone piers. Trevor Dannatt wrote that 'this was one of the few jobs where I had an instant mental vision of the design'.

Several of the recurring themes for worship spaces that Dannatt explored can be seen here: an entry transition sequence (from street to step to porch with a turn to the church hall); a balanced asymmetry (both pulpit and ridge beam were off-centre); and separation of different components (the roof and the deep horizontal window frame).[249]

Dannatt's family were Congregationalists and his father attended this church. Dannatt had been involved with other projects for local congregations, including the conversion of a school room into a temporary chapel at Maze Hill in 1954 and an earlier project for a full church that was never built. His work at Independents Road led to another major commission – the adjacent Quaker Friends Meeting House.[250]

The building was much altered following the amalgamation of the Presbyterian and Congregational union, which ultimately led to its closure in 1974. At this time, Dannatt considered moving his practice offices into the now deconsecrated building but it was eventually sold to chartered surveyors Watts and Partners, who converted the space into offices, adding a first floor and relocating the front door.[251] Since 2002, the offices have been used by the Blackheath Hospital.

Front elevation and canopy from the entrance court, with some of the original stone walls

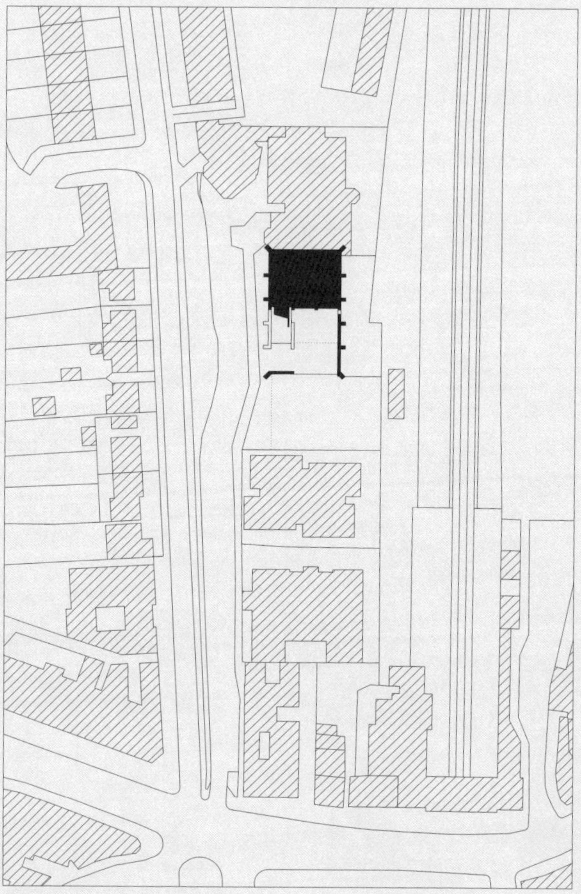

Site location

1:2000 50m

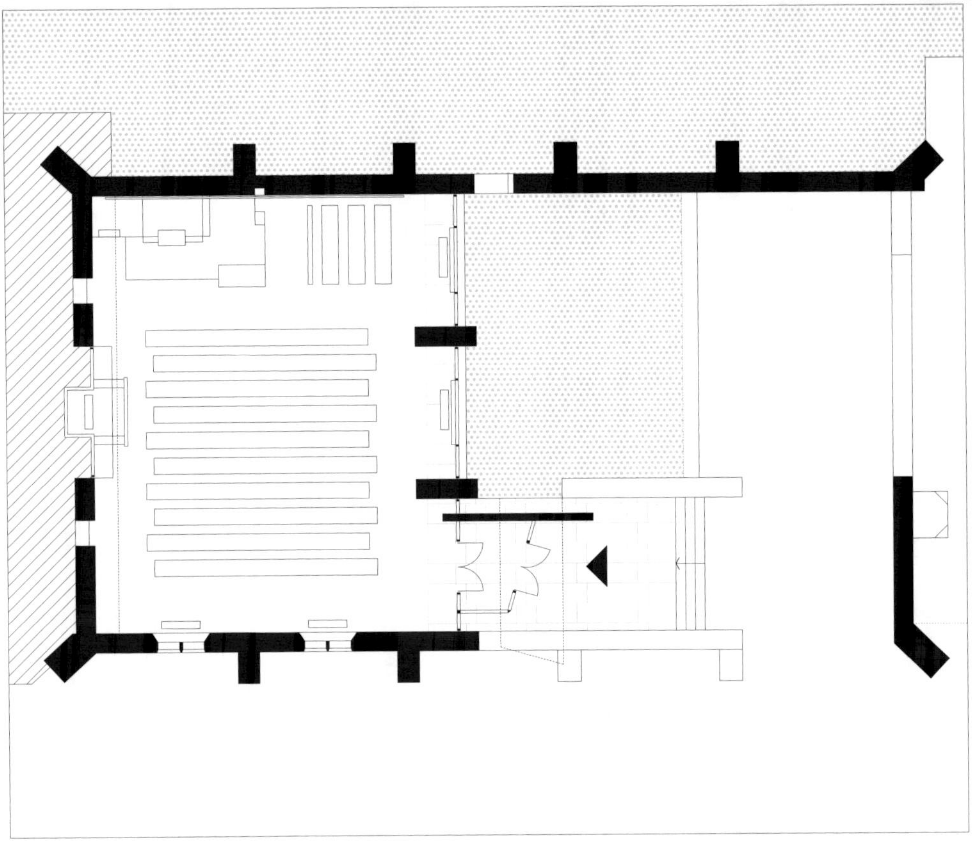

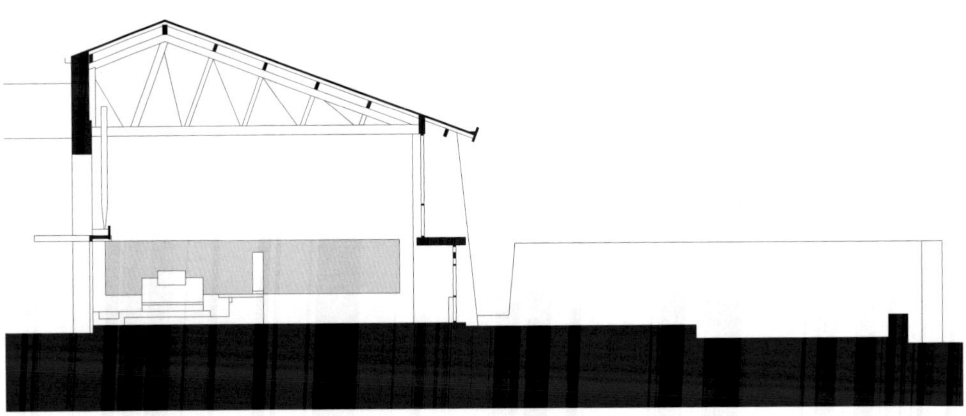

Above: ground floor plan, as originally built
Below: section, as originally built

10m

1957

56

Project	Blackheath Quaker Meeting House
Architect	Trevor Dannatt
Completed	1972
Status	Grade II Listed
Awards	Civic Trust Award 1973 Concrete Society Commendation 1974

Described by the Concrete Society as ‘a small, jewel-like brutalist design’[252], the Blackheath Quaker Meeting House is believed to be the only Quaker meeting house built in this style. Dannatt was not pleased with the label, as he considered the idea of ‘brutal’ as the exact opposite of this delicately detailed building,[253] notable for the carefully composed timber board markings on its exposed concrete walls and finely expressed roof structure.

Site location 1:2000 50m

347 The entrance from Lawn Terrace

56 Designed as 'a modern building to fit in with the forward-looking community around it',[254] with its square and centralised form, the Meeting House takes inspiration from medieval chapter houses. The two-storey structure is lit by a square central lantern over the main meeting room together with four additional lanterns, one in each corner of the room. These lanterns are created by the chamfered corners of the otherwise square roof, creating a gap with the walls of the meeting room below and allowing light to filter down. Externally the lanterns are expressed as small turrets.

The building actively utilises the changes in level on the site and is also connected to the adjacent Victorian congregational hall on two levels. The open undercroft (or crypt) elevates the building and accommodates parking for four cars, a planning requirement. On the upper level, the main entrance from Lawn Terrace leads visitors through a spiralling open reception hall to the main prayer room. This 'spin' or rotation is set in play by the 45-degree placing of the building relative to the existing church hall and road.

Dannatt worked closely with the structural engineer Ted Happold of Ove Arup, a Quaker himself.[255] They had previously collaborated on the 400-seat assembly hall at the Society of Friends' Bootham School in York – another brutalist building, which was finished in 1971.

Inside the Meeting House, the entrance hall has low ceilings, exposed concrete walls and quarry tiles on the floor. The hall leads to the uplifting volume of the main room – a calm and reflective space with its timber ceiling above simple plastered walls. The central square lantern on the roof filters light into the inner space; the constructional beauty and structural logic of the roof structure – a combination of timber in compression and steel rods in tension – is left exposed.

'Good architecture nourishes and refreshes, as with Dannatt's Blackheath Meeting House, where silence is maintained within, the concrete walls speak quietly of strength, and its bright timber roof lantern feeds, to use a favourite Quaker expression, the inward light.'[256]

348

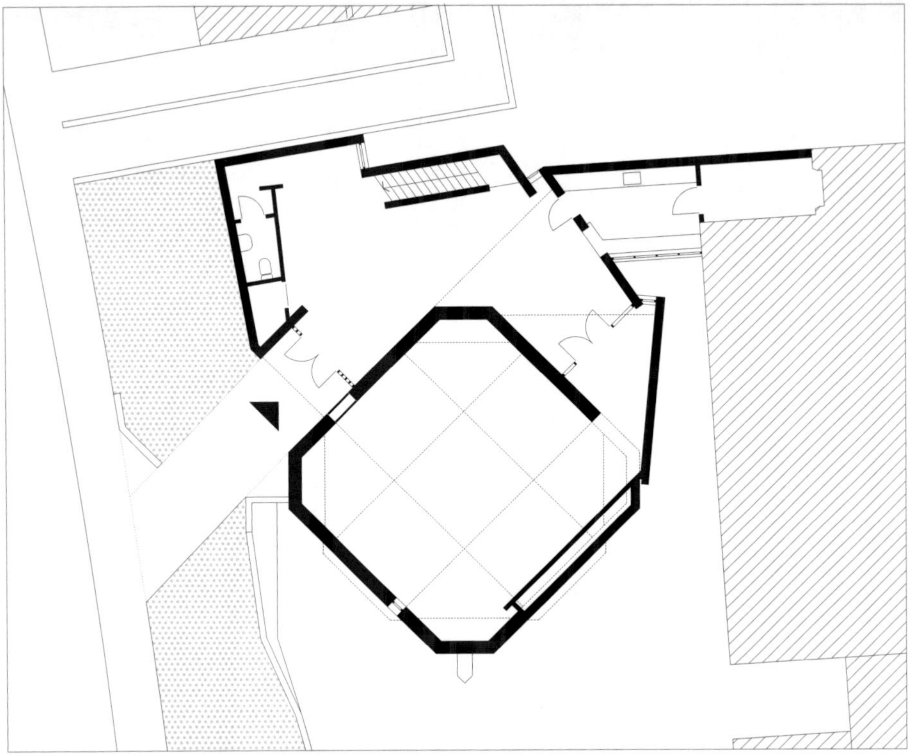

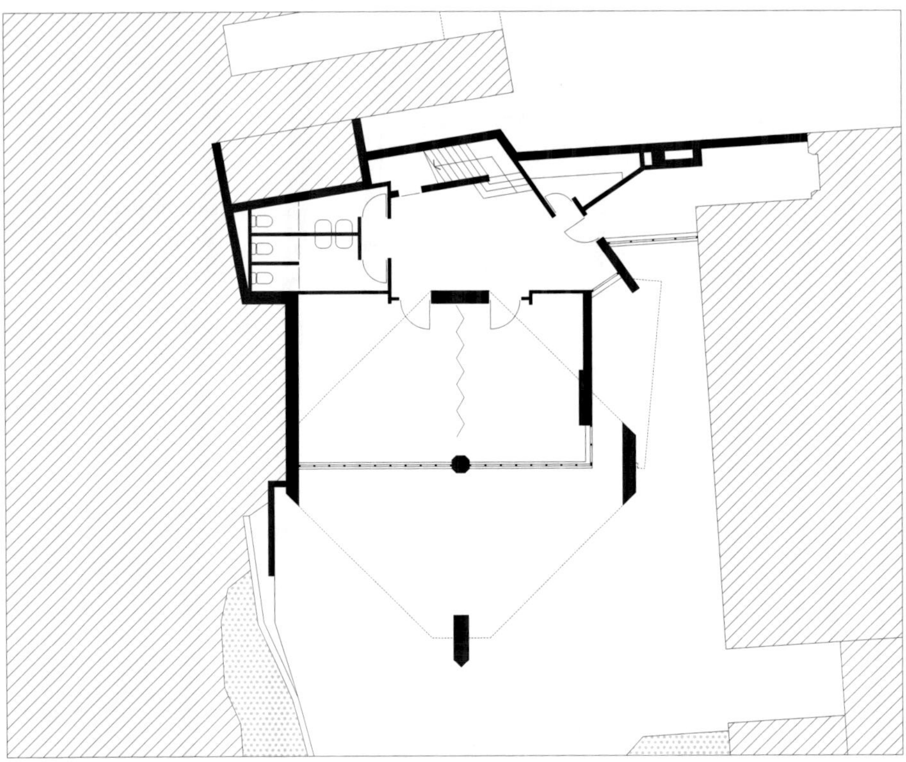

Opposite: the exposed timber and steel structure of the central roof lantern
Above: ground floor plan
Below: lower ground floor plan

10m

Meeting room entrance to the left lit by one of the corner skylights

BLACKHEATH QUAKER MEETING HOUSE

 Meeting room interior with slot window towards the street

1972

57

Project	Greenwich Building Society
Architect	Trevor Dannatt
Completed	1958 and 1974
Client	Greenwich Building Society
Awards	Civic Trust Award 1960

The offices for the Greenwich Building Society at 279–283 Greenwich High Road have had three incarnations. The original building was a nineteenth-century three-storey block occupied by the Industrial Building Society, with a shop at ground level. In 1958, Dannatt's first intervention was an extension at the side and rear including a striking modern reworking of the reception and office space.

The second transformation was made in the early 1970s, retaining the original building with its well-proportioned front of great sentimental value to the building society and wrapping a new three-storey building around. This was built from matching red brick but with a concrete frame construction, unadorned surfaces and modern detailing.

The rear façade aligns with the railway cutting. A generous staircase provides a transition from old to new and sits in the triangular shape at the centre of the plan, separating the later open-plan offices from the original spaces. Vertical glazed slots on the front façade clearly differentiate the old from the new. The glazed corner windows to the right of the building face towards St Alfege Church tower (designed by Hawksmoor). The separation between old and new is continued on the top floor with glazed slots surrounding the boardroom.

In 1997, The Greenwich Building Society merged with Portman, which was later absorbed by the Nationwide Building Society. During the 2000s the building was occupied by a succession of smaller businesses and it is currently a branch office of the estate agents, Winkworths. The persistent changes in occupancy have resulted in some unfortunate alterations at the street level, which have undermined the integrity of Dannatt's original design.[257]

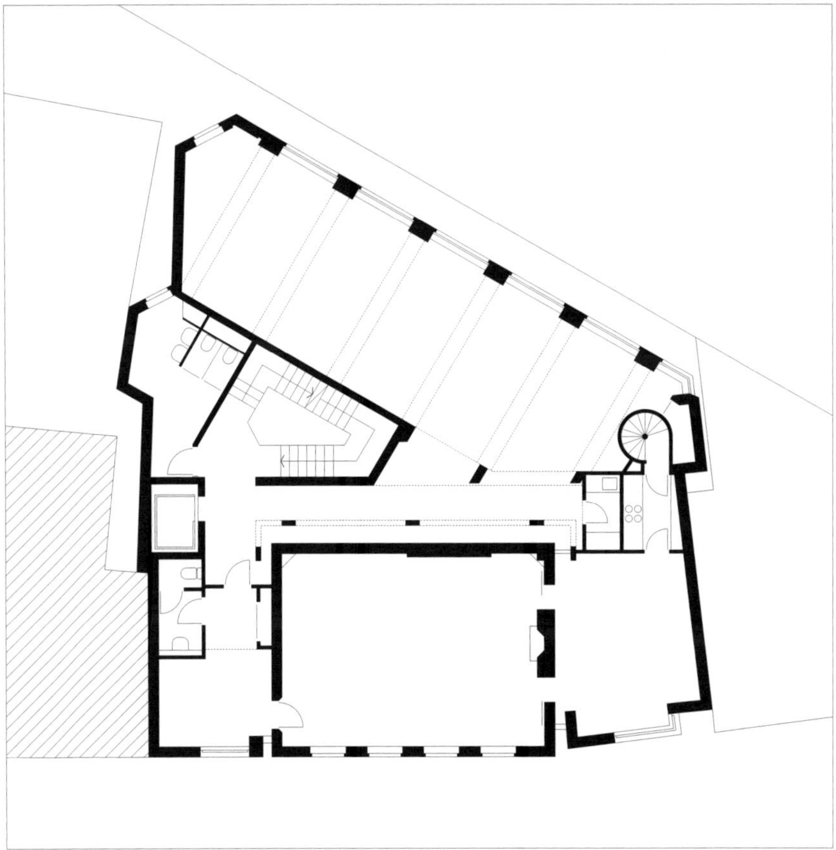

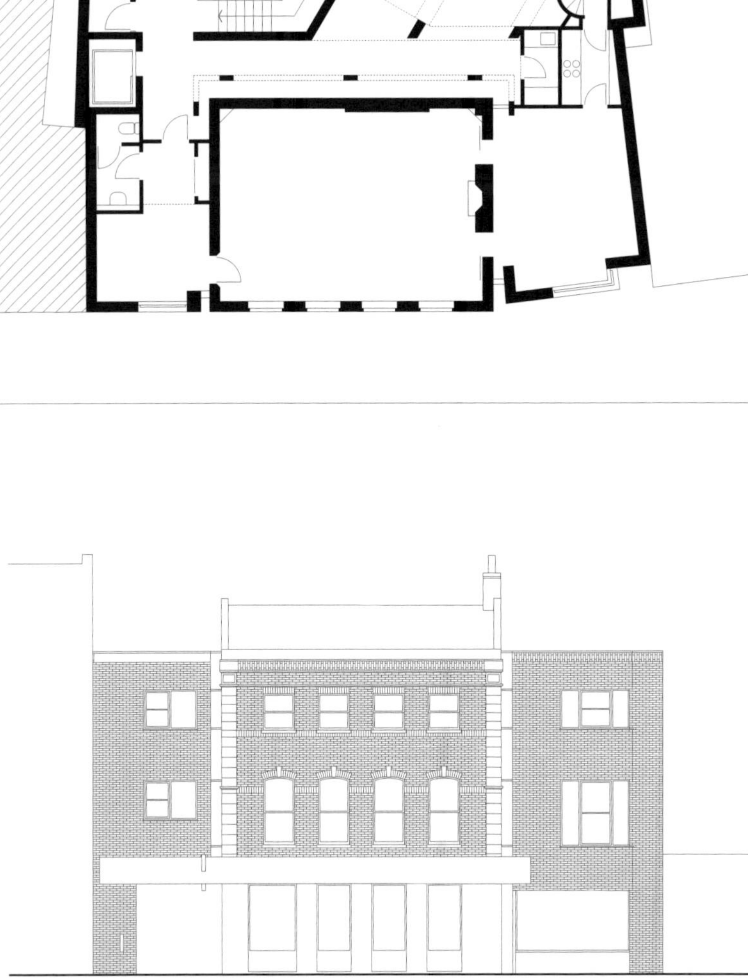

Above: second floor plan, as originally built
Below: street elevation, as originally built

10m

The 1958 street elevation showing the new entrance lobby to the right

 The street elevation in 1974 showing the wrap-around three-storey extension

58

Project	8 Lloyds Place
Architect	Trevor Dannatt
Completed	2001[258]
Client	Morden College Charity

This house is part of a set of three commissioned by Morden College, sited on a secluded sloping site near Blackheath village. The first two houses had planning constraints that limited their design, but this third building, Southbank Cottage, provided the opportunity to create something more exciting – a unique split-level house with a central staircase that also serves a top floor terrace, providing extensive views over London.[259]

Making the most of the site's natural contours, the entrance is on a half-landing with living rooms on the ground floor below and three bedrooms on the first floor and upper half-landing. This novel layout removes the need for corridor circulation as all rooms are accessed from the landings. It was one of Dannatt's favourite house designs.[260] The house is of London stock brick with white painted windows. Canopies at the entrance, in the living room and on the roof terrace, have red painted posts that add interest to the composition.

The house from the top of the steeply sloping site

Entrance porch

2001

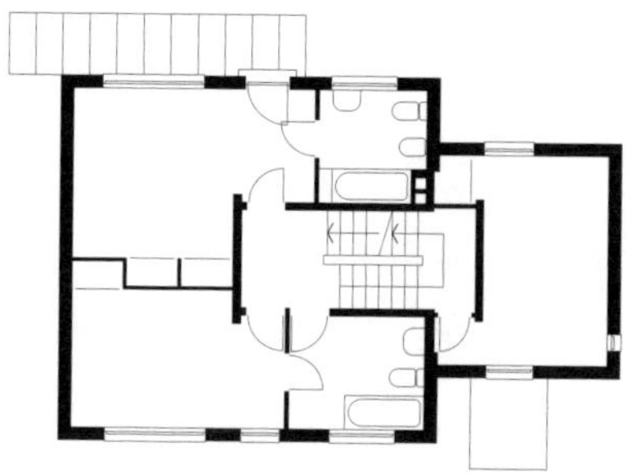

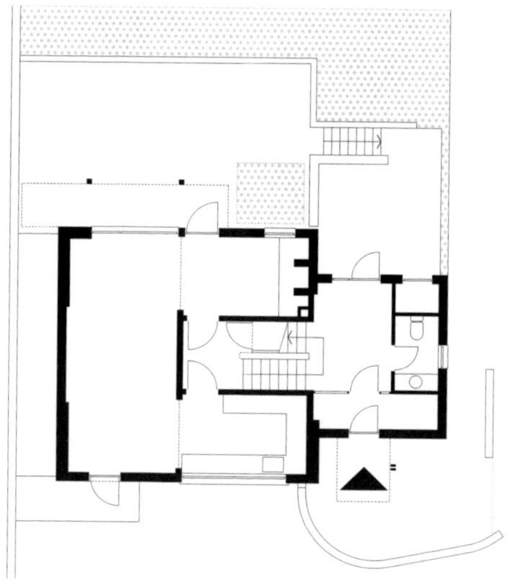

Above: first floor plan
Below: ground floor plan

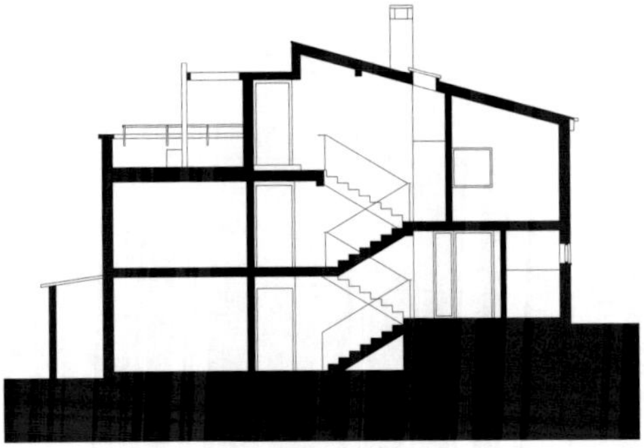

Above: section showing
the split-level arrangement
Below: garden elevation

10m

Albert Victor Heal (1887 – 1975) built a practice that served several banking clients including Lazard and the Bank of England. His track record may have helped persuade Grindlay's Bank to commission him to design its housing development in Sweyn Place, off Blackheath Park.

Heal worked for Cambridge-based builders Rattee and Kett from 1904 to 1906 and as an assistant to George Frederick Bodley and Cecil G. Hare at Bodley and Hare, from 1906 to 1913. He became assistant to Richard T. Creed in 1913 and took over the practice after Creed's death in 1914.

Until 1927, Heal ran an independent practice, which included Cecil G. Hare as a partner from 1919 to 1924. He became a RIBA fellow in 1927 and during the 1950s joined forces with R. V. Smith as Victor Heal & Partners.

During his early career, Heal worked on a number of significant projects, including Little Bardfield Hall, Essex (1920, restoration); 32 Grosvenor Square, W1 (1923, interior replanning and fitout); Parham Park, Sussex (1925, restoration); and Lazard Bank, 10 – 12 Old Broad Street (1926, new building).

His later work focused on churches, offices and residential projects, mainly in London and the southeast of England.

Local projects	Sweyn Place	1969
Other London projects	New Change Buildings (demolished 2007)	1953–1960
	St Paul's House, Warwick Lane	1964

59

Project	Sweyn Place
Architect	Victor Heal and Partners
Completed	[illegible]
Client	National Overseas & Grindlays Bank

Neil Rhind has noted that Sweyn Place takes its name from one of the Danish invaders who sailed up the Thames in 1011 and killed Alfege, Archbishop of Canterbury. The development was built on the site of three houses on Blackheath Park, which were damaged during the Second World War. 111 Blackheath Park was a large red brick villa (Mohun House, 1898) which had been owned by the National Bank of India since the 1940s and used as a clubhouse to serve the sports fields, which were leased by the bank as far back as the 1920s.[261]

Sweyn Place had a unique brief: to provide a mix of detached, terraced houses and flats with associated garaging for sale, along with two facilities to be retained by the bank. The facilities were a block of studio flats, named Minerva Lodge, to accommodate visiting staff and students from overseas as well as a social club to cater for visitors and for those using the playing fields opposite at weekends.[262] The resulting scheme faced onto Blackheath Park but also created a new secluded landscaped court. Four detached houses and the social club block line the street, while a central lawned court is enclosed by the two blocks of flats (18 flats in total) and two rows of 10 terrace houses.[263]

The social club, a concrete and brick two-storey building, originally raised on pilotis, housed a bar, restaurant, games room and staff training rooms. This building was named Aldington House, in honour of the Chairman of the bank at the time. Adlington House was converted into a care home in the 1980s, with a basement excavated to provide additional space. The ground floor's covered terrace was infilled to provide six extra bedrooms, which spoiled the open character of block. Planning permission for its conversion into nine flats plus a third-floor penthouse was granted in March 2023.

The bespoke concrete nameplates at the entrances to Sweyn Place all feature an elephant – the bank's logo and a reference to its connection with the Indian sub-continent.

A sculpture of the Roman goddess *Minerva* by Alan Collins (1928–2016) was specially commissioned and placed in the estate gardens at the front of Aldington House. It was removed in 1983, following the bank's sale to an Australian financial group. The sculpture was eventually relocated to the front of Minerva House in Montague Close, by Southwark Cathedral.[264] Minerva House (1983) was the bank's purpose-built headquarters. Alan Collins also created a frieze to another of the practices' project, at St Pauls House, Warwick Lane (1964).

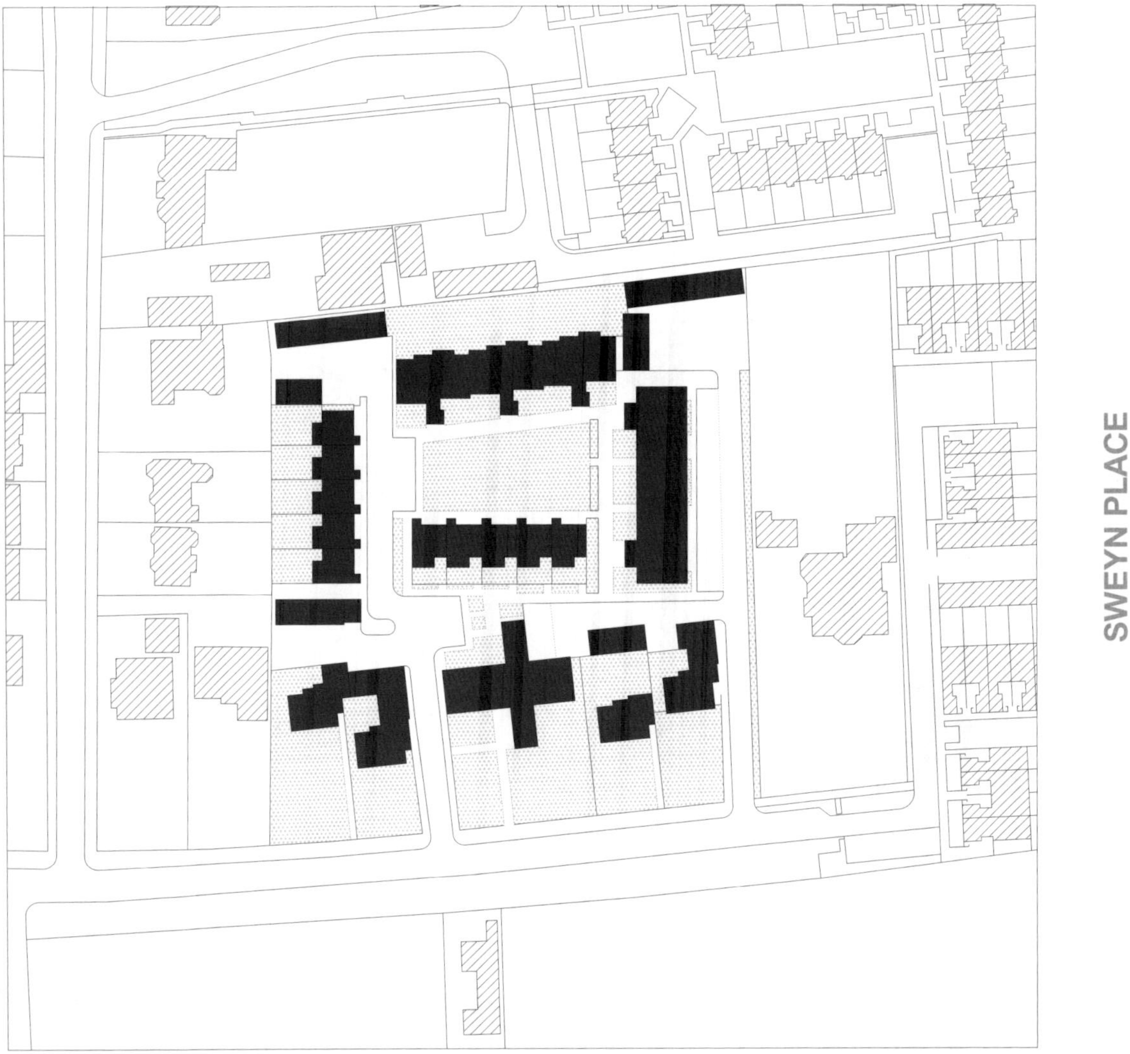

363 Site location 1:2000 50m

1969

The front garden of one of the detached houses

The living room of one of the detached houses

Walter Greaves (1924–2004) and his family lived in Blackheath from the mid-1950s to 1968 at 57 Lee Road, a derelict house that Greaves renovated and extended with modern additions.[265]

Greaves started his career working with Peter Moro on the 1951 Royal Festival Hall project; a talented designer and skilful artist, he was responsible for most of the building's published architectural drawings. He then went on to develop his own practice, specialising in private houses and housing projects. He also collaborated with Peter Moro, who lived at 20 Blackheath Park and had been his teacher at the Regent Street Polytechnic during the 1940s.

In the early 1950s, Greaves was recommended by Peter Moro to the Tawse family. The Tawses had previously commissioned Moro to design their house in Chichester, Harbour Meadow (1940), which is now recognised as Moro's seminal work. Mrs Tawse asked Moro to design a holiday house nearby but he was unavailable and recommended Greaves. Greaves met his future wife, Annabel Tawse, the client's daughter, while working on the project.

In the late 1960s Greaves and his family moved from Blackheath to Chichester in Sussex. He handed over several projects to E Morton Wright, including 1 Leycroft Close, Canterbury, Kent (listed grade II) and 24 and 26 Morden Road Mews. By the 1970s, Greaves's work had shifted away from commissions for private houses to larger housing schemes, including the Jubilee Trust housing in Greenwich and Red Lion Lane off Shooters Hill. By the end of the 1970s, finding it harder to travel to London for site visits due to worsening multiple sclerosis, Greaves wound down his work in the capital to concentrate on local projects, including his own home, Severels (1981), which is one of very few late twentieth-century houses to attain Grade II* listing.

Henry Greaves recalls watching his father at work: 'Sometimes he would let me come into the office and watch him draw, which was fascinating even to me as a child, because he drew freehand, never with a square or ruler, and rarely with a compass. He had a sheet of square grid graph paper under the tracing paper, and he could draw such straight lines that he often added slight wiggles to make the lines look more natural. Kenneth Grange, who shared the office in Charing Cross and later went on to found Pentagram, considers Dad to have produced the best architectural drawings he has ever seen.'

Local projects		
	57 Lee Road, own house (much altered)	1957
	26 to 32 Meadowcourt Road (much altered)	
	11a Morden Road Mews	1960
	64 Corner Green (with Peter Moro)	1962
	9 and 11 Manor Way (with Peter Moro)	1960 + 1963
	20a Blackheath Park, alterations	1962
	Bennett Park and Blackheath Village[266] (unbuilt)	1963
	12a Blackheath Park, alterations[267]	1964
	1 to 3 Rocque Lane	1968
	21 Morden Road (demolished 2006)	1968
	24 and 26 Morden Road Mews (with E Morton Wright)	1968
	Jubilee Trust housing, Egerton Drive, Greenwich	1974
	Red Lion Lane housing, Woolwich	

Walter Greaves with his son Henry

60

Project	11a Morden Road Mews
Architect	Walter Greaves
Completed	19[illegible]0
Client	Leslie Bilsby

The site was previously occupied by an old coach house linked with the gardener's cottage at number 11 (altered and extended in 2010 by Nick Wilson Architects), on the adjacent plot.

The house was designed for Leslie Bilsby and purchased when under construction for Greaves's brother-in-law, James Tawse, after his return from a period in Canada.[268] The building presents a rather closed façade to the street with an inner courtyard providing light to the rooms. The northern end of the plot is an open patio for carparking and the southern end a small entrance court.

Accessed down the unmade mews lane, the brick house has three bedrooms, two bathrooms and two reception rooms. The first-floor roof terrace railings were a later addition. The building features curved brick walls, a curved stair enclosure with an expressed timber clad turret recessed from the outer brick wall and an integrated garage, later converted for extra accommodation.

The curved turret to the staircase, clad in timber and painted white, evokes a ship's funnel. This nautical reference is a recurring theme in Greaves' work, as is the use of curved brick walls.[269] He went on to explore these concepts further at his own house, Severels (1981), in West Sussex.

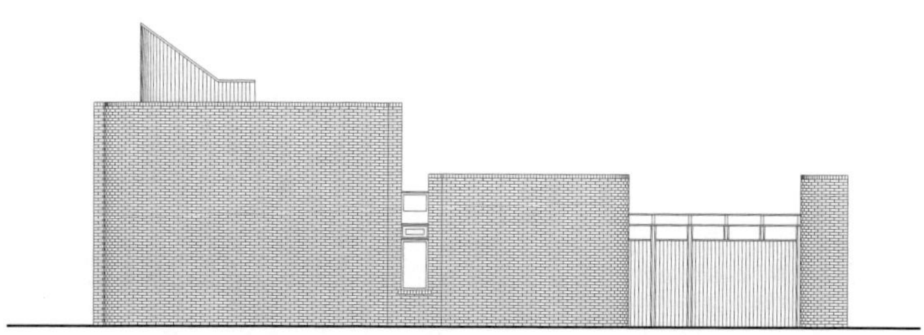

West elevation, as originally built

10m

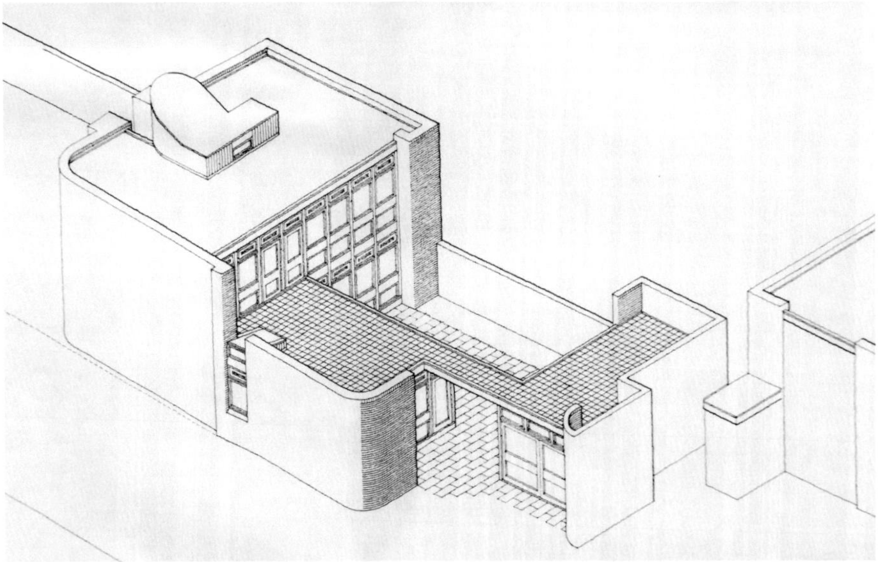

Above: freehand axonometric drawing by Walter Greaves
Below: the entrance court with the original garage in 1970

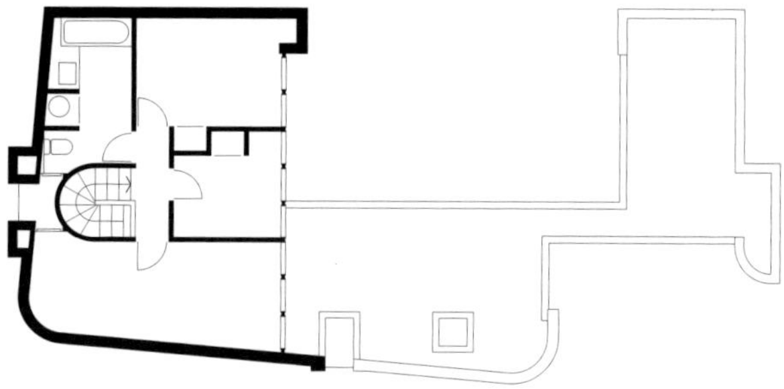

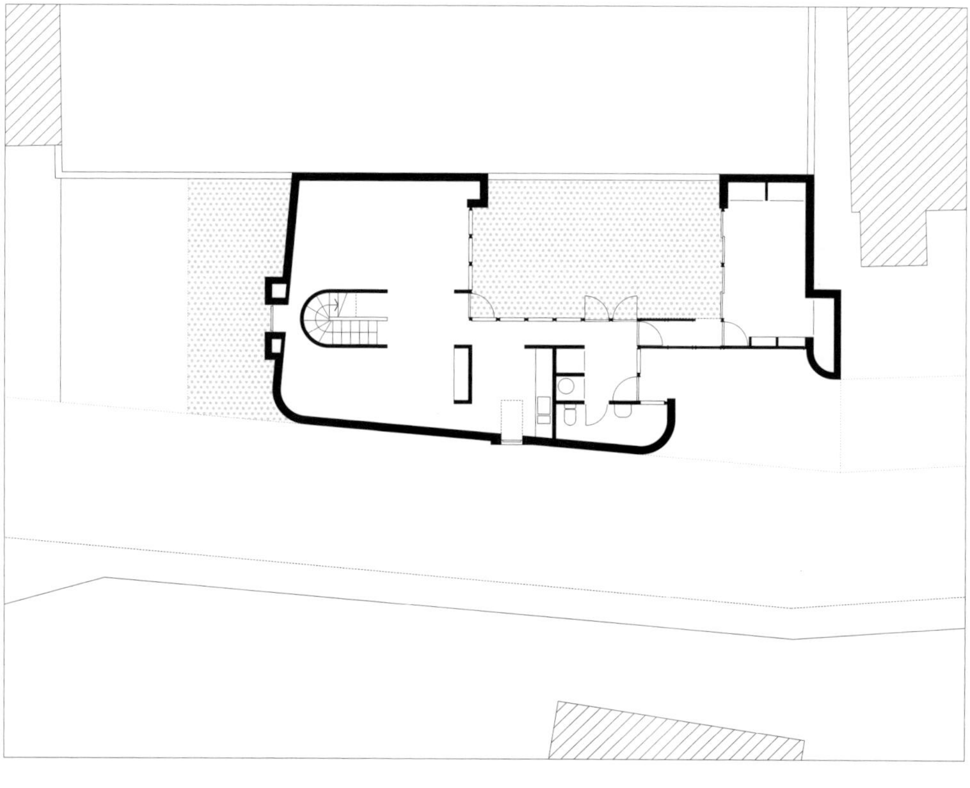

Above: first floor plan, as originally built
Below: ground floor plan, as originally built

10m

11A MORDEN ROAD MEWS

The sculptural staircase volume from Morden Road Mews

1960

61

Project	64 Corner Green
Architect	Walter Greaves
Completed	1962
Client	Mr and Mrs O'Keefe

The twisting lane of Corner Green was created in the mid-1950s to provide access to two Span estates – The Keep and Corner Green. The lane ran through market gardens, linking Pond Road to Morden Road Mews and Blackheath Park.[270] Number 64 Corner Green is a single-storey house with a split-level, designed by Greaves, in association with Peter Moro.

The original dark brick house consisted of two equally sized square pavilions. Conceived as functionally separate blocks, one for living and one for sleeping, these squares are offset in plan and connected by a glazed entrance hall. Their heights also vary and this is reflected internally; the living block has a tall section containing the sitting room and fireplace overlooked by the kitchen and dining areas, which are at a higher level and are accessed by a few steps. This dynamic space is framed by the exposed brick fireplace. The ceilings originally had strip pine cladding and the dark brick with grey mortar was left exposed internally.

Greaves' son Henry recalls: 'Mum and Dad remained good friends with his clients after their houses were finished, so I spent time in most of them. The O'Keefe's house was one of my favourites, and I remember the big party they held when they left to go to live in Thailand.'[271]

The house is now much altered, with a rear extension accommodating a large bedroom in another square footprint. A fence has also been added on the road front and further rear extensions were completed in 2013.

64 CORNER GREEN

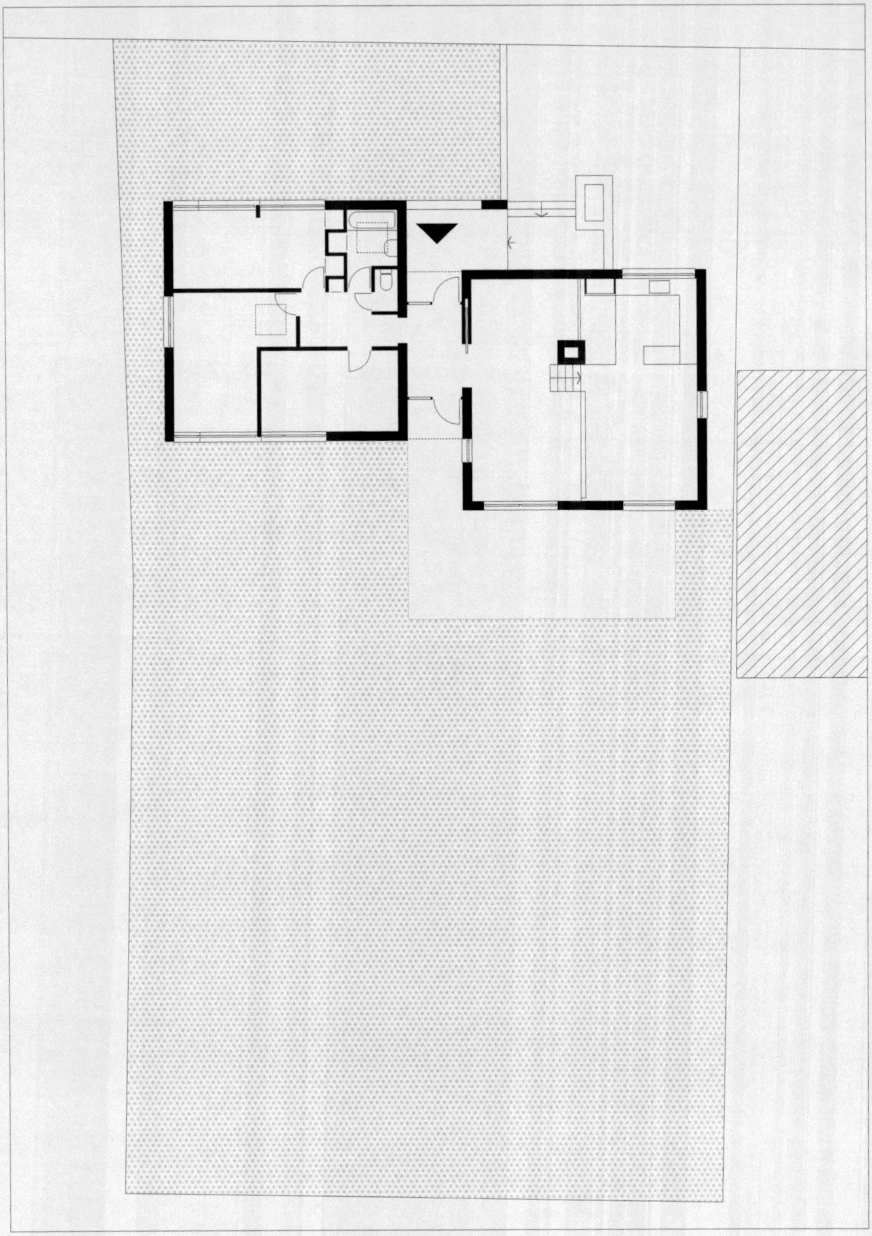

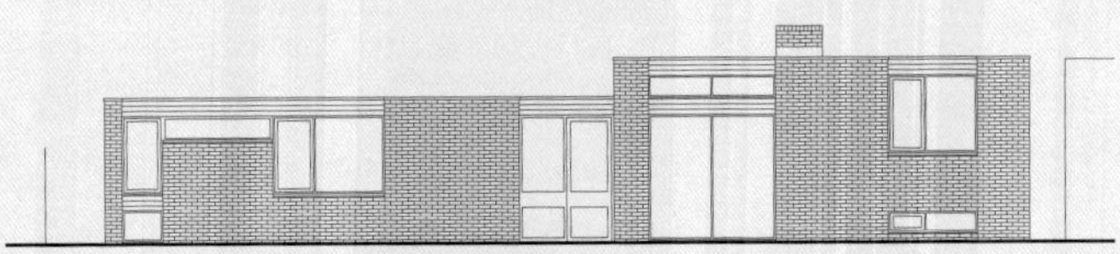

Above: ground floor plan,
as originally built
Below: garden elevation,
as originally built

10m

1962

The garden elevation in 1962

 The split-level living room spaces

62

Project	9 and 11 Manor Way
Architect	Walter Greaves
Completed	1960 for number 11 and 1963 for number 9
Client	Ernst Gorge for number 11 and Bryce Knox for number 9

A pair of detached single-storey courtyard houses set back from the street behind high walls that contain private front gardens and patios. The houses were built on what was once the rear garden and orchard of 95 Lee Road.

Number 11 Manor Way was designed by Peter Moro, with Walter Greaves managing the construction stage and delivering the project on site. It was commissioned by Ernst Gorge, a wine merchant born in Czechoslovakia and lifelong friend of Moro. Greaves' son, Henry recalls that 'Ernst Gorge paid Dad in wine, which lasted our family a very long time.'[272]

Number 11, built in a distinctive off-white brickwork, retains the original layout and many original features. The plan is arranged with the bedrooms to the rear and the kitchen, dining and living room to the front. All the rooms benefit from large windows or floor-to-ceiling glazed doors and clerestory windows. Original features include pine cladding to the walls and ceilings.

In typical Greaves style, the door handles align with the light switches, at a lower than usual height, making them more accessible to children and creating a pleasing visual alignment. The corridor has a lowered ceiling, allowing high-level windows in the bedrooms and living room. The layout is extremely fluid with most rooms opening onto an inner court or towards the perimeter walls, which are softened by the use of climbing plants.[273]

As the first house was under way, Greaves was separately appointed to design number 9, which is of a darker brown brickwork. Of the pair, it has suffered more alterations over the years. The original layout was centred on a courtyard with open views from the front garden. Over the years, Greaves produced three studies for extending the house including a new block to the front. Eventually part of the courtyard was enclosed to be used as a dining room. Carefully detailed windows and internal joinery were complemented by dark green terrazzo floors.

In 1993, Ernst and Hazel Gorge commissioned David Branch, local architect and family friend, to carry out an extensive refurbishment project of number 11 that fully respected the original designs. The garden was redesigned by Joanna Herald in 2005.

Opposite
Above, left to right: no. 9 and no. 11 ground floor plan, as originally built
Below: garden elevation, as originally built

9 AND 11 MANOR WAY

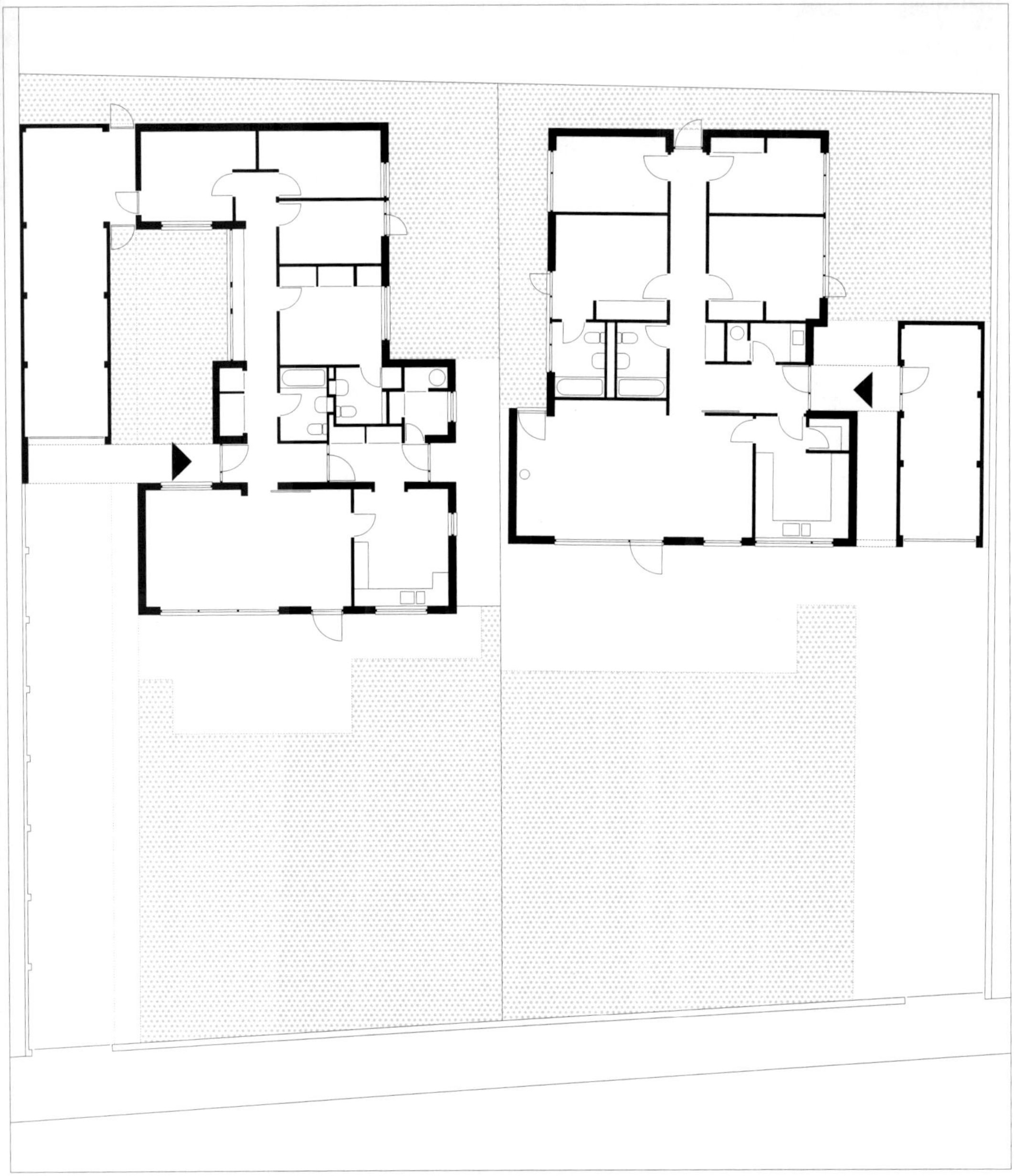

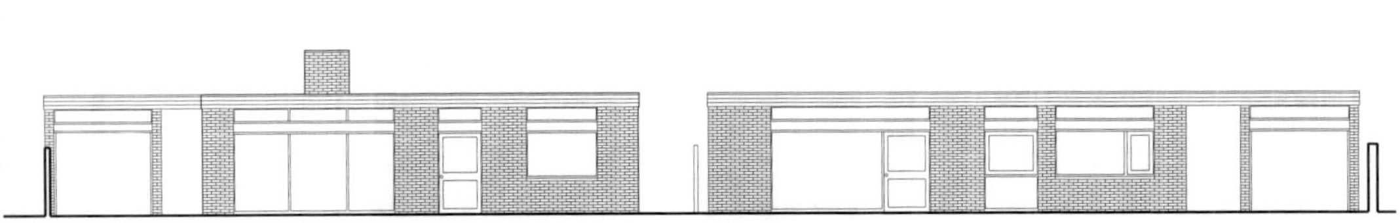

10m

1960, 1963

The front garden of no. 11 with no. 9 to the left

 The living room of no. 11 in 1962

63

Project	21 Morden Road
Architect	Walter Greaves
Completed	1960, demolished 2006
Client	Leslie Bilsby

A single-storey courtyard house, built on a constricted site that was acquired by Leslie Bilsby when he secured land for The Plantation in 1960.[274]

The house made experimental use of prefabricated and modular construction techniques, which Bilsby was interested in exploring at the time.[275] The exquisite plan was highly articulated and incorporated complex connections and vistas, which blurred the distinction between inside and outside. Low-level windows emphasised this continuity. The planting design was by Ivor Cunningham and the garden was arranged around the grid of the house in a series of patios. There were also two small ponds.[276]

Site location 1:2000 50m

The modular panels contained a high level of asbestos, which was not unusual at the time it was built. However, this material caused problems when the house exchanged hands and required renovation during the early 2000s. The house was eventually demolished in 2006 and a flat roofed two storey Huf Haus built in its place.

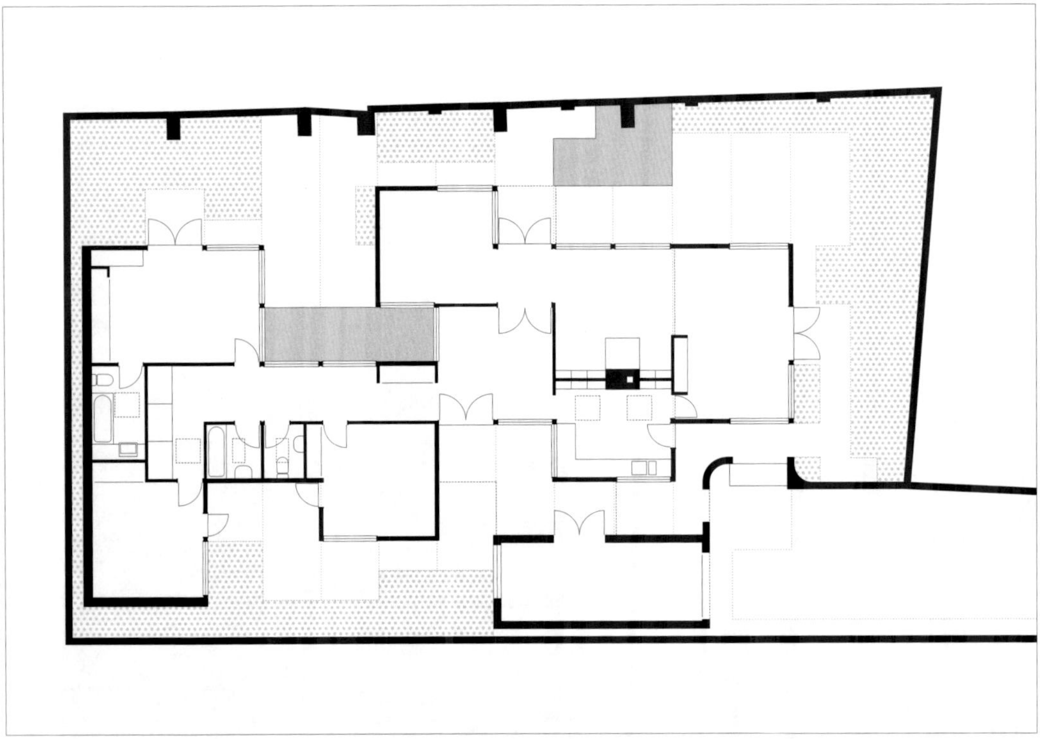

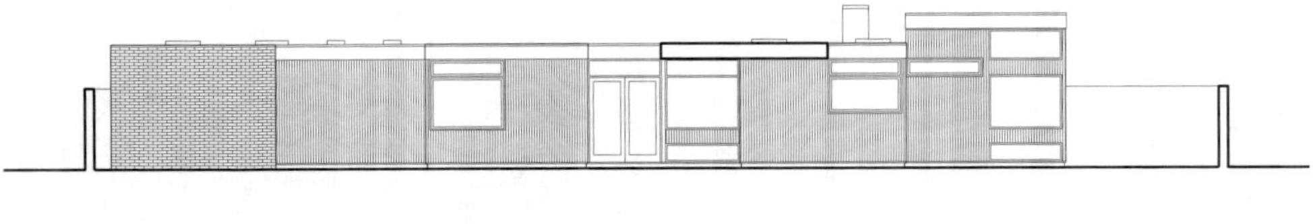

Above: ground floor plan, as originally built
Below: northwest elevation, as originally built

10m

Layered spaces: courtyard with pond from the entrance lobby and bedroom beyond

 Inside and outside blurred: double-height living room and garden

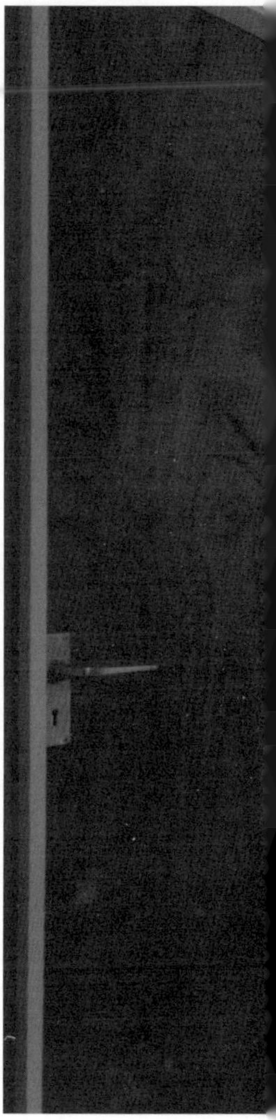

WALTER GREAVES

The double-height living room volume from the garden

21 MORDEN ROAD

Corridor to the bedrooms looking towards the entrance lobby

1968

Project	1–3 Rocque Lane
Architect	Walter Greaves
Completed	1968
Client	Annabel Greaves

Number 1–3 Rocque Lane is a development of three three-storey houses, built on land following the demolition of number 1 Pond Road, a Victorian villa built in 1862.[277] The development was named after the cartographer John Rocque, who is best known for his 1745 map of London. The name was proposed by John Roberts, the architect for the site at the rear of the plot.

The site was acquired through Leslie Bilsby and Walter Greaves' wife, Annabel, acted as the client for the project, since RIBA members were not permitted to act as developers at that time. Greaves considered this to be one of his best schemes.[278]

The houses each have five or six bedrooms, all with extensive views of St Michael's Church and the long rear gardens along Pond Road. They also have three roof terraces and double-aspect, open-plan reception rooms. The various terraces, at first and second floor, create a highly sculptural scheme of stepped volumes. Inside, the rooms have exposed brick, full height windows, built-in storage and timber-panelled walls.

The floorplan for each storey is the same, but is ingeniously rotated, first by 90 degrees and then by 180 degrees, creating a tower-like tiered single volume and an intimate entrance court at the heart of the scheme. The architectural drawings for the project are particularly beautiful, especially the shaded site plan and the elevations that show the layering of brick piers.[279]

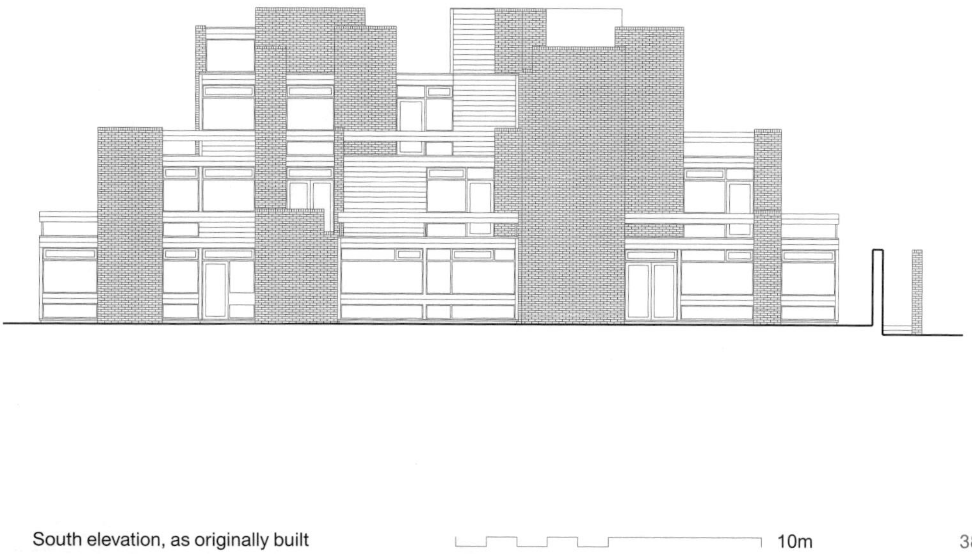

South elevation, as originally built

1–3 ROCQUE LANE

Site location 1:2000 50m

1968

The entrance hall to one of the houses

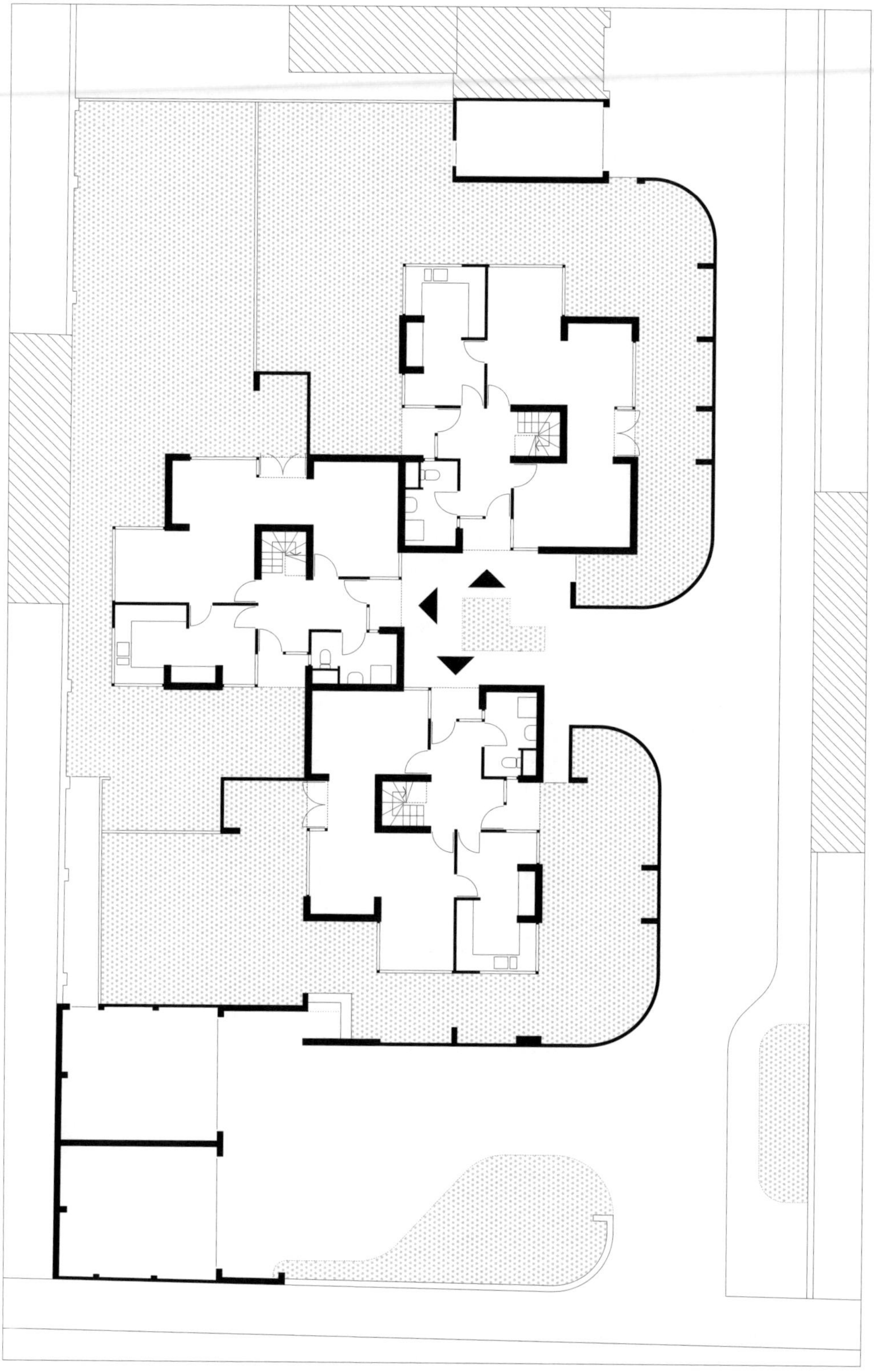

Ground floor plan, as originally built

10m

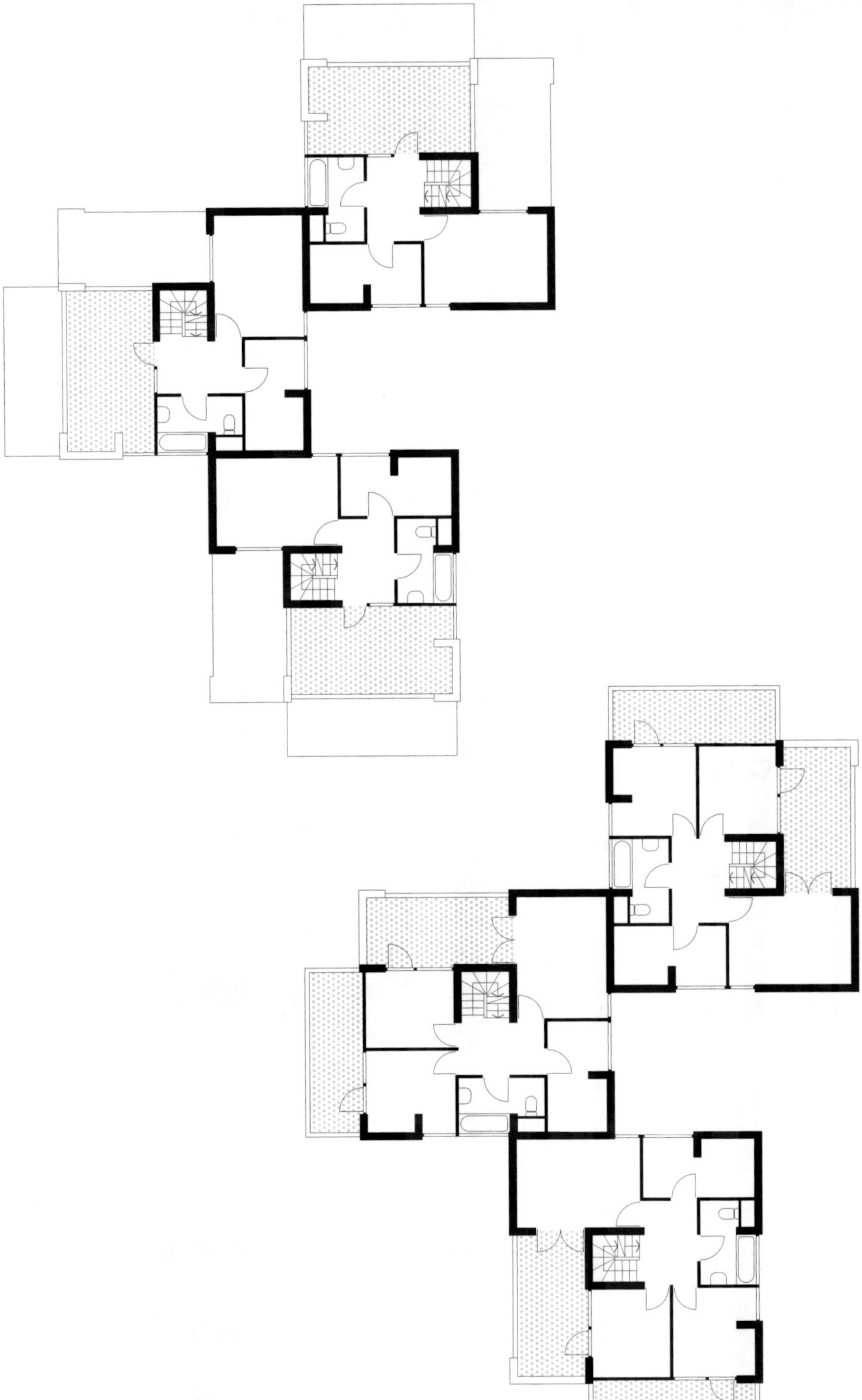

1–3 ROCQUE LANE

Above: second floor plan, as originally built
Below: first floor plan, as originally built

10m

1968

The stepped massing of the three houses from Pond Road

1–3 ROCQUE LANE

1968

MODERN BUILDINGS

01 Oak Yard, The Keep
02 6–16 Morden Road and 14–18 Morden Road Mews
03 Rangers Square
04 85–104 Vanbrugh Park
05 Church Army Chapel
06 66 Greenwich Park Street
07 Greenwich Theatre, Crooms Hill
08 6 Paragon Place
09 Vanbrugh Park Estate
10 8 Meadowbank
11 24 and 26 Morden Road Mews
12 Christ Church Forum, East Greenwich
13 The Priory, Priory Park and Park Row
14 Corner Green and 24–33 Corner Green
15 The Keep
16 Spangate
17 Hallgate, The Hall, Foxes Dale and Brooklands Park
18 The Plantation and Parkend
19 South Row
20 The Lane and Streetfield Mews
21 Holm Walk
22 17 and 17a Montpelier Row
23 2 Langton Way
24 Lyndale Close
25 Trafalgar Road Housing
26 St Michael and All Angels Church Hall
27 10 and 11 Park Row
28 4–7 Rocque Lane
29 Meridian West, Diamond Terrace
30 Brooklands Park Estate
31 85 Brooklands Park
32 11 Westgrove Lane
33 5a–5e St Germans Place
34 57a Blackheath Park
35 129 Maze Hill
36 115 Blackheath Park
37 House in Blackheath, unbuilt project
38 10 Blackheath Park
39 22 Parkgate
40 14 Baizdon Road
41 81–88 Ashburnham Grove
42 31 Langton Way
43 20 Blackheath Park
44 Chatfield House, 21 Westgrove Lane
45 21 Park Vista
46 37 Park Vista
47 4 and 4a Langton Way
48 35a Hyde Vale
49 28 and 30 Heathway
50 47a Blackheath Park
51 40 Heath Lane
52 North Several, Orchard Drive
53 16 Baizdon Road
54 17 Langton Way
55 Blackheath Congregational Church
56 Blackheath Quaker Meeting House
57 Greenwich Building Society
58 8 Lloyds Place
59 Sweyn Place
60 11a Morden Road Mews
61 64 Corner Green
62 9 and 11 Manor Way
63 21 Morden Road
64 1–3 Rocque Lane

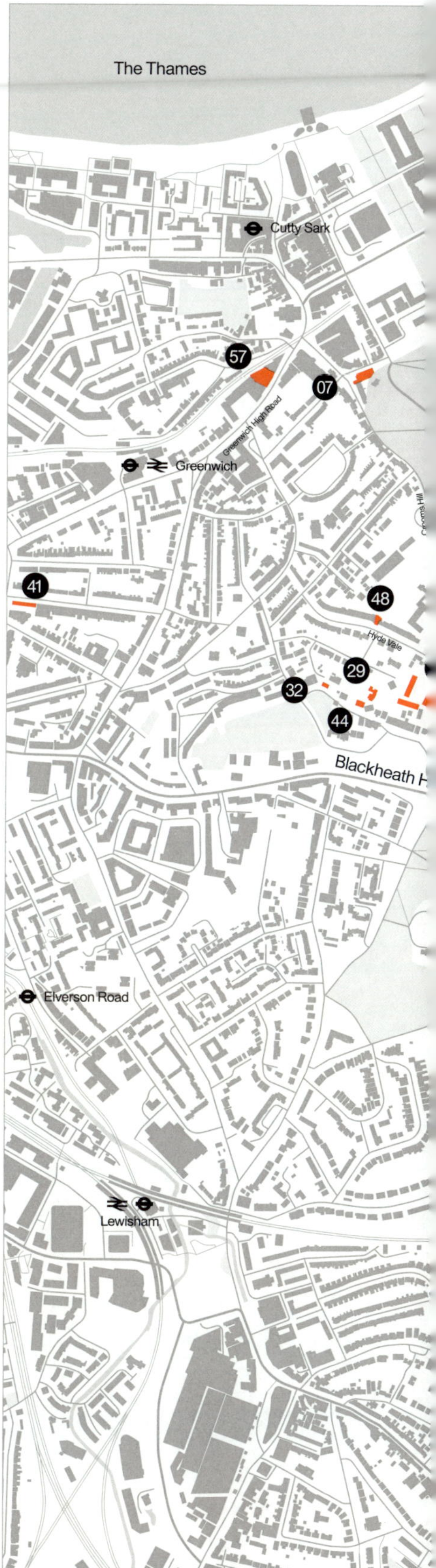

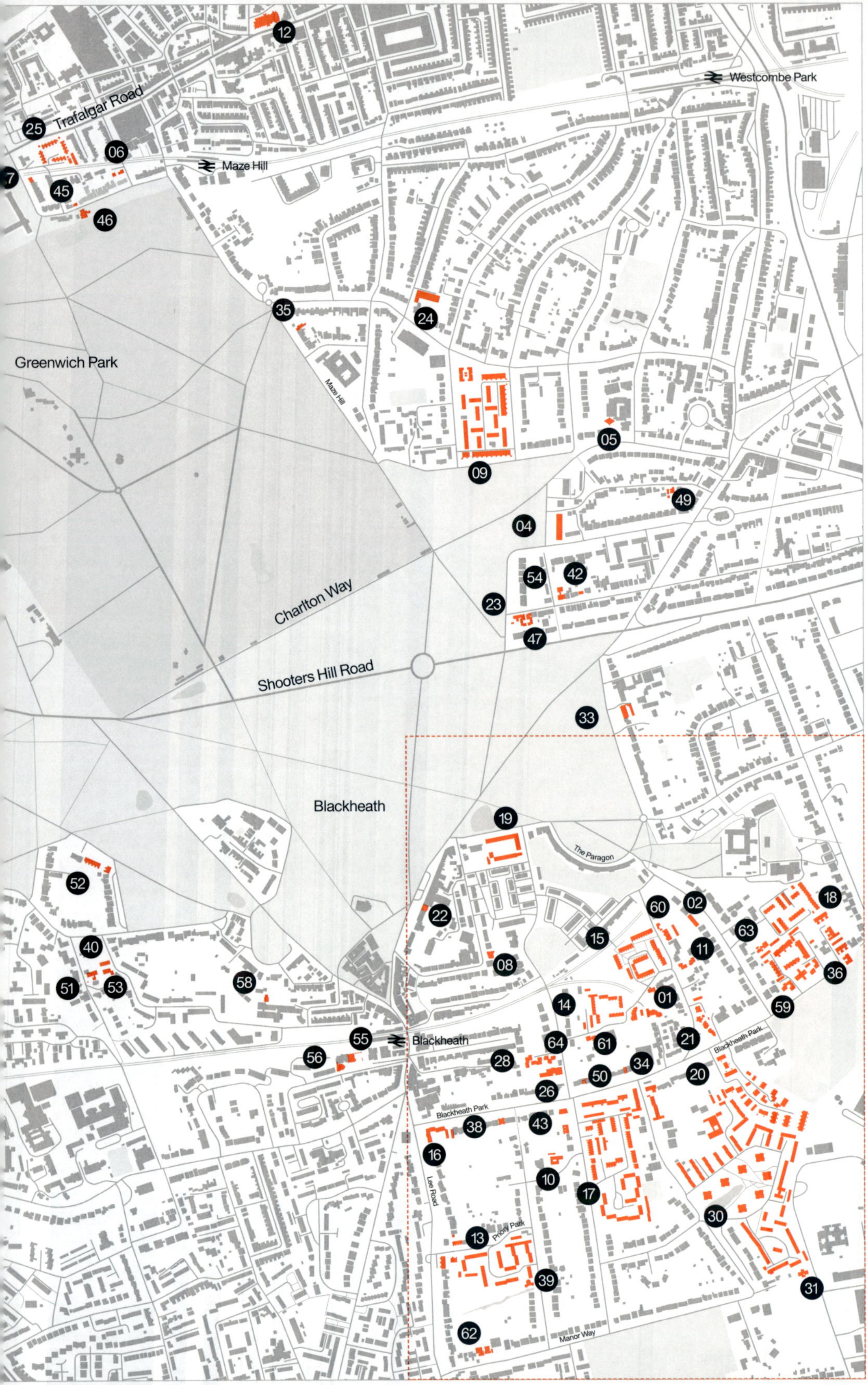
Trafalgar Road
Maze Hill
Westcombe Park
Greenwich Park
Maze Hill
Charlton Way
Shooters Hill Road
Blackheath
The Paragon
Blackheath
Blackheath Park
Blackheath Park
Lee Road
Priory Park
Manor Way
12
25
06
7
45
46
35
24
09
05
49
04
54
42
23
47
33
19
52
40
51
53
58
22
08
15
60
02
11
63
18
36
01
14
59
64
61
21
55
56
28
34
50
20
26
43
38
16
10
17
30
13
39
31
62

THE CATOR ESTATE

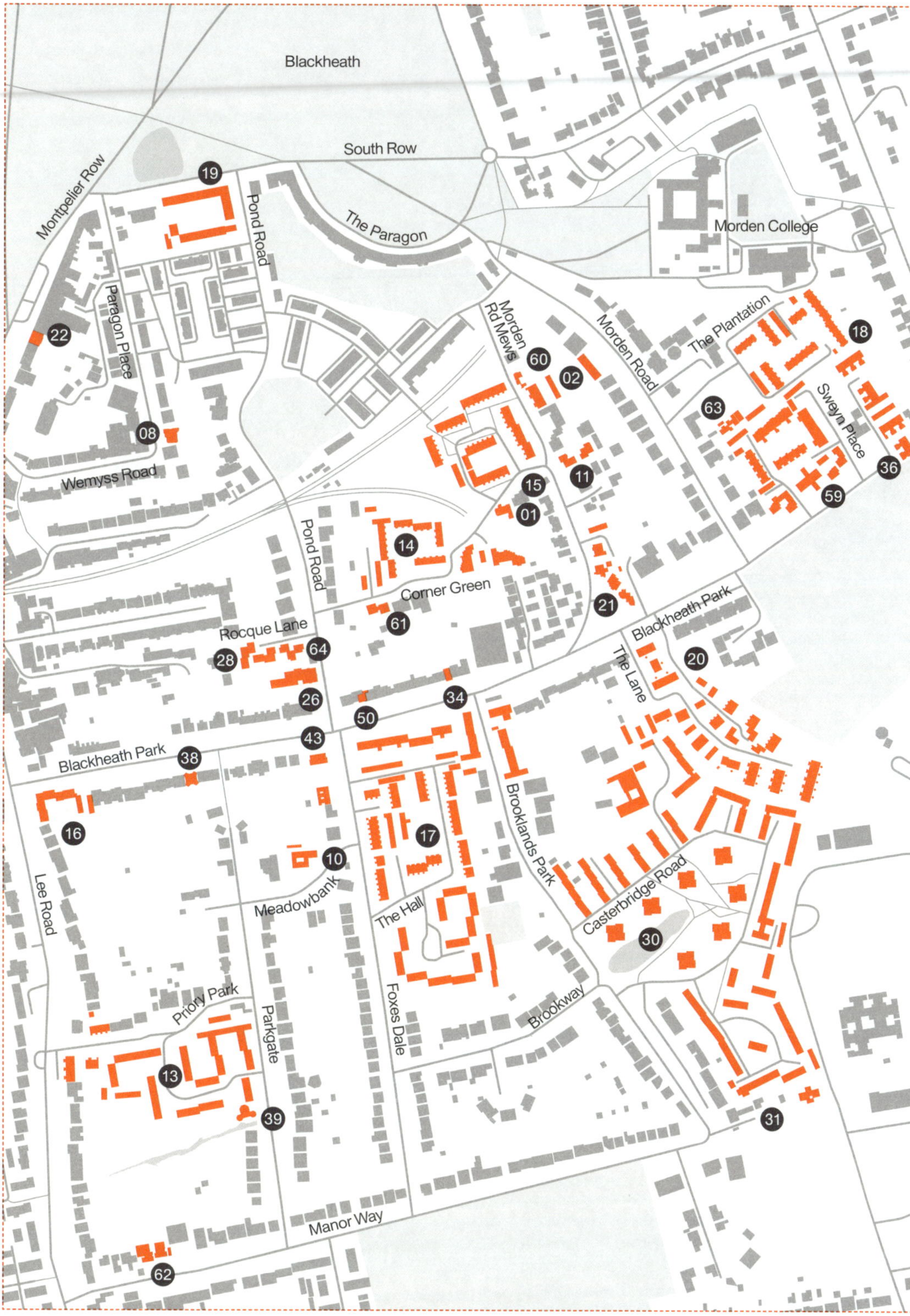

The inclusion of a building in this map does not mean it is accessible.
Please respect the privacy of the residents.

OTHER BUILDINGS OF INTEREST

CATOR ESTATE

2a Pond Road
A timber-clad artist's studio over a garage, with concrete details and an external spiral staircase.

32 Morden Road
Architect: Douglas Evan Cook, 1958
Alterations by David Bush, 1970s
A coach house conversion, with bespoke joinery and a terrazzo and metal sculptural fireplace.

Bernersmede, 61 Blackheath Park
Two blocks of flats with inset balconies and a large shared garden, 1965.

Birchmere, Pond Road
Developer: Span
A late Span development of six houses in two terraces, 1982.

Papillons Walk, Blackheath Park
Developer: Barratt Homes
26 two- and three-storey houses, in a dense scheme, initially planned by Royston Summers, 1981.

BLACKHEATH

2a Vanbrugh Hill
A two-storey red brick house with pitched roofs.

3 Dartmouth Grove
A single-storey courtyard house with integrated garage.

11 Kidbrooke Gardens
Architect: Ruth Oldacres (of Martindale and Oldacres, Deal, Kent), 1970s
Owner and builder: Richard Brown
A neo-Georgian gem, designed by the owner's great-aunt. Originally a two-storey design, Brown eventually built a three-storey house. A printer by trade with 'building houses' as a hobby, he was assisted by the technical knowledge and guidance of the Building Control surveyors. He built the house himself by hand from the foundations to the windows, woodwork, roofing and brickwork; the adventure took 10 years to complete. During this time, the family lived at 16 Corner Green, where Brown built a two-storey side extension.

29 Langton Way
Architect: Norman Plastow, 1964
A two-storey timber-clad house with large glazed areas and steeply pitched roofs.

45 and 47 Langton Way
A pair of courtyard houses, with integrated garages facing the street.

83a Mycenae Road
A detached house of light brickwork set in a row of older houses.

113 Mycenae Road
A two-storey corner house of light brick.

Allison Court, Blackheath Hill
A development of 13 houses and a four-storey block of flats, at the top of Blackheath Hill, accessed from Dartmouth Hill, 1970. Built on the site of the demolished Green Man Pub, previously a hotel and assembly rooms (originally of 1629, rebuilt in 1688 and 1868).

Baizdon Road
A Lewisham Council estate of three-story and four-storey blocks, with expressive concrete balconies and entrance canopies, 1950s.

Church of Jesus Christ of the Latter-Day Saints, 2–4 Lee Road
Architect: Gareth Wright & Colin Dixie, 1980

19 Dacre Place
Architect: Sarson and Greenway, 1970s. A courtyard house with interesting use of angled rooflights.

Drewery Court, The Glebe
A three-storey block of flats, with balconies and two-tone brickwork.

Dunstable and Bradbury Court, St John's Park
Three three-storey L-shaped blocks of flats and associated garages creating a formal private courtyard garden.

Greyladies Garden, Wat Tyler Road
Two three-storey blocks of flats arranged around landscaped gardens. The buildings are of brickwork and painted render, with expressive balconies and glazed staircase blocks.

Grove House and Wyatt House, Blackheath Grove and Wemyss Road
Two Lewisham Council blocks of flats of four storeys and five storeys, with expressive entrance canopies. Built by Leslie Bilsby's construction company.

Hatcliffe Close and Lee Park
Developer: Gough Cooper
An extensive development of three-storey terraced houses and two-storey detached houses with low-pitched roofs.

Lawn Terrace and Prendergast Road
A Lewisham Council estate of three- and four-storey blocks, with expressive concrete balconies.

Lynher Lodge, St Germans Place
A Greenwich Council block of flats, of three storeys in dark brickwork, facing the Heath with access from the large shared garden at the back .

Michael's Close, off Belmont Park
Four terraces of three-storey and two-storey houses inspired by Span. The three-storey types on Brandram Road accommodate a flat on the ground floor and a maisonette above.

Regents Place, Kidbrooke Gardens
A three-storey-inward looking scheme of five detached houses with steep slate roofs, overlooking the Paragon.

Spencer House (interiors only), Dartmouth Row
Architects: Geoffrey and June Holroyd.
An interesting mezzanine inserted into a listed building (demolished).

St James Court, Wricklemarsh Road
A three-storey block of flats in brick with exposed concrete horizontal bands.

Tristan Square, off Lee Terrace
Three blocks of three-storey terraced houses with tile-hung façades.

Varma Court, 11 Kidbrooke Grove
An end of terrace block of flats with projecting bays, informed by the adjacent Victorian houses.

GREENWICH

2–5 Hawk Mews, off Luton Place
Architect: John Bradbury
A terrace of four two-storey mews houses, early 1970s.

6 – 9 Catherine Grove
Architect: John Winter
A block of four terraced houses, 1960s.

11a Westgrove Lane
Architect: Joyce Lowman
A two- to three-storey house with a large terrace.

12 and 13 St Alfege Passage
Architects: Andrew Jackson, Susan Miles and Tom Jestico, 1973
Engineer: Anthony Hunt Associates
Builder: JW Page
A pair of four-storey new-build houses; a replacement for disused shops which were demolished pre-Second World War. Externally they continue the arrangement of the adjacent terrace, internally each house has a mezzanine and extensive glazed roofs to the rear. Architects Andrew Jackson (associate at Zeev Aram + Associates) and Susan Miles (of Gordon and Ursula Bowyer) with Tom Jestico (later of Jestico + Whiles) bought the site from John Roberts (see entry) in 1971. The mezzanine sitting area is on the top floor and enjoys views both over the park and St Alfege Church. There is a small shared garden at the rear. No. 13 originally had a striking spiral staircase in the middle, this was removed when the interior was reorganised by Gus Alexander in 2002.

Bernard Angell House, Trafalgar Road with Park Row
A Greenwich Council four-storey block of flats, of brick and concrete, 1970s.

East Greenwich Fire Station, Woolwich Road
Architects: GLC Department of Architecture and Civic Design (Jack Lambert and Peter Smith), 1985
Part of the 1980s GLC updated facilities for the London Fire Brigade. This is a steel and brick building, with bright red finishes and curved brick walls and windows. Its expressive red metal roof line evokes the roof of the earlier LCC East Greenwich Fire Station from 1902 in nearby Tunnel Avenue. North Kensington's station and the Fire Command Center in Albert Embankment were also built in the same year by the GLC.

Greenwich District Hospital, Vanbrugh Hill (demolished)
Architect: Michael Bench, leader of the Hospital Design Unit of the Ministry of Health, on-site 1965 – 1972
A large hospital with experimental mechanical solutions including a trolley conveyor system, air-conditioning and escalators. The building proved too expensive to maintain. Closed in 2001 and demolished in 2006.

Greenwich Police Station, Royal Hill
Swanne House (police accommodation), Gloucester Circus
Architect: John Innes Elliott
Chief architect of the Metropolitan Police, 1960
Part demolished; part converted into flats in 2022.

Maribor Estate
A Greenwich Council estate formed of two blocks: a five-storey block at 1 – 24 Burney Street and a six-storey block at 25 – 54 Gloucester Circus accommodating maisonettes. Named after Greenwich's twin town in Slovenia.

Maze Hill Lodge, Greenwich Park Street
12 flats in a three-storey block over garages. Built from red brick and horizontal bands of exposed concrete.

Maze Hill School, Woodland Crescent (demolished)
Architect: Architects Co-Partnership, 1971

National Maritime Museum, Neptune Court
Architect: Rick Mather, 1995 – 1999
A large glazed courtyard with lifts and stairs and reorganised circulation, galleries and displays.

Peabody Close, off Devonshire Drive
A part three- and part two-storey block of flats at the centre of the Ashburnham Triangle, of brick and concrete with generous communal areas. The block and a colonnade enclose a landscaped courtyard.

Picturehouse Cinema, Greenwich High Street
Architects: Howard & Unick, 1989 (closed 2002)
Transformation architects: Panter Hudspith (2005)

Royal Hill Estate
LCC Architects Department, 1958
A large municipal estate including three six-storey point-blocks – Topham House, Darnhall House and Renbold House.

Sussex Court, Roan Street
Architects: Hemingway Cumbo, 1993
Developer: Roy Jones and Ward Homes
A mews scheme of 10 houses over two terraces, built on a tight site, between Roan Street and St Alfege Park. The houses feature generous entrance atriums, double-height spaces and decorative stained-glass panels. Accessed by a gateway with a decorative wind vane. Local scaffolding business owner Roy Jones bought the old Roan School headmaster's house and employing architects Hemingway Cumbo, of Chiswick, developed the site to the rear. The project was eventually delivered by Ward, builders and developers.

The John Roan Lower School, Westcombe Park (demolished)
Architects: GLC's Ann Webb and Geoff Denison, 1981. Replaced in 2015 by a larger building by John McAslan + Partners.

Tom Smith Close, by Maze Hill train station
A Greenwich Council estate of 72 flats in three six-storey blocks with striking horizontal bands of red brick and aluminium cladding.

West Greenwich Methodist Church,
142 Greenwich High Street
Architect: Edward D. Mills, 1954

ABBREVIATIONS AND SCHOOLS OF ARCHITECTURE

AA Architectural Association School of Architecture, founded in 1847.

Brixton School of Building Active from 1943 to 1970. Originally the London County Council School of Building opened in 1904. It became part of the Polytechnic of the South Bank in 1970, now the London South Bank University.

GLC Greater London Council, active from 1965 to 1986, the London-wide general municipal authority, responsible for a larger area than its predecessor the LCC. Between 1986 and 2000 most of the powers of the GLC were devolved to the London boroughs and other bodies. The GLA, Greater London Authority, was created in 2000.

Kingston Polytechnic Founded as Kingston Technical Institute in 1899, renamed Kingston Polytechnic in 1970 and then again in 1993 as Kingston University School of Architecture.

LCC London County Council, active from 1889 to 1965, London-wide general municipal authority.

Northern Polytechnic Active from 1896 to 1971. It was founded in 1848 as The Metropolitan Evening Classes for Young Men. It became the London Guildhall University in 1992 and since 2002 the London Metropolitan University.

Regent Street Polytechnic Founded as the Royal Polytechnic Institution in 1838, later the Polytechnic of Central London and since 1992, the University of Westminster.

RIBA Royal Institute of British Architects, founded in 1834.

South West Essex Technical College Founded in 1938. It became Waltham Forest Technical College in 1966 and North East London Polytechnic in 1970 which would later become the University of East London.

The Bartlet The Bartlet School of Architecture is part of University College London. It has been named as such since 1919 whilst the UCL had a chair of architecture since 1841.

Woolwich Polytechnic Founded in 1891, renamed Thames Polytechnic in 1970, and then in 1993 as University of Greenwich.

ENDNOTES

INTRODUCTION

1 Marshall Berman, *All that is solid melts into air: the experience of modernity* (New York: Verso, 1982)
2 Le Corbusier, *Towards a New Architecture* (London: The Architectural Press, 1978)
3 Justin McGuirk, *Charlotte Perriand, the modern life* (London: The Design Museum, 2021)
4 Further reading: Alan Powers, *The Modern Movement in Britain* (Merrell, 2005)
5 Charles Jencks, *Late-modern Architecture* (Academy Editions, 1980)
6 www.blackheathartsociety.org.uk
7 Felix Barker and Tony Aldous, *Guardians of the Heath* (The Blackheath Society, 2009)
8 John Henry Forshaw and Patrick Abercrombie, *County of London Plan* (London: Macmillan, 1943)
9 Corporation of London, Court of Common Council, *Report of the Preliminary Draft Proposals for Post War Reconstruction in the City of London* (London: HMSO, 1944)
10 Patrick Abercrombie, *Greater London Plan 1944* (London: HMSO, 1944)
11 Frank Mort, *Fantasies of Metropolitan Life: Planning London in the 1940s*, Journal of British Studies, 43(1), 120–151, 2004
12 H. Myles Wright, *The First Ten Years: Post-War Planning and Development in England*, The Town Planning Review 26, no. 2, 1955
13 Felix Barker and Tony Aldous, *Guardians of the Heath* (The Blackheath Society, 2009)
14 Elain Harwood and Alan Powers (Edit.), *Festival of Britain*, The Twentieth Century Society Journal, 2001
15 Henry Greaves in correspondence 28 March 2022
16 Paul Wright, *Road Rage! 50 years of plans for motorways through Blackheath* (The Blackheath Society, 2019)
17 Ian Nairn, *Nairn's London* (London: Penguin, 1966). Nairn was referring to the corner of Blackheath Park with Pond Road, where one can see St Michael's Church (1830), Peter Moro's own house (1957), Hallgate by Span (1958) and Georgian villas (1827).
18 Neil Rhind, *A Fair Estate* (Blackheath Cator Estate Residents Ltd, 2007)
19 Felix Barker, *Greenwich and Blackheath Past* (Historical Publications, 1993)
20 Neil Rhind, *The Heath* (Bookshop Blackheath, 2002)
21 *Morden College, a Brief Guide and Handbook* (Trustees of Morden College, 1984)
22 Neil Rhind and Roger Marshall, *Walking the Heath* (The Blackheath Society, 2013)
23 Extract from *National Life Story Collection, Architect's Lives, Peter Moro*. Interview by Louise Brodie, 1996
24 Dannatt, Johnson Architects, *The University of Greenwich, Maritime Greenwich Campus* (Dannatt, Johnson Architects, 2002)
25 Gill Frayn, Jackie Hicks and Peter Kent, *A Brief History of the Greenwich Society, 50 years of challenge & change*, 2011
26 Bridget Cherry and Nikolaus Pevsner, *Buildings of England: London 2: South* (London: Penguin, 1983) p.252
27 Neil Rhind, *The Paragon and South Row* (The Bookshop on the Heath, 2012)
28 Charles Bernard Brown, *The conversion of old buildings into new homes for occupation and investment* (London: Batsford, 1955)
29 Elizabeth McKellar, *You Didn't Know it was Neo-Georgian*, Historic England website, 30 September 2016
30 Neil Rhind, *Blackheath Village & Environs* – 3 volumes – (Bookshop Blackheath, 1976, 1983 and 2020)
31 *Blackheath Preservation Trust 1938–2016* (Blackheath Society, 2017)
32 John Bold, *Dannatt, Johnson Architects, 2000–2018* (Dannatt, Johnson Architects 2018) p. 20
33 Edwin Heathcote, in *Modernist dreams, the architectural future that never was*, Financial Times Weekend, 28 March 2022
34 Walter Benjamin, *Berlin Childhood around 1900* (Harvard University Press, 2006)
35 Michael de Certeau, *The Practice of Everyday Life* (Berkeley: University of California Press, 1984)

ARCHITECTS AND PROJECTS

Allies and Morrison to E Morton Wright

36 Barbara Simms (Edit.), *Eric Lyons and Span* (London: RIBA Publishing, 2006)
37 www.alliesandmorrison.com
38 Ian Latham (Edit.), *Allies and Morrison* (London: Right Angle Publishing, 2011) pp. 50–53
39 Pamela Buxton, 'Allies and Morrison on 40 years of sitting side by side', in *RIBA Journal*, 5 July 2021
40 Later Andrews Sherlock & Partners
41 Harley Sherlock, *An Architect in Society* (The Islington Society, 2006) p.21
42 Harley Sherlock, *An Architect in Society* (The Islington Society, 2006)
43 Barbara Simms (Edit.), *Eric Lyons and Span* (London: RIBA Publishing, 2006)
44 Harley Sherlock, *An Architect in Society* (The Islington Society, 2006) pp. 52–53
45 Harley Sherlock, *An Architect in Society* (The Islington Society, 2006) p. 46
46 www.myheritage.com
47 Bernard Hartley in conversation, 18 January 2023
48 RIBA Library in correspondence, 10 January 2023
49 Arthur worked on a similar scheme of ten interlocking maisonettes in Clarendon Road, Notting Hill, whilst at Rubinstein & Hartley (Bernard Hartley in conversation)
50 Norman Parkinson in conversation, 17 July 2020
51 Ian McInnes in correspondence, 28 December 2022
52 Paul Davis, Ian McInnes and Catherine Samy,
53 *Dulwich Mid-Century Oasis* (London: IMcI, 2021)
54 Paul Davis, Ian McInnes and Catherine Samy, *Dulwich Mid-Century Oasis* (London: IMcI, 2021)
55 Chapel opening programme, 1965

56 Linda O'Carroll in correspondence, 28 December 2022

57 Edna Meeking in conversation, 17 October 2020

58 John Cox in conversation, 21 June 2022

59 A terrace of three connected two-storey houses, with loft. All have different floorplans and a varied roofline of monopitch roofs. The garden walls were built reusing materials from the coach house that previously stood on the site. Iain Heardman in conversation, 8 May 2022

60 A house-folly combining the remnants of a small church tower with additional brickwork wings and timber-clad overhanging balconies.

61 Alice Hope, *Town Houses* (New York: Hayden Book Company, 1965) pp.44–47

62 *Architect & Builder*, vol 22, no. 12 (December 1972) pp. 24–25

63 Edna Meeking in conversation, 2021

64 John Cox in conversation, 21 June 2022

65 *The Architects' Journal* (5 April 1967) p. 818

66 *Interior Design* (July 1970) pp. 424–425

67 Bridget Cherry and Nikolaus Pevsner, *The Buildings of England: London 2, South* (London: Penguin Books 1983) p. 266

68 David Lawson, *And then there was light* in The Independent, House & Home (9 January 1993)

69 *Town-house Terraces, 6 Paragon Place* in Concrete Quarterly 154 (July-September 1987) pp. 2–5

70 Elain Harwood, *Chamberlin, Powell & Bon* (London: RIBA Publishing, 2016) pp. 73–74

71 *Architectural Design* (November 1965) pp. 550–554

72 *Architectural Review* (November 1965) pp.326–332

73 *Architectural Review* (November 1965) pp.326–332

74 Bridget Cherry and Nikolaus Pevsner, *The Buildings of England: London 2, South* (London: Penguin Books, 1983) p.274

75 Miranda H. Newton, *Architects' London Houses: The Homes of Thirty Architects since the 1930s* (London: Butterworth Architecture, 1992) pp. 76–81

76 Miranda H. Newton, *Architects' London Houses: The Homes of Thirty Architects since the* 1930s (London: Butterworth Architecture, 1992) p. 76

77 'How to Make a Dream-House Really Work' in *House & Garden*, vol.28, no.282 (September 1973) pp. 104–105

78 E Morton Wright in conversation, 6 July 2020

79 E Morton Wright in conversation, 6 July 2020

Eric Lyons to Julian Sofaer

80 Neil Bingham, 'The Architect in Society: Eric Lyons, his circle and his values', in *Eric Lyons and Span* (London: RIBA Publishing, 2006)

81 Leslie Bilsby, A lifetime's devotion, in *RIBA Journal* (November 1981) p.53

82 Felix Barker and Tony Aldous, *Guardians of the Heath* (Blackheath Society, 2009) pp. 51–56

83 Span pamphlet, 1960s, in *The Spirit of Span Housing*, James Strike, 2005, p.8

84 Ian Nairn, *Modern Buildings in London*, London: Notting Hill Editions, 2023 reprint, p.119

85 Further reading: Barbara Simms (Edit.), *Eric Lyons and Span* (RIBA Publishing, 2006)

86 Eric Lyons, 'Private Housing', in *RIBA Journal* (May 1977) p. 182

87 Subtopia refers to a concept by Ian Nairn describing unchecked development resulting in monotonous low-density suburban housing, blurring the distinction between town and country.

88 *The Span T8 house*, promotional brochure, n.d.

89 Michael Frayn, in *Among Others, Friendships and Encounters*, Faber & Faber, 2023

90 *Span – living with new ideas*, promotional brochure, mid-1960s

91 Bridget Cherry and Nikolaus Pevsner, *The Buildings of England: London 2, South*, Penguin Books, London 1983, p.277

92 *Omnibus: The more we are together*, BBC documentary, 1969

93 Ian Nairn, Modern Buildings in London, Notting Hill Editions, 2023 reprint, p.120

94 Neil Rhind, *Blackheath Village & Environs* 1790–1970, *volume* 2, Bookshop Blackheath, 1983, p.157

95 Edna Meeking in conversation, 17 October 2020

96 Rob Whitlock, *Building of the month, Corner Green, Blackheath*, in C20 Society Journal, April 2013

97 Eric Lyons, 'Back to Blackheath' in *The Architect* (July 1971) pp. 36–41

98 Neil Rhind, *Blackheath Village & Environs 1790–1970, volume 2* (Bookshop Blackheath, 1983) p. 128

99 Neil Rhind, *Blackheath Village & Environs 1790–1970, volume 2* (Bookshop Blackheath, 1983) p. 128

100 Eric Lyons, 'Back to Blackheath' in *The Architect* (July 1971) pp. 36–41

101 Ian Nairn, *Modern Buildings in London* (Kendal: Notting Hill Editions, 2023 reprint) p.120

102 Neil Rhind, *Blackheath Village & Environs 1790–1970, volume 2* (Bookshop Blackheath, 1983, p. 153

103 Bridget Cherry and Nikolaus Pevsner, *The Buildings of England: London 2, South*, Penguin Books, 1983, pp. 276–277

104 Neil Rhind, *Blackheath Village & Environs 1790-1970, volume 2*, Bookshop Blackheath, 1983, p. 38

105 Elain Harwood, *Mid-century Britain, Modern Architecture 1938–1963*, Batsford, 2021, pp. 62–63

106 Geraldine Betts in conversation 30 June 2021

107 House & Garden, *The House of Ideas*, June 1957, pp. 36–41

108 Elain Harwood and James O. Davies, *England's Post-War Listed Buildings*, Batsford, 2015, pp. 560 and 571

109 Susan and Geoffrey Jellicoe, *Modern Private Gardens*, London 1968, pp. 17–19

110 Felix Barker and Tony Aldous, *Guardians of the Heath*, The Blackheath Society, 2009

111 Felix Barker and Tony Aldous, *Guardians of the Heath*, The Blackheath Society, 2009

112 Eric Lyons, *Back to Blackheath* in The Architect, July 1971, pp. 36–41

113 The Builder, *A Successful Planning Appeal*, 20 May 1960

114 Elain Harwood and James O. Davies, *England's Post-War Listed Buildings*, Batsford, 2015, p. 580

115 Ivor Cunningham, August 1994, Span Archives, RIBA

116 Bridget Cherry and Nikolaus Pevsner, *The Buildings of England: London 2, South*, Penguin Books, 1983, p.423

117 National Life Story Collection – Architect's Lives – Gordon Bowyer interviewed by Niamh Dillon, 2013–14

118 Iain Langlands in conversation

119 Neil Rhind, *Blackheath Village & Environs 1790-1970, volume 2*, Bookshop Blackheath, 1983, p. 74

120 *Uncommon neighbourliness: An architect and an MP build two houses and cultivate one garden in Blackheath*, in House & Garden Book of Small Houses, Robert Harling (Edit.), London: Condé Nast, 1961, pp. 82–83

121 Michael Mellish in conversation 21 February 2022

122 *Mrs James Callaghan on her new life in No. 11*, House & Garden, vol 20, no.2, February 1965, pp. 21–23, as quoted in Neil Bingham: *A Second Skin: Houses and Housing* by Gordon and Ursula Bowyer in Houses: Regional Practice and Local Character, Twentieth Century Architecture 12, The Journal of the Twentieth Century Society, 2015

123 Neil Bingham: *A Second Skin: Houses and Housing* by Gordon and Ursula Bowyer in Houses: Regional Practice and Local Character, Twentieth Century Architecture 12, The Journal of the Twentieth Century Society, 2015, p. 91

124 Graham Lane in conversation, 2023

125 Neil Rhind, *Blackheath Village & Environs 1790–1970, volume 2*, Bookshop Blackheath, 1983, p. 304

126 Neil Bingham, *A Second Skin: Houses and Housing* by Gordon and Ursula Bowyer in Houses: Regional Practice and Local Character, Twentieth Century Architecture 12, The Journal of the Twentieth Century Society, 2015, pp. 92–93

127 *The Architectural Review*, MANPLAN 8, Vol 148 No. 883, September 1970

128 Charles McKean and Tom Jestico, *Guide to Modern Buildings in London 1965–75*, Warehouse Publishing, 1976, p.69

129 Ellis Woodman, Modernity and Reinvention, *The Architecture of James Gowan*, London: Black Dog Publishing, 2008, pp. 97–113 and 209–211

130 Sue Burden in correspondence 9 February 2022

131 Sue Burden in correspondence 9 February 2022

132 Elizabeth Wiggans in conversation 2 September 2020

133 Sue Burden in correspondence 9 February 2022

134 William Lowe in correspondence 30 March 2020

135 John Newton in correspondence 31 May 2022

136 John Newton in correspondence 7 July 2022

137 National Life Story Collection – Architect's Lives – John Roberts. Interview by Cathy Courtney, 2002

138 Michael Hook in conversation 26 April 2022

139 *Julian Sofaer Obituary*, www.aaschool.ac.uk, 30 January 2020

140 E Morton Wright, *Meridian West and Pictures*, unpublished, priv. coll.

141 English Heritage, official list entry no. 1392348, 2007

142 *The architect from Baghdad who rebuilt his life in London*, Jewish Renaissance, Summer 2022

143 *On the slope of Blackheath*, in *Architectural Review*, August 1968, pp.110–111

LCC to Pierre D'Avoine

144 Lynne Dixon, *Annotated personal and professional CV*, unpublished, priv. coll., June 2021

145 Elizabeth Darling in correspondence, 4 January 2023

146 Elizabeth Darling, *Rosemary Stjernstedt [née Smith], Rosemary Owen*, in Oxford Dictionary of National Biography online, 9 February 2023

147 Tom Butler, *Raffaele Monti sculpture on Brooklands Pond*, in Blackheath Cator Estate Newsletter, Summer 2022

148 Old Emanuels Newsletter, Len Lewis Obituary, Summer 1999

149 E Morton Wright in conversation, 6 June 2020

150 Barbara and Oliver Froome-Lewis in correspondence, 26 April 2023

151 Paul Harpin in conversation, 6 May 2020

152 The Barbican hand rinse basin has a compact square form, a high integrated splashback and is recessed into the wall with concealed pipework. An exercise in compact design, it also integrates a soap dish area and toilet roll holder as well as a concealed mixer fitting.

153 Stefan Hohmann in correspondence 2023

154 Bernard Hartley in conversation, 2023

155 Bernard Hartley in conversation, 2023

156 Stefan Hohmann in correspondence, 2023

157 Mary Couper in conversation, 2023

158 Lorenzo Masini in conversation, 2022

159 Lorenzo Masini in correspondence 4 April 2022

160 Roger Marshall in conversation 25 June 2020

161 Myles Dove in correspondence 8 June 2020

162 Our Ladye Star of the Sea is a Gothic-revival church by William W. Wardell of c.1850 in Crooms Hill, Greenwich. The alterations by Myles and Deirdre Dove included the insertion of a timber choir gallery with a new organ and porch below.

163 Myles Dove in correspondence, 28 June 2020

164 *Architects Journal*, vol. 15, 1971, pp. 144–145

165 Brochure produced for Open House, 2018

166 Neil Bingham, The Homewood guidebook (National Trust, 2004)

167 Further reading: Neil Bingham, Patrick Gwynne, Twentieth Century Architects series, 2023 and Neil Bingham, *The houses of Patrick Gwynne*, in Twentieth Century Architecture 4, Post-war Houses, The Journal of the Twentieth Century Society, 2000, pp. 32, 33

168 This project was completed in 1949, which deviates from the time-frame of the book. It is included here for completeness regarding Patrick Gwynne's work for Leslie Bilsby in the area.

169 *House at Blackheath*, in Architect & Building News, 16 June 1955, pp. 724–728

170 *The Architectural Review*, vol. 117, number 700, April 1955, pp. 258–259

171 *Conversion of a Victorian House*, in Ideal Home, July 1955, pp. 64 – 69

172 Neil Bingham, T*he houses of Patrick Gwynne*, in Post-war Houses, Twentieth Century Architecture 4, The Journal

of the Twentieth Century Society (Twentieth Century Society: 2000) pp. 32–33

173 Patrick Gwynne, *Houses by Patrick Gwynne 1938–1979* (privately printed, c.1980)

174 Bridget Cherry and Nikolaus Pevsner, *Buildings of England: London 2: South* (London: Penguin, 1983) p.276

175 Patrick Gwynne, *Houses by Patrick Gwynne 1938–1979* (privately printed, c.1980)

176 Neil Bingham, *The houses of Patrick Gwynne*, in Post-war Houses, Twentieth Century Architecture 4, The Journal of the Twentieth Century Society (Twentieth Century Society: 2000) pp. 37–38

177 Elain Harwood and James O. Davies, *England's Post-War Listed Buildings* (London: Batsford, 2015) p. 588

178 Project architect Bob King in conversation, 10 May 2023

179 Felix Barker and Tony Aldous, *Guardians of the Heath* (Blackheath Society, 2009) pp. 51–57

180 Patrick Gwynne, *Houses by Patrick Gwynne 1938-1979* (privately printed, c.1980)

181 Paul Harpin in correspondence, May 2022

182 Sylvie Tvrtkovic in conversation, November 2021

183 Paul Tvrtkovic monograph (self-published, priv. coll., 2008)

184 Paul Tvrtkovic monograph (self-published, priv. coll., 2008)

185 Paul Mayo in correspondence, 19 January 2023

186 Philip Curtin in correspondence, 16 January 2023

187 *Peter Foggo Architect*, Memorial Exhibition catalogue, 1994

188 Caroline Banks in correspondence, 24 March 2022

189 John Welsh, 'Saved?' in *RIBA Journal*, vol 101, no.8 (August 1994) pp. 16–19

190 *Modern House* sales brochure, Langton Way

191 Peter Moro memories (unpublished/ priv. col.)

192 Michael Mellish in correspondence, 26 June 2023

193 Alistair Fair, *Peter Moro and Partners*, Twentieth Century Architects series (Liverpool University Press, Historic England and The Twentieth Century Society, 2021)

194 Neil Rhind, *Blackheath Village & Environs 1790-1970, volume 2* (Bookshop Blackheath, 1983) p. 108

195 National Life Story Collection – Architect's Lives – Peter Moro. Interview by Louise Brodie, 1996

196 June Park, *Houses and Bungalows* (London: Batsford, 1958) pp. 83–88

197 Dinah Moro in conversation, 7 February 2023

198 Michael Mellish in conversation, 25 April 2023

199 'Me and My House, Moro House' in *C20, The Magazine of the Twentieth Century Society* (Issue 2021/2) pp. 34–44

200 Tony Bevan and Glenys Johnson in conversation, 2023

201 This project was completed in 2009, which deviates from the time-frame of the book. It is included here for its relevance in relation to Meridian West and as an exemplary reconfiguration of a mid-1960s house.

202 E Morton Wright in conversation, 2020

203 'Lightness of touch' in *Architecture Today*, no.198 (May 2009) pp. 20–29

Ray Smith to Royston Summers

204 See Edward Denison, *McMorran & Whitby*, Twentieth Century Architects series, 2009

205 Peter Smith in correspondence, 28 June 2022

206 Robert Harling (Edit.), *House & Garden Book of Small Houses* (London: Condé Nast, 1961)

207 Alice Hope, 'New House at Greenwich' in Town Houses (London: Batsford, 1963) pp. 67–69

208 Peter Smith in correspondence, 28 June 2022

209 Faith Clarke in conversation, 2022

210 Peter Smith in correspondence, 28 July 2022

211 Sales brochure, 1973

212 Peter Bell in correspondence, 21 March 2022

213 *The Architectural Review*, Vol 158, No. 941 (July 1975) pp.33–34

214 'Within these walls…', in *Ideal Home* (August 1981) pp. 7–9

215 Anne Burton in conversation, 8 February 2022

216 Peter Bell in correspondence, 21 March 2022

217 'The frustrated architects waiting for a call' in *The Daily Telegraph*, 1991

218 'Little Boxes' in *Ideal Home* vol. 109, no.2 (February 1975)

219 Mark Simpson in correspondence, 15 November 2021

220 Russel + May Associates, *Planning Statement* (June 2016)

221 Ronald Coleman in conversation, 22 February 2023

222 Ronald Coleman in conversation, 22 February 2023

223 Nick Cuddon in conversation, 21 February 2023

224 *'A small house-cum-flat is added to a late Georgian house in Blackheath'* in *House & Garden Book of Modern Houses and Conversions* (London: Condé Nast, 1966)

225 John-Michael O'Sullivan, 'Habitat at 50: a new way of living' in *The Observer* (4 May 2014)

226 Nick Cuddon in conversation, 21 February 2023

227 Andrew Webley and Kim Brazill in correspondence, 23 November 2021

228 Michael Frayn in conversation, 5 April 2023

229 Justin Summers, 'Royston Summers obituary' in *The Independent* (11 June 2012)

230 'Royston Summers obituary' in *RIBA Journal*, vol 86, no.10 (October 1979) p.459–460

231 Tyler's Yard Ltd comprised of architect Royston Summers, author and playwright Michael Frayn, publisher Michael Wace, geologist Ian Forrest, dentist Shyam Khanna, solicitor James Dolman and builder Peter Dobbs (trading as Pace Developments).

232 Michael and Jose Manser, 'Seven Homes for seven families' in *Sunday Times* (undated newspaper cuttings)

233 Ian Forrest in conversation, 25 March 2022

234 David Wilcox, 'Families win top design award' in the *Evening Standard* (18 September 1969)

235 Michael Frayn in conversation, 5 April 2023

236 'A house built for warmth' (newspaper cutting, 1971)

237 Jennifer and Alan Lee Williams in conversation, 19 April 2022

238 Michael O'Halloran, 'An inexact science' in *The Financial Times* (1969)

239 Rebecca Frayn, 'The glasshouse dream that shattered' in *The Times* (5 June 2000)

Stephen Gardiner to Walter Greaves

240 Joan Scotson in conversation, 10 February 2023
241 Monica Pidgeon and Theo Crosby (Edit.), *An Anthology of Houses* (London: Batsford) 1960
242 Robert Harling (Edit.), *House & Garden Book of Small Houses* (London: Condé Nast, 1961) pp. 104–105
243 Jane Gardner in conversation, 19 November 2021
244 Teresa Forrest, *Life after Lucy* (self-published, 2016)
245 Teresa Forrest in conversation, 24 June 2020
246 Neil Bingham, 'Trevor Dannatt Obituary', *20C Society Magazine* (Issue 2021/1) p.76
247 The extensive works at the Maritime Greenwich Campus, for the University of Greenwich, included master planning, restoration, conversion, introduction of new stairs, lifts and lecture theatres to the Queen Anne, King William and Queen Mary Buildings; as well as the University Library and Learning Centre, later Student Hub at the Dreadnought Seamen's Hospital building and a TV studio at the Stephen Lawrence Building.
248 Neil Rhind and Roger Marshall, *Walking the Village* (The Blackheath Society, 2017) p.15
249 Roger Stonehouse, *Trevor Dannatt works and words* (London: Black Dog Publishing, 2008) pp.182–191
250 Trevor Dannatt in conversation, 8 October 2020
251 Adrian Dannatt in conversation, 27 September 2022
252 *Blackheath Quaker Meeting House*, leaflet, 2018
253 Trevor Dannatt in conversation, 8 October 2020
254 Roger Stonehouse, *Trevor Dannatt works and words* (London: Black Dog Publishing, 2008) pp.198–201
255 *The Arup Journal* (March 1974) pp. 21–23
256 Neil Bingham, 'Blackheath Meeting House' in *20C Society Journal* (May 2019)
257 Roger Stonehouse, *Trevor Dannatt works and words* (London: Black Dog Publishing, 2008) pp.104–107
258 This project was completed in 2001, which deviates from the time-frame of the book. It is included here for its relevance regarding Trevor Dannatt's work in the area.
259 Roger Stonehouse, *Trevor Dannatt works and words* (London: Black Dog Publishing, 2008) pp.70-71
260 Trevor Dannatt in conversation, 8 October 2020
261 Neil Rhind, *Blackheath Village & Environs 1790–1970, volume 2* (Bookshop Blackheath, 1983) p. 102
262 Lise Peat and Liz Rodin in conversation, 20 June 2020
263 Sweyn Place Sales brochure, 1969
264 Joy Langridge in conversation, 2022
265 *House & Garden*, vol 39, no.1 (January 1984) pp. 39–48
266 The 1963 unbuilt proposals at Bennett Park and Blackheath Village were for a large 4 storey block of shops, offices and flats; the client was developer Leslie Bilsby.
267 The 12a Blackheath Park project was for alterations and the addition of garages for Leslie Bilsby in 1964. The modern additions were later removed and the building was altered to match the adjacent Victorian houses of 1830–40.
268 Henry Greaves in correspondence, 28 March 2022
269 Neil Bingham, *Record of visit to Severels* (unpublished, 21 November 1993)
270 Neil Rhind, *Blackheath Village & Environs 1790–1970, volume 2* (Bookshop Blackheath, 1983) p. 128
271 Henry Greaves in correspondence, 28 March 2022
272 Henry Greaves in correspondence, 28 March 2022
273 Hazel Gorge in conversation, 19 June 2020
274 Neil Bingham, *Record of visit to Severels* (unpublished, 21 November 1993)
275 Rosemary Connor in conversation, 2020
276 Henry Greaves in correspondence, 28 March 2022
277 Neil Rhind, *Blackheath Village & Environs 1790-1970, volume 2* (Bookshop Blackheath, 1983) p. 121
278 Neil Bingham, *Record of visit to Severels* (unpublished, 21 November 1993)
279 Denise Blunn in conversation, 17 January 2023

SELECTED BIBLIOGRAPHY

Abbott, Joshua *MiM Mini Guide No. 2: L.C.C. & G.L.C. Selected Projects 1946–86* (London: Mod in Metro Publishing, 2022)

Allinson, Ken, *Architects and Architecture of London* (London: Architectural Press, 2008)

Barker, Felix and Aldous, Tony, *Guardians of the Heath, A chronicle of battles fought by the Blackheath Society from* 1937 *to* 2008 (The Blackheath Society, 2009)

Barker, Felix, *Greenwich and Blackheath Past* (Historical Publications, 1993)

Bingham, Neil, *Patrick Gwynne*, Twentieth Century Architects series (Liverpool Architectural Press and History England, 2023)

Blackheath Preservation Trust 1938–2016 (The Blackheath Society: 2017)

Bold, John, *Dannatt, Johnson Architects 2000–2018*, (London: Dannatt, Johnson Architects, 2018)

Brown, Charles Bernard, *The conversion of old buildings into New Homes for occupation and investment* (London: Batsford, 1955)

Cherry, Bridget and Pevsner, Nikolaus, *The Buildings of England: London 2, South* (London: Penguin Books, 1983)

Dannatt, Johnson Architects, *The University of Greenwich, Maritime Greenwich Campus* (London: Dannatt, Johnson Architects, 2002)

Dannatt, Trevor, *Modern Architecture in Britain: selected examples of recent buildings* (London: Batsford, 1959)

Davis, Paul, McInnes, Ian, Samy, Catherine, *Dulwich Mid-Century Oasis* (London: IMcI Publishing, 2021)

Daybelge, Leyla and Englund, Magnus, *Isokon and the Bauhaus in Britain* (London: Batsford, 2019)

Fair, Alistair: *Peter Moro and Partners*, Twentieth Century Architects series (Liverpool Architectural Press and History England, 2021)

Forrest, Teresa, *Life after Lucy* (self-published, Oxfordshire: 2016)

Harling, Robert (editor), *House & Garden Book of Modern Houses and Conversions* (London: Condé Nast, 1966)

Harling, Robert (editor), *House & Garden Book of Small Houses* (London: Condé Nast, 1961)

Harwood, Elain and O. Davies, James, *England's Post-War Listed Buildings* (London: Batsford, 2015)

Harwood, Elain, *Chamberlin, Powell & Bon*, Twentieth Century Architects series (London: RIBA Publishing, 2011)

Harwood, Elain, *Mid-Century Britain, Modern Architecture 1938-1963* (London: Batsford, 2021)

Hatherley, Owen, *Modern Buildings in Britain, A Gazetteer* (London: Particular Books, 2022)

Hope, Alice, *Town Houses* (New York: Hayden Book Company, 1965)

Jackson, Iain and Holland, Jessica, *The architecture of Edwin Maxwell Fry and Jane Drew, Twentieth Century Architecture, Pioneer Modernism and the Tropics* (London: Routledge, 2016)

Jencks, Charles, *Late-modern Architecture* (Academy Editions, 1980)

Jones, Edward and Woodward, Christopher, *A Guide to the Architecture of London* (London: Book Club Associates, 1983)

MacCarthy, Fiona, *Walter Gropius Visionary Founder of the Bauhaus* (London: Faber & Faber, 2019)

McKean, Charles and Jestico, Tom, *Guide to Modern Buildings in London 1965–75* (London: Warehouse Publishing, 1976)

Middleton, Michael (editor), *House & Garden Book of 30 better houses* (London: Condé Nast, 1955)

Nairn, Ian, *Nairn's London* (London: Penguin Books, 2014 – original edition 1966)

Nairn, Ian, *Modern Buildings in London* (Kendal: Notting Hill Editions, 2023 – original edition 1964)

Newton, Miranda H., *Architects' London Houses: the homes of thirty architects since the 1930s* (London: Butterworth Architecture, 1992)

Park, June, *Houses and Bungalows* (London: Batsford, 1958)

Park, June, *Houses of Today* (London: Batsford, 1971)

Pidgeon, Monica and Crosby, Theo (editors), *An Anthology of houses* (London: Batsford, 1960)

Powers, Alan, *The Modern Movement in Britain* (Merrell, 2005)

Rhind, Neil and Marshall, Roger, *Walking the Village, An Introduction to its History* (The Blackheath Society, 2017)

Rhind, Neil and Marshall, Roger, *Walking the Heath, An Introduction to its History* (The Blackheath Society, 2013)

Rhind, Neil, *A Fair Estate* (Blackheath Cator Estate Residents Ltd, 2007)

Rhind, Neil, *Blackheath Village & Environs 1790–1970, volume 2* (Bookshop Blackheath, 1983)

Rhind, Neil, *Blackheath Village & Environs 1790–2000, volume 3* (The Blackheath Society, 2020)

Rhind, Neil, *The Heath, A companion volume to Blackheath Village & Environs* (Bookshop Blackheath, 2002)

Rhind, Neil, *The Paragon and South Row*,Blackheath (The Bookshop on the Heath for the Blackheath Society, 2012)

Sherlock, Harley, *An Architect in Islington* (The Islington Society, 2006)

Simms, Barbara (editor), *Eric Lyons and Span* (London: RIBA Publishing, 2006)

Stonehouse, Roger, *Trevor Dannatt works and words* (London: Black Dog Publishing, 2008)

Strike, James, *The Spirit of Span Housing* (Strike Print, 2005)

Twentieth Century Architecture 2, *The Modern House revisited*, The Journal of the 20C Society (The 20C Society, 1996)

Twentieth Century Architecture 4, *Post-War Houses*, The Journal of the 20C Society (The 20C Society, 2000)

Twentieth Century Architecture 5, *Festival of Britain*, The Journal of the 20C Society (The 20C Society, 2007)

Twentieth Century Architecture 8, *British Modern, Architecture and Design in the 1930s*, The Journal of the 20C Society (The 20C Society, 2015)
Twentieth Century Architecture 12, *Regional Practice and Local Character*, The Journal of the 20C Society (The 20C Society, 2015)
Wright, Paul, *Road Rage! 50 years of plans for motorways through Blackheath* (The Blackheath Society, online)
Yorke, F. R. S., *The Modern House in England* (London: The Architectural Press, 1937)

WEBSITES

www.historicengland.org.uk
www.layersoflondon.org
www.c20society.org.uk
www.ukmoho.co.uk
https://sounds.bl.uk/oral-history/architects-lives
Lewisham Council and Royal Borough of Greenwich online planning records

IMAGE CREDITS

The author and publisher have made every effort to contact copyright holders and will be happy to correct, in subsequent editions, any errors or omissions that are brought to their attention.

© Allies and Morrison 31
© Architectural Press Archive / RIBA Collections 97, 151, 153, 157, 158, 166, 167
© ARUP 257
© Jason Bell 289 (Peter Bell)
Courtesy of Peter Bell 290, 293, 294, 295
© Valerie Bennett / National Portrait Gallery, London 289 (Sir Richard Cornelius MacCormac)
Courtesy of Neil Bingham 229
The Blackheath Society Archive 12 (Selwyn Court, Nurses Home), 14, 108, 121, 198, 216, 231
CC by Bornhard 74 12 (Genesta Road)
© Kayte Brimacombe 61
© Mann Bros 242, 243
Courtesy of the Burden family 169, 172
Courtesy of Louise Carrabba 81, 84 (patio)
Courtesy of Faith Clarke 286
Courtesy of Ronald Coleman 303
Courtesy of Nick Cuddon 309, 310, 311, 313
CC by Dalbera 10 (Villa Savoie)
Courtesy of Ann Dannatt 341
Trevor Dannatt archives 356, 357
Courtesy of Pierre d'Avoine 275
Courtesy of Lynne Dixon 195
© John Donat / RIBA Collections 99, 148, 236, 239, 241, 245
Courtesy of the Dove family 221, 222, 226, 227
© Jonathan Dove 221 (Myles Dove)
© AChP/ Courtesy of Mme Perriand-Barsac 10
Courtesy of Teresa Forrest 335
© Rachel Germaine 278
Courtesy of Henry and Hannah Greaves 363 (drawing), 367, 382, 383, 384, 385
Courtesy of Stefan Hohman 207, 212, 213
Courtesy of Simon Latham 315
Courtesy of Alan and Jenny Lee Wiliams 325, 328
Courtesy of the Lewis family 201
© Sandra Lousada, Mary Evans Picture Gallery 161
© John Maltby / RIBA Collections 237, 375
Courtesy of Lorenzo Masini 215
Courtesy of Paul Mayo 25, 253
CC by MCAD Library 10 (Bauhaus Dessau)
Brian Meeking archives 63, 68
© Metropolitan Archives 199
© The Modern House 260, 261
Dinah Moro 263, 265, 270
Courtesy of E Morton Wright 92, 93, 95
Courtesy of John Newton, 175, 176
CC by Ninara 10 (Villa Mairea)
Courtesy of Linda O'Carroll 53
CC by Pabsanch 10 (Fallingwater)
©Tony Ray-Jones / RIBA Collections 84, 369
© RIBA Collections 58, 71, 140, 141, 142, 354, 355, 379, 392, 393
Courtesy of the Roberts family 179
Courtesy of Joan Scotson 331
© Pierce Scourfield 33, 39, 43, 49, 55, 56, 65, 66, 73, 74, 79, 103, 105, 107, 110, 111, 112, 116, 117, 119, 122, 123, 126, 127, 128, 129, 130, 131, 136, 137, 139, 143, 155, 171, 181, 185, 192, 193, 203, 205, 210, 211, 217, 242, 255, 266, 267, 271, 272, 273, 299, 300, 305, 317, 319, 324, 329, 338, 339, 347, 348, 350, 351, 364, 365, 371, 388, 389
Courtesy of Sarah Jane Sherlock 37
Courtesy of Mark Simpson 297
Courtesy of Peter Smith 281, 284 (top)
© Henk Snoek / RIBA Collections 133
Courtesy of Julian Sofaer's family/Sephardi Voices UK 187
Courtesy of the Summers family 321
© Ana Francisco Sutherland 12 (Greenwich Town Hall), 16, 18, 100, 188, 241 (above), 249, 276, 378
© Thomas Francisco Sutherland 20, 21
© Ian Sutherland 147
© Ian C. Taylor, Courtesy of E Morton Wright 87, 88, 89, 91
CC by Timffl 12 (Willow Road)
Courtesy of Sylvie Tvrtkovic 247, 251
© Philip Wiggans BSc, MICE, Courtesy of Elizabeth Wiggans 171 (1965)
CC by David Wilson 1949 10 (Farnsworth House)

ACKNOWLEDGMENTS

This book was only possible through the financial donations of many individuals and the following main sponsors:

John Payne

THE BLACKHEATH SOCIETY

THE GREENWICH SOCIETY

WATES FAMILY ENTERPRISE TRUST

I am also indebted to the following:

Ian Sutherland for the initial idea for this book, in 2015, the continued support, editing and finalising the drawings.

Neil Bingham for the guidance, mentoring, editing, enthusiasm and friendship.

Neil Rhind for his blessing and help.

Heidi Seetzen, all at Studio Blackburn, Pierce Scourfield, Fraser Southey and Rita Peres Pereira who contributed to the book and made it possible.

Nara Paiva, Angela Pallaro and Neil Ditte who created the initial drawings.

David Landau, Victoria Yates and Carolina Thorbert for assisting with research and proofreading on early drafts.

Philip Binns and Rosemary Clements, for invaluable detailed feedback on early drafts.

Jocelyn Rodin, Susan and Roger Taylor for the friendship and local connections.

The staff at the RIBA Drawings & Archives Collection and at the RIBA British Architectural Library, especially Cathy Wilson.

Stefi Orazi, Richard Young, Ralph Henderson and Elain Harwood for their help in researching the Rubinstein brothers' history.

The Blackheath Society for the support with archive photos and the invitation to talk on the subject in March 2021.

The staff at Blackheath High School, Quaker Meeting House's staff and Simon Francis at the Greenwich Theatre, for granting access to their buildings.

Trevor Dannatt, William Lowe, E Morton Wright, Michael Mellish, Myles Dove, Lorenzo Masini, Brian Meeking, Suzanne Brewer, Joyce Lowman, Teresa Forrest, Richard Frewer, Michael Hook, Iain Langlands, Geraldine Betts, John Kelsey, Ian McInnes, Ursula Bowyer, Bernard Hartley, Ronald Coleman, Peter Carolin, Sophie Potter and David Johnson, Susan Miles and Andrew Jackson – architects for their time and generosity sharing views and information.

Hazel Gorge, Ann Woolf, Roger Marshall, Elizabeth Wiggans, Mark Helm, Geraldine Betts, Norman Parkinson, Lorna Lloyd, Anne Burton, Michael Dibley, Tony Bevan and Glenys Johnson, Lisa Peat, Liz Rodin, Jenny and Alan Lee-Williams, Sarah Buckley, Pete and Jess Sampson, Louise and Richard Farrow, Jocasta Kelsey, John Cox, Iain Herdman, Denise Blunn, Andrew Webley and Kim Brazill, Jane Gardner, Michael Frayn, Phil Eisenberg, Paul and Clare Harpin, Helen Doris, Felix Mason, Patrick Morrissey, Joy Langridge, Trudi Lawrence, John O'Mahony, Hugh Sainsbury, Philip Smith, Sonja Moore, Keir McGuinness and Dr Alex Hooi – current and/or original homeowners who shared stories and documents relating to their properties, most of whom also invited me into their homes.

Henry and Hannah Greaves, Oliver and Deborah Froome-Lewis, Peter Smith, Dinah and Alice Moro, Mark Simpson, Jonathan, Simon and Caroline Dove, Edna Meeking, Sylvie Tvrtkovic, Rosemary Connor, Nick Cuddon, Louise Branch Carrabba, Linda O'Carroll, Paul Mayo, Anne and Adrian Dannatt, Peter and Joanna Roberts, Stefan Hohmann, Ben Summers, Simon and Rachel Latham, Victoria, Rob and Daniel Newton – architects' family members who helped with information on the work of their relatives.

Portuguese architects Helder Carita and Alexandra Miguel, who inspired my own path into architecture sometime in the early 1990s and my parents and family for everything else.

INDEX

Photographs and drawings are not indicated separately when within, or adjacent to, the relevant text. Otherwise they are identified by an italic page number, e.g. 23.

Ana Francisco Sutherland is a Portuguese architect based in London. Trained in Lisbon, she set up Francisco Sutherland Architects in 2015 after 12 years at Allies and Morrison and a period in the Netherlands. Her practice has worked on the refurbishment of several Span houses, as well as flats on the Barbican Estate, the Alexandra Road Estate and other modernist buildings. Her interest in British post-war architecture sprang from these experiences and from exploring Blackheath, where she has lived since 2006.

CONTRIBUTORS

Dr Heidi Seetzen is an artist and urban sociologist. She lectures in Sociology at Kingston University and has previously worked as a researcher at the Centre for Urban and Community Research at Goldsmiths College, University of London. She has written about and researched community politics and regeneration. She lived in Blackheath for almost 20 years.

Studio Blackburn is an international brand strategy and design studio, inspiring desire for brands and businesses that makes people's lives better, more enjoyable and more beautiful. Studio Blackburn's founders have lived in Greenwich and Blackheath since 2004.

Pierce Scourfield is a London-based architectural photographer who learned his craft in Vietnam. He gravitates towards contextual design and a subtle colour palette. Weaving these elements with his pared-down approach he aims to create a calm sense of connection and intrigue between viewer and image.

Fraser Southey is a writer and editor for brands and businesses, with particular expertise in sustainability and social responsibility. He lives in a Span flat in The Hall.

Dr Neil Bingham has lived in a Span house in Blackheath for more than 35 years. He is an architectural historian and former curator of architectural collections at the Victoria and Albert Museum, the Royal Academy of Arts, and the Royal Institute of British Architects. He has published on the architects Patrick Gwynneand Eric Lyons, who both made major contributions to Blackheath's modernism.

Ian Sutherland studied engineering and architecture at Cambridge University and was a director for over 20 years at Allies and Morrison Architects. His architectural drawings were displayed at the Line Work exhibition in 2015 and have been published widely. In 2023, he joined Francisco Sutherland Architects to focus on residential projects.

Author: Ana Francisco Sutherland

Introduction co-author: Heidi Seetzen
Research assistance: Carolina Thorbert,
Ian Sutherland
Copy editing: Neil Bingham, Ian Sutherland,
Fraser Southey
Photography: Pierce Scourfield
Drawings: Ian Sutherland assisted by Neil Ditte,
Angela Pallaro and Nara Paiva
Proofreading: Jose do Carmo Francisco,
JJ Purthill
Index: Sharon Laverick

Design:
Studio Blackburn
Paul Blackburn
Mark Jones
Adam Moore
Will Cooper
Jen Wong
Višnja Milošević
Susie Blackburn
Rita Peres Pereira

Studio Blackburn
12 Printing House Yard
London E2 7PR
United Kingdom
www.studioblackburn.com

Image processing, printing, and binding:
Longo AG, Bolzano

Park Books
Niederdorfstrasse 54
8001 Zurich
Switzerland
www.park-books.com

Park Books is being supported by the Federal
Office of Culture with a general subsidy
for the years 2021–2024.

ISBN 978-3-03860-342-9

FOREWORD
by Neil Bingham

MODERN BUILDINGS

ANA FRANCISCO
SUTHERLAND

BLACKHEATH
AND GREENWICH

LONDON 1950–2000

PARK BOOKS

MODERN BUILDINGS

BLACKHEATH AND GREENWICH

LONDON 1950–2000